96 Days of Unbroken Time with God

A Devotional

David Andrew Thomas

Printed in the United States of America

ISBN 979-8-837-35511-0

96 Days of Unbroken Prayer
Copyright © 2019 David Andrew Thomas
All rights reserved

Cover art by the author

To Joseph,
my son and ministry partner,
without whose initiative and generosity this book would not exist

Introduction

Jeremiah says this, *"Can a virgin forget her ornaments, or a bride her attire? Yet my people have forgotten me days without number."* (Jeremiah 2:32)

This is a piercing commentary, not just regarding the inhabitants of Judah and Jerusalem in the prophet's day, but rather about God's people across all of history. It is a characteristic of fallen human nature that we suffer from a sort of "spiritual amnesia"—we quickly forget our God, and we often do so for days on end. It is a *spiritual* forgetfulness we deal with; even if God comes to mind, His love, power, and holiness are "forgotten" as present realities to us, and soon we wander like straying sheep.

This book is an attempt to push back against that human tendency. In the pages that follow, you will find prayerful, scriptural reflection on the ups and downs of what it means to be a God seeker in today's world. But before you get started, let me make a couple of comments for the sake of orientation.

If the book feels a bit "organic," it's because it is. These reflections were first written, one each day, between January 1st, 2019 and Easter Sunday about three and a half months later as part of a time of spiritual renewal at NorthLake Church in Camas, Washington. The goal for a self-selected group of people (known as the *Corps of 24*—named for the 24 hours in each day as well as the number of people in the group) was to spend at least an hour a day with God, unbroken, for that entire 111 day stretch. I personally began this season on an extended fast, and I was challenged to write something every day that would impact those participating in the challenge. The chapters that follow have been somewhat modified from the original, but they are essentially what I wrote during that period. Some chapters will be longer, some shorter. Some read more like encouragements while others like teaching. None of them are "canned," and some definitely retain their "shoot from the hip" feel. They reflect a transformative spiritual journey I was taking along with the people of my church who joined me at that time. The "rest of the story" is that by year's end the Lord had sovereignly swept us back into the missionary work we had greatly desired for years. God's arm is bared in great power, and the impossible becomes the norm, when we *pray*.

But while the book was birthed through that season, daily prayer as a personal emphasis is nothing new to me. I've been hammering the importance of a robust, consistent time of prayer and Scripture reading and meditation for years, in every context I've ministered in, from informal campus ministry while in college, to academic settings, to pastoring, to our missionary work. And, knowing my own weaknesses, I am keenly aware of the importance of Hebrews 3:13, *"But exhort one another every day, as long as it is called 'today,' that none of you may be hardened by the deceitfulness of sin."* We all need constant encouragement, and my prayer is that these pages will encourage you.

Why 96 reflections? As I've shared, the original challenge was 111 days. (Most know that a new habit can be established by consistency over about a month's time; days added thereafter help cement the pattern even more firmly within us.) But some of those original reflections were so specific to our church context that they wouldn't work well in a book intended for a wider audience. In the end I settled on 96 days as a symbolic number: the Greek word for God (*theos*) occurs *96 times* in the Book of Revelation— intentionally, I believe, and representative of God's worthiness to be worshipped by all of creation and all of God's people (represented through the 24 elders compounded by the 4 living creatures worshipping before the throne). Revelation is a book about God's eternal nature colliding with human time. My most powerful seasons of prayer have experienced precisely this sense of being lost in God's presence. The more we seek God within the time we've been given, the more He lifts us and the more we can experience the blessings of eternity, even while we still walk out our days in this life. Psalm 90:12 comes to mind: *"So teach us to number our days, that we may get a heart of wisdom."* By being a good steward over *time*, somehow we are over into *timelessness*. The challenge of this book, therefore, is found in the title: "unbroken"—seek to be in God's presence through daily prayer and time in the Word, as an unbroken chain. For at least 96 days; these meditations are meant to help you in that effort.

I would like to thank Joanne Messinger, who was a big help with proofing and suggestions for clarity; remaining errors are my responsibility. To my wife, Patti, and my daughter, Eden, I am grateful for their patience during the time this was written, putting up with my drive to produce something every day and losing time with me in the process. But I offer the biggest thanks to my son, Joseph, whose help and intervention made a rough-cut collection of emails into a book for many to enjoy.

A final thought: as we begin this journey together, let me encourage you: be a surrendered worshipper. As part of your daily time, make sure you worship the Lord. Sing to Him (or hum if you can't sing!), lift your hands, tell Him you love Him and trust Him and want Him. Ask for grace to be more surrendered to Him than ever. Saint of God, if you do nothing else in His presence, do this each day. Jesus tells us in John 4:23 that *God is seeking worshippers* who will worship Him in Spirit and in truth. That is a remarkable truth indeed, because it tells me that when we worship God daily, consistently, untiringly, our seeking of God intersects with His seeking of us. And in that intersection, my brothers and sisters, is power, revival, and miraculous transformation—for us and for His church.

God be with you, Father, Son, and Holy Spirit, as you begin your pilgrimage.

David Andrew Thomas

Day 1

And one of the scribes came up and heard them disputing with one another, and seeing that he answered them well, asked him, "Which commandment is the most important of all?"

Jesus answered, "The most important is, 'Hear, O Israel: The Lord our God, the Lord is one. And you shall love the Lord your God with all your heart and with all your soul and with all your mind and with all your strength...' ~ Mark 12:28-30

Although this exchange between Jesus and an unnamed scribe is actually a quotation of that holy declaration known as the *Shema* (or *Sh'ma*), I find it very powerful for how Jesus cites it and how the question gave rise to it in the first place. First found in Deuteronomy 6:4-5, this passage is still considered the very essence of what it means to be an observant Jew, and scrolls with this passage inscribed upon them fill the Scripture boxes called the *mezuzah* that Jewish people use to adorn the entrance to their homes (see Deuteronomy 6:9). That there is one true God, and that all the different aspects of our duty to Him boil down to loving Him, is the core of this passage. Jesus not only affirms this command, He exalts it by calling it "the most important." In a way, every one of Jesus' injunctions to "hear" (i.e., "he who has an ear...") points back to this command, since the first Hebrew word in the verse is the verb for *listen* (*sh'ma*).

As we begin this journey of prayer and scriptural focus on our relationship with God, I feel it central that we understand and establish proper motivation in our hearts. God wants us to walk victoriously, confidently, steadily in Him. He wants our faith to be strong, He wants to see us take hold of the blessings that Jesus paid so dearly on the cross that we might have. But life is about peaks and valleys, even for those mighty in the faith, no matter what anyone might say. We all have down days from time to time, and sometimes down stretches. As I grasp that truth in one hand

and a determination to seek God daily in the other, I find that the simple command to *love God* to be a steadying force for me. Whether I am shouting (Joshua 6:16) or moaning like a dove (Isaiah 38:14)—and I have done both—I know I can love God in either state.

The world, our social environment, is mightily confused about what love even is. Lost people (and even many Christians, or folks who claim to be Christians) are turned around over what love between people is supposed to look like; they are utterly upside down when it comes to loving God. Love has been reduced to sentimental attachment, to romantic feelings, to political agreement, to sex. People walk away from marriage, intended to be a lifetime covenant, because things don't "feel" the way they used to, and similarly walk into disastrous relationships over a fleeting emotion. People are told they are devoid of "love" simply because their stance differs from the passionately held views of their accuser. These distortions splash over into people's view of God, for whom some express undying love but are incensed when their starkly unbiblical lifestyle is challenged by Scripture; for them, loving Jesus seems to be more sentiment than substance.

But there is no need for the confusion. *Love* for God, Jesus makes clear, is *obedience* to God. *"If you love me, you will keep my commandments."* (John 14:15) This is not even remotely intended to be a mechanical, heartless rule-keeping; the Psalms vividly express the kind of heartfelt passion God's dearest servants offered Him through the ages. God is not sitting enthroned in heaven "keeping score" at a cold and remote distance. Rather, we love God as His children, just as sincerely obedient children today love their parents. Obedience is the outgrowth of love, the evidence of its authenticity. This is the posture we can take and must take towards God, regardless of how we feel on a given day. And it is the common denominator in every effort, no matter what form it takes, to draw close to God daily.

I am convinced that if we love God, we will want to spend time with Him, just as in the human sphere love often boils down to time spent with someone. In the same way, the more I spend time with someone, the more I grow to love and appreciate them. Of course, such a scenario requires a person who is sufficiently outward-focused to be able to appreciate something in someone else, as well as a person worthy of that appreciation. And God is infinitely worthy. His worthiness and our desire to love Him in obedience to what Jesus calls the most important commandment are the deepest assumptions behind this book and its quest for a long stretch of unbroken time with God.

Let us remember what the Apostle Paul assures us: "*What no eye has seen, nor ear heard, nor the heart of man imagined, **what God has prepared for those who love him.**"* (1 Corinthians 2:9)

Love for God is what we are created for, love for God undergirds all true devotion to Him, and love for God carries great reward in this life and the life to come. Let us *hear*, and answer by loving the Lord our God with all our heart, and soul, and mind, and strength.

Day 2

In the year that King Uzziah died I saw the Lord sitting upon a throne, high and lifted up; and the train of his robe filled the temple. ² Above him stood the seraphim. Each had six wings: with two he covered his face, and with two he covered his feet, and with two he flew. ³ And one called to another and said: "Holy, holy, holy is the LORD of hosts; the whole earth is full of his glory!"⁴ And the foundations of the thresholds shook at the voice of him who called, and the house was filled with smoke. ⁵ And I said: "Woe is me! For I am lost; for I am a man of unclean lips, and I dwell in the midst of a people of unclean lips; for my eyes have seen the King, the LORD of host!" ˉ Isaiah 6:1-5

There's a lot to say about this passage, but I'll focus on one aspect: as Isaiah beholds the Lord in an open vision of heavenly *worship*, he is immediately moved to *brokenness and repentance*. My view of this passage, in fact, is that it is simultaneously one of the Bible's most powerful passages about both worship and repentance, and powerfully demonstrates the connection between them.

This is a different understanding of repentance than many have. Most people see repentance as something that sinners who don't know God do as part of their conversion, or something Christians do to say they're sorry for a specific sin. Most view repentance (if they do it at all) as an unpleasant necessity to get past as quickly as possible. But Isaiah's brokenness and repentance doesn't come from any single "sin event" in his life, but instead from the revelation that God is divine, holy, and heavenly, while Isaiah himself is mortal, sinful, and earthly. In other words, Isaiah is contrite because he has first *seen God* and His awesomeness in worship, not because he is suffering from a "worm mentality" about himself. For Isaiah, his "woe is me" *is worship*. In the following verses it leads to him being cleansed by a coal from the altar, and him being called as a prophet.

If we are going to be effective people of prayer, we need to repent. Better said, we need to become people of repentance. We need to clothe ourselves in repentance. We need to embrace repentance as a *way of life*, the natural effect of spending time in God's presence. The more we behold the Lord, the more we will realize that God is *other*, while we are *common*. But as we find Him in that holy place, we will not be driven away or made to feel unwelcome, but we will be drawn in closer like Isaiah was. True worship leads to true repentance, which in turn deepens worship even more. Repentance is the gateway to intimacy with God. God's greatest saints paradoxically walked in great closeness to the Lord even as they recognized how exalted God is compared to their own lowliness. Human religion cannot grasp that paradox. It tends to either exalt God beyond reach or make God into some sort of buddy to chat with; He is neither. He is the Almighty God who is holy beyond our comprehension, but He dwells with the humble, and the broken and contrite heart He will not despise.

We must *repent* if our prayers are to get any traction. Consider David's words...

If I had cherished iniquity in my heart, the Lord would not have listened. [19] But truly God has listened; he has attended to the voice of my prayer. ̄ Psalm 66:18-19

It's pretty simple, if we love a sin and refuse to let it go, God cannot hear us. We are in idolatry; we see our idol and therefore cannot behold the Lord as Isaiah did. This hard but redemptive truth obviously makes repentance a priority. For this reason, David also prays...

Search me, O God, and know my heart! Try me and know my thoughts! [24] And see if there be any grievous way in me, and lead me in the way everlasting! ̄ Psalm 139:23-24

True, Holy Spirit-driven repentance is a process that comes in waves, or like peeling an onion. In God's light, we see light. The more we seek Him, the more we turn to Him; the more we ask Him to reveal our own heart to us in His presence, the more He will; the more we are cleansed, the closer we will draw to Him. And so it goes. Think of the effect of Isaiah's repentance, the ministry that was born in him. Let us imitate his example and cry out for a coal from God's altar to cleanse us.

Day 3

Regarding today's encouragement, I would like to continue with the theme of *repentance and forgiveness.* Today, however, I want to touch on the matter of us forgiving others. As with the truths regarding worship and repentance, the matter of forgiveness is extraordinarily fundamental to effective prayer. To pursue a pilgrimage into deeper waters without addressing forgiveness is essentially an attempt to sharpen a rock; until this spiritual fundamental is dealt with, the fine-tuning stuff is a lesson in futility.

Jesus told us, *"And when you stand praying, forgive..."*(Mark 11:25). His stated reason in the rest of the verse mirrors exhortations found in Matthew 6 (the Lord's Prayer passage in vv. 7-15), Luke 6:37, and many others elsewhere in Scripture: *"...if you have anything against anyone, so that your Father also who is in heaven may forgive you your trespasses."*

What Jesus tells us, in effect, is that if we refuse to forgive the sins of others against us, we nullify our own repentance. In other words, regardless of our own tears of repentance towards God, He is *unable* to forgive us our sins if we refuse to forgive those who've sinned against us. Our unforgiveness blocks the forgiveness of God in our lives. It is fairly common in the secular realm to hear people dramatically declare that they can never and will never forgive such-and-such an offense, or that they consider a certain sin against them unforgivable, or even that the one who hurt them so badly should burn in hell. This kind of talk has no place in the life of a Christian.

The Scriptures are full of powerful passages that illustrate Jesus' point. In my mind, the Parable of the Unjust Servant in Matthew 18 is one of the most powerful:

Then Peter came up and said to him, "Lord, how often will my brother sin against me, and I forgive him? As many as seven times?"²² Jesus said to him, "I do not say to you seven times, but seventy-seven times. ²³ "Therefore the kingdom of heaven may be compared to a king who wished to settle accounts with his servants. ²⁴ When he began to settle, one was brought to him who owed him ten thousand talents. ²⁵ And since he could not pay, his master ordered him to be sold, with his wife and children and all that he had, and payment to be made. ²⁶ So the servant fell on his knees, imploring him, 'Have patience with me, and I will pay you everything.' ²⁷ And out of pity for him, the master of that servant released him and forgave him the debt. ²⁸ But when that same servant went out, he found one of his fellow servants who owed him a hundred denarii, and seizing him, he began to choke him, saying, 'Pay what you owe.' ²⁹ So his fellow servant fell down and pleaded with him, 'Have patience with me, and I will pay you.' ³⁰ He refused and went and put him in prison until he should pay the debt. ³¹ When his fellow servants saw what had taken place, they were greatly distressed, and they went and reported to their master all that had taken place. ³² Then his master summoned him and said to him, 'You wicked servant! I forgave you all that debt because you pleaded with me. ³³ And should not you have had mercy on your fellow servant, as I had mercy on you?' ³⁴ And in anger his master delivered him to the jailers, until he should pay all his debt. ³⁵ So also my heavenly Father will do to every one of you, if you do not forgive your brother from your heart." ¯Matthew 18:21-35

I also recommend the story of Joseph in Genesis, especially Genesis 45:1ff, and Genesis 50:15ff. These passages are too long to include here, but they are extremely powerful passages of grace found in the Old Testament.

I have some basic observations about forgiving others:

1) *Unforgiveness blinds us.* Note how the unjust servant in Jesus' parable has lost all perspective. The debt he was forgiven is the equivalent of *200,000 years* of wages, and yet he chokes and imprisons another for a debt worth a *few months*. Until we forgive, we will not be able to see clearly and our prayers will be muddled and ineffective.

2) *Refusing to forgive another binds their sin to us.* As a corollary to the last point, people who refuse to forgive basically end up becoming what they hate. Bitterness over a sin spawns that same sin inside of us. For a narrative to this effect, read 2 Samuel chapters 11-18, wherein Absalom hates his father David for his moral turpitude but then tragically becomes worse than David himself.

3) *Forgiveness opens the gates of heaven.* When Stephen forgave those who stoned him to death (story found at the end of Acts 7), especially a young man named *Saul,* who had taken charge of the lynching, *he released the hand of God to do things no one could have anticipated* in Saul's life. We should see a direct line between Stephen begging God not to charge Saul with the sin and Saul's conversion two chapters later. We have no guarantee that our forgiving another will produce another Apostle Paul, but we do know God can do things greater than we have imagined.

4) *Don't wait for an apology.* Your forgiving others is dependent upon God's forgiveness of you, *not* upon someone else asking you to forgive them. A little thought on the matter will help us realize how liberating this is: to forgive another frees not only them, but also us in a profound way. If that freedom is dependent upon the humility of another person or their ability to admit their sin, then we will be continually bound, because most people don't have that ability. Furthermore, many offenses incurred against us are perpetrated by strangers, rank sinners, or in some cases by people who have died. Getting an apology from them is not only impractical, but sometimes impossible. The power of Jesus' forgiveness from the cross in Luke 23:34 is that he forgave men who hadn't an ounce of contrition in them (the same goes for the aforementioned passage about Stephen in Acts 7:60).

5) *Pray for those who have hurt you.* Jesus does this, and tells us to do it ourselves (Luke 6:28). When we pray for those who've hurt us, we reverse the flow; instead of bitterness flowing from the

thoughts we have about that person into our spirit, sweetness flows from our spirit into our thoughts about them. This has a powerful healing effect if done persistently.

6) *Forgiveness is not glossing over things.* If the way we deal with an offense is to belittle it or otherwise pretend it wasn't a big deal after all, we miss the point. God is not asking that we be dishonest with ourselves or others over a deep hurt we've suffered. He is not requiring us to declare a profound offense was "not that bad" or "no big deal" when it was, in fact, *that bad.* If we try to do this we are actually dodging the core issue and simply putting off the painful necessity of dealing with the offense in our spirit. The fact is, we need to call an offense what it is and *forgive it,* not pretend that it wasn't an offense in the first place. Only when we do this can we be free and can the grace of God flow.

7) *Forgiveness liberates us from the victim mentality.* People who do not forgive end up nursing a sense of victimhood. In terms of restoration, this is the repentance/forgiveness version of giving to be seen by others (Matthew 6:1)—you have used your own power to receive your reward, rather than trusting God for an unseen (but infinitely more valuable) heavenly reward. Simply put, you may be a victim, or you may be free. You may not be both.

8) *Do not confuse forgiveness with reconciliation.* These are related, but not exactly the same thing. If we are aware of a rift between us and someone else—particularly another Christian—we should attempt to reconcile with them in the context of prayer (Matthew 5:23-24, also Matthew 18:15-17). But strictly speaking, God does not *require* reconciliation (although He does require us to attempt it), because reconciliation involves willingness and sincerity by both parties. Sometimes reconciliation is not possible at the moment, and sometimes even in this lifetime. Forgiveness, on the other hand, requires only *you.*

God's forgiveness in us provides the grace to forgive others. As you pray, understand that God has really forgiven you, and His forgiveness will then flow through you to others. This can be a process. With "life level" offenses—serious offenses against us that change the course of our lives—sometimes we need to pray for days, weeks, and even years to be fully free. But if we persist, God's grace will be sufficient for us, and the result will be an uncluttered, sweet spirit within us that God can flow through and use.

Day 4

I'm not finished with fundamentals, but a posture of worship, along with a clear spirit (repentance and forgiveness), are "out of the blocks" sort of material just so we can have some sense of an open heaven and sincere communication with God.

Now I want to lay down another foundation stone, this time arming you with more focused power for prayer. At issue is the question of God's Word. There are countless passages that teach of the power of God's Word, but consider these from Jesus Himself regarding the Word and prayer:

In that day you will ask in my name, and I do not say to you that I will ask the Father on your behalf; ²⁷ for the Father himself loves you, because you have loved me and have believed that I came from God. ⁻John 16:26-27

Here Jesus speaks stunning words about the Father's receptivity to our prayers, and why: we love Jesus and have believed on Him. But what is love for Jesus? He's already covered that, a couple chapters earlier:

"If anyone loves me, he will keep my word, and my Father will love him, and we will come to him and make our home with him. ²⁴ Whoever does not love me does not keep my words. And the word that you hear is not mine but the Father's who sent me."
⁻John 14:23-24

Simply put, if we love Jesus we obey His Word. Living this way opens the heavens to us in terms of our prayers. It behooves us, therefore, to saturate ourselves in God's Word unto obedience.

There is a reason the Bible is called "canon." The word canon (one "n" in the middle—not a field weapon) means standard, or measure, like a yardstick. The Scriptures set the standard for truth and teaching for all believers. It is through the Scriptures that we conform to that standard, become more sensitive to God's voice, and bring stability to our spiritual life.

In respect to a rounded prayer life, permit me to make some observations...

1) *God's Word is not merely information, it is living truth that works within us.* Paul refers to *"...the word of God, which is at work in you believers..."* (1 Thessalonians 2:13), and Hebrews 4:12 speaks of the *"word of God as "living and active, sharper than any two-edged sword."* As informational as God's Word can be (indeed, like nothing else), its power lies in the living Holy Spirit who accompanies us as we read and meditate in it. Prayer facilitates this power, just as rain falling on seed helps it penetrate the ground, germinate, and bring forth a harvest.

2) *Those who fill themselves with the written Word become more sensitive to the leading of the Holy Spirit.* David says, *"I have more understanding than all my teachers, for your testimonies are my meditation. I understand more than the aged, for I keep your precepts."* (Psalm 119:99-100) This observation connects the discipline of spending time in God's written Word with the inner promptings that make the difference between mediocre religion and victorious faith. The principle is simple: the more we fill ourselves with God's written Word, the more attuned our inner (spiritual) ear will be to the promptings of the Holy Spirit who inspired it. Most of the time I have felt God speak specifically into my life, He has done so by passages I am already familiar with, whether by directing me to them in the Bible or by bringing them to my memory.

3) *Reading the Word of God brings stability and balance.* People who *only pray*, and don't spend time grounding themselves in God's Word, well, they can get weird. Why? Because there is no person who is so mature in Christ that they no longer need guidance; we all naturally crave it. If we do not get it from the Bible (where it should come from), we will fill the void, and that

will come from what we "feel" in prayer. I'm not knocking promptings (I just wrote of them!), but left to ourselves with the canon, the yardstick, the standard, we will drift. We become goofy mystics in the worst sense. Some entire (false) movements have been birthed and resulted in (or still produce) false doctrines and broken lives, all because someone got a "private revelation" through prayer that deviates from the standard of truth. Paul tells us *"not to go beyond what is written"* (1 Corinthians 4:6), while John says bluntly, *"Everyone who goes on ahead and does not abide in the teaching of Christ, does not have God."* (2 John 9). Prayer and God's Word should be done in balance, and in relation to each other.

4) *The Word of God guides our prayers so that they might be answered.* 1 John 5:14-15 tells us this: *And this is the confidence that we have toward him, that if we ask anything according to his will he hears us. And if we know that he hears us in whatever we ask, we know that we have the requests that we have asked of him.* God cannot and will not answer a prayer that does not conform to His will. How do we know His will? His Word. The more we are in the Word, the more we will know God, and the more we will know His will. Sometimes this knowing can be articulated in chapter and verse precision. Sometimes it is a growing discernment that a mature Christian develops by long experience (see Hebrews 5:14). But the simple truth is that those who fill themselves with God's Word increasingly know God's will, conform to God's will, and experience success in prayer.

5) *Prayer produces faith, and by faith we pray and are heard.* Romans 10:17 tells us that *faith comes from hearing, and hearing through the word of Christ."* The more we take in God's word, the more we will grow in faith. My personal experience in this, and I believe the context bears it out, is that we grow in faith as we receive God's Word, act upon it, live in a faith relationship with God through prayer, and walk out our pilgrimage in the world. Just as prayer alone leads to misguided mysticism, just reading the Bible but never developing a prayer life defies Paul's intent in this

statement. The faith God's Word births in us finds its feet in the place of prayer. Together, a healthy habit of time in God's word, along with a living prayer life (not merely "saying prayers") leads to tremendous spiritual growth and results.

May God empower and anoint you as you spend time hearing from Him and making yourself heard.

Day 5

From beginning to end, the Scriptures are replete with admonitions, warnings, and encouragements about our words. In the Old Testament, Genesis records Adam's first words to God after the Fall as being a slander of Eve, the Exodus and desert wanderings of Israel are packed with warnings about the Israelites' murmurings and grumblings against God and His chosen leaders, the story of the monarchy period tell us of the dangers of false prophets, Psalms and Proverbs go on and on about guarding our lips, the Prophets teach us the power of words to speak truth, life, and hope. In the New Testament, from Jesus to the epistles, we are warned and guided about how we speak, and the Scriptures end with a severe warning to all liars.

It would be impossible to cover all these things here, so I will restrict my comments to two salient points drawn from key Scriptures, again in relation to prayer.

1) Do not grieve the Holy Spirit. The Apostle Paul says this straight up in Ephesians 4:30. But the larger context tells us precisely what he is thinking when he writes it:

Let no corrupting talk come out of your mouths, but only such as is good for building up, as fits the occasion, that it may give grace to those who hear.[30] And do not grieve the Holy Spirit of God, by whom you were sealed for the day of redemption.[31] Let all bitterness and wrath and anger and clamor and slander be put away from you, along with all malice.[32] Be kind to one another, tenderhearted, forgiving one another, as God in Christ forgave you. ¯ Ephesians 4:29-32

If we grieve the Holy Spirit with our words, we alienate the very Person through whom we offer our prayers to God. We shoot ourselves in the foot, spiritually speaking. People who speak as Paul is describing ("corrupting talk," bitterness, clamor, slander, etc., rather than edifying others by their words) impede their own prayers because they have driven away God's Spirit. In the long run, the Holy Spirit who anoints us to pray becomes increasingly absent, and such a Christian ceases to feel the prompting to pray and the confidence to pray, leading to a spiritual tailspin.

James says this:

With [the tongue] we bless our Lord and Father, and with it we curse people who are made in the likeness of God. From the same mouth come blessing and cursing. My brothers, these things ought not to be so. ¯ *James 3:9–10*

James' clear message, coupled with Paul's, is that God is forced to take into account our cursing as something that nullifies our blessing, just as mixing fresh water and salt water results in more salt water, not more fresh. The contradiction is not just mental, but deeply spiritual. It is a collision within us that impedes our prayers.

2) Do not curse your own prayers. Cursing our own prayers can happen more easily than we think, often we are in the regular habit of doing so, and breaking that habit takes discipline. What do I mean by this?

Proverbs 18:21 says, *"Death and life are in the power of the tongue, and those who love it will eat its fruits."* What we say with our mouths has direct and serious consequences—either good or bad—for our lives and the lives of those around us. This proverb has broad application (even to the previous point), but I'm applying it in the sense of Romans 10:10.... *¯ For with the heart one believes and is justified, and with the mouth one confesses and is saved."* If we speak according to the faith in our heart, salvation results. If our speech does not conform to the faith we profess, the result is destruction. Paul means that here in the absolute sense, but it is a truth that applies to lesser things as well.

This incontrovertible truth has been distorted in the past. Some folks took it to an extreme, claiming we have next to Godlike powers to create with the tongue, and we should so use it (i.e., "I have a Cadillac, I have a Cadillac, I have a Cadillac..." etc.). That application of this truth is a distortion of God's intent. But we shouldn't throw the baby out with the bathwater. When speaking to others about matters important to us—matters we are praying about and asking others to pray for—let our conversation conform to our prayers of faith. Let us not *pray* one thing and *say* another—fresh water and salt water from the same spring. Nobody is more convincing to you about serious things than *yourself*. If you pray one thing in the morning and in the afternoon curse your own prayers by speaking doubt, doom, and gloom, you are working against yourself, sowing doubt at one moment after striving in prayer to speak faith to the same thing. This doesn't mean you create a fable or become neurotic in respect to a struggle you are having, and how you speak of it (i.e., "I'm a millionaire, I'm a millionaire!" when in fact you are having a hard time making ends meet). But it is fine to pray in faith and yet say, "This is hard, I don't know the way forward of myself, but God is with us." Let us seek to become people of faith is all aspects of our lives, not sequester faith to our times of prayer, or during a church service.

I deeply appreciate the words of Thomas à Kempis in the *Imitation of Christ* (Book I, chapter 10) on this subject:

Shun the gossip of men as much as possible, for discussion of worldly affairs, even though sincere, is a great distraction inasmuch as we are quickly ensnared and captivated by vanity. Many a time I wish that I had held my peace and had not associated with men. Why, indeed, do we converse and gossip among ourselves when we so seldom part without a troubled conscience? We do so because we seek comfort from one another's conversation and wish to ease the mind wearied by diverse thoughts. Hence, we talk and think quite fondly of things we like very much or of things we dislike intensely. But, sad to say, we often talk vainly and to no purpose; for this external pleasure effectively bars inward and divine consolation. Therefore we must watch and pray lest time pass idly. When the right and opportune moment comes for speaking, say something that will edify.

Let the words of my mouth and the meditation of my heart be acceptable in your sight, O Lord, my rock and my redeemer.
¯Psalm 19:4

Day 6

Beloved, if our heart does not condemn us, we have confidence before God; [22] and whatever we ask we receive from him, because we keep his commandments and do what pleases him. [23] And this is his commandment, that we believe in the name of his Son Jesus Christ and love one another, just as he has commanded us. [24] Whoever keeps his commandments **abides in God, and God in him.** *̄ 1 John 3:21-24*

He continues these thoughts in the next chapter...

God is love, and **whoever abides in love abides in God, and God abides in him**... *If anyone says, "I love God," and hates his brother, he is a liar; for he who does not love his brother whom he has seen cannot love God whom he has not seen. [21] And this commandment we have from him: whoever loves God must also love his brother. ̄ 1 John 4:16, 20-21*

The full richness of John's thought under the inspiration of the Spirit is not to be missed; 1 John is short and direct, and I suggest you read the whole of it as soon as possible. But these excerpts will serve us for this chapter.

John speaks of an *abiding in Christ*—an abiding in God's love. The mature person of prayer recognizes that successful prayer is achieved not as a worm crying into the Throne Room from outside, but rather by humbly recognizing we have been invited into the presence of God, we do all we can to abide there, and from a place of security and God-given confidence we present our petitions to God and believe we receive as we ask. As Jesus tells us:

If you abide in me, *and my words abide in you, ask whatever you wish, and it will be done for you. ̄ John 15:7*

How does one abide, then? If it is such a key to answered prayer, we should certainly be asking that question. I believe abiding is a way of life that involves seeking Christ consistently in the setting of a believing community, repenting, obeying, and serving. But John puts a serious point on things in his letter that I am driving at here: *we must love one another.* Abiding is impossible without love for one another, and answered prayer is impossible apart from abiding.

Now, I gave my heart to Christ when I was 15. That was over forty years ago (you can do the math), and I've been around Christians ever since. And knowing myself and others, I can say from experience that Christians tend to think Christians hating other Christians is something that *other people do*—not themselves. No matter how mean, how sharp-tongued, how apathetic, how contentious and exclusive, somehow those attitudes end up getting "sanctified" in our minds to excuse us of our sin. This creates a blindness in us when John has the audacity to tell us we need to repent of hating one another, and buckle down and love one another. But this passage is written for us all, because we tend to want to love on *our terms,* which, of course, ends up being something entirely other than the love God requires of us; authentic love always includes an element of *sacrifice.*

In the future I will circle back to this theme and what it means to be a church community of love. For now let it be a matter of concerted prayer, of asking God to work in us as we worship, and repent, and forgive, and watch our tongues. Oh Lord Jesus, make me a person of profound love—not a hypothetical love, not a "spiritual" love, but rather cords of human kindness, tender words, genuine concern and generosity, turning the other cheek, mildness and sweetness of spirit. Let us be, as Jesus said we could be and would be, known by all people as His disciples *by our love* (John 13:35).

What is it to be the church of Jesus Christ? Again, He speaks, this time from Revelation 2:2-4...

I know your works, your toil and your patient endurance, and how you cannot bear with those who are evil, but have tested those who call themselves apostles and are not, and found them to be false. I know you are enduring patiently and bearing up for my name's sake, and you have not grown weary. But I have this against you, that you have abandoned the love you had at first.

Many have spoken of this passage as referring to our first love for God. But the truth is that the text of Scripture makes no such restriction. Jesus is concerned about the love of the Ephesians church across the board. After reading 1 John, we already know that from God's perspective there is no authentic love for Him if we do not love one another. So Jesus reproved the Ephesian church—powerful, influential, numerous, strong in works and doctrine—for one reason and one reason alone: they lacked love.

These things are given us because by God's power we are able. After all, John also tells us God's commands are not burdensome. Let us be in earnest, seek the Lord, and love one another deeply, from the heart (1 Peter 4:8).

Day 7

To cite à Kempis once again, he remarks shortly, *"Curb your appetite and you will more easily curb every inclination of the flesh.*"(*Imitation of Christ*, Book 1, chapter 19). There is a great deal of truth in these words. Note that à Kempis does not speak of *hunger*, which is a God-given and natural bodily function. Rather, he speaks of *appetite*. Appetite is connected to our emotions and desires as much, and in some cases more, than it is to our body. There have been many times when I was fully satisfied by a meal, but was tempted to eat a rich dessert, not because I needed it or even felt the slightest bit hungry for it, but because of the visual and emotional delight that it promised me (and almost never delivers on, by the way). Giving unbridled leave to our appetite never strengthens us spiritually; it almost invariably enables those aspects of our character that run counter to sound and mature spirituality.

It is unbridled appetite, not hunger, that is the driving force behind what has been named throughout Christian history as one of the Seven Deadly Sins: *Gluttony*. Referring back to previous chapters, if a critical tongue has gotten something of a "bye" in our Christian culture, gluttony is nearly forgotten altogether. What is gluttony? Gluttony, like all sins, is the distortion of a good thing beyond the limits of its God-given intention. Earning a fair wage to support our family and be generous is good; *greed* is the distortion of that good; a healthy, moral sexual relationship within marriage as God intended is good; *lust* is a distortion of that good; eating and drinking tasty food for sustenance, fellowship, and enjoyment is good; *gluttony* is a distortion of that good.

I have observed from both Christian writings and experience over the years that there are two basic kinds of gluttony. First, there is simply eating *too much*. Second, there's the "dainty" kind of gluttony—not eating too much necessarily, but being absurdly picky to a fault, being an "eating prima donna." (And based on this, *one must never judge by appearances*; one person may appear larger than another, but for all we know the thinner person is a "dainty glutton" while the heavier person is simply genetically prone or has health issues we do not know about.) When these become entrenched in our lives, both of these forms of gluttony are essentially gastronomical lust, and lust is a form of idolatry. Idolatry is the exaltation of the created order to a place of lordship over us, a position only the Creator should have, and idolatry blocks the blessing of God in our lives.

God has given us food, delicious food, and we are grateful for it. He enjoys that we enjoy His creation. But the hard truth is that no one bound by gluttony truly enjoys food, because food has become their master and they its slave.

True joy comes through liberty. Ecclesiastes 10:17 declares, *"Happy are you, O land, when your king is the son of the nobility, and your princes feast at the proper time, for strength, and not for drunkenness!"*

Fasting is not about abstaining from gluttony for a time, but rather breaking gluttony off of our lives—fasting and prayer liberates. God does not desire or require us to fast all the time, but He does require that we shun gluttony all the time, as He does any other sin. A fast "hits the reset button" on this issue by refocusing our affections on Christ, revealing gluttony for what it is, and opening the way for God to work a deep and refreshing repentance in our lives. Sometimes a fast serves as a guard to us: we may not be gluttons in the sense most understand, but fasting strengthens us and builds perspective in us.

I encourage you to fast as God leads you. And I encourage you to expect a breakthrough.

Day 8

Today, the subject is *faith*, which I've already mentioned when writing about the Word of God a few days ago. Faith is the currency of our relationship with God; it is how we are saved, and it is how prayer is answered. A friend of mine observed that, practically speaking, the difference between an authentic New Testament Christian and a mere religious churchgoer is the sense that God is hearing the genuine believer and answering their prayers. This doesn't mean all prayers are answered like an order for Combo #1 at the McDonalds Drive Thru (i.e., to our timing and taste), but they are being answered.

How can this subject be adequately addressed? It is the theme of all Scripture. I have opted to list a series of passages I find particularly powerful and helpful on the subject. My only remark will be this, before I present my litany: faith is not an abstract ability to believe that something will happen, like a spiritual superpower. Faith is fundamentally relational trust. Pharaoh told Moses (Exodus5:2), *"Who is the LORD, that I should obey his voice and let Israel go? I do not know the LORD, and moreover, I will not let Israel go,"* while Paul tells us that, *"obedience comes from faith"* (Romans 1:5). The more we *know* the Lord, the more we will *obey* Him, because knowledge of God ultimately equates to *faith*. Think of how a small child trusts her own father over against a stranger, and you get the idea.

This is a time of drawing near to God, to know Him better. As you desire the Lord relationally, He will answer, and your faith will grow.

Here are the verses to edify your spirit...

And he believed the LORD, and he counted it to him as righteousness. ~ Genesis 15:6

And Jesus answered them, "Have faith in God. [23] Truly, I say to you, whoever says to this mountain, 'Be taken up and thrown into the sea,' and does not doubt in his heart, but believes that what he says will come to pass, it will be done for him. ˜ Mark 11:22-23

Trust in the LORD with all your heart, and do not lean on your own understanding. [6] In all your ways acknowledge him, and he will make straight your paths. ˜ Proverbs 3:5-6

Now faith is the assurance of things hoped for, the conviction of things not seen. ˜ Hebrews 11:1

And without faith it is impossible to please him, for whoever would draw near to God must believe that he exists and that he rewards those who seek him. ˜ Hebrews 11:6

We walk by faith, not by sight. ˜ 2 Corinthians 5:7

And Jesus said to him, "'If you can'! All things are possible for one who believes." ˜ Mark 9:23

"Let not your hearts be troubled. Believe in God; believe also in me. ˜ John 14:1

For in it the righteousness of God is revealed from faith for faith, as it is written, "The righteous shall live by faith." ˜ Romans 1:17

"Behold, God is my salvation; I will trust, and will not be afraid; for the LORD GOD is my strength and my song, and he has become my salvation." ˜ Isaiah 12:2

May the God of hope fill you with all joy and peace in believing, so that by the power of the Holy Spirit you may abound in hope.
˜ Romans 15:13

Day 9

The prayer of a righteous person has great power as it is working. [17] Elijah was a man with a nature like ours, and he prayed fervently that it might not rain, and for three years and six months it did not rain on the earth. [18] Then he prayed again, and heaven gave rain, and the earth bore its fruit. ⁻*James 5:16–18*

So much could be said about this passage, and perhaps I will revisit some of its other aspects in the future. At this point, however, I want to touch on the *character* of Elijah's prayer. Elijah prayed *fervently* (or as other versions render it, *earnestly*). The Greek more literally reads something like "he prayed with *prayer*," or maybe even "he prayed *prayingly*" (not good English, but it gets the point across). The whole passage refers to the commonness of Elijah's human nature, his righteous standing with God, and the power of his prayer when he offered it *fervently*.

I believe this passage should give us pause, so that we step out of the "biblical world" and give thought to our "real world"—and realize that there should be no distinction between the two. God's Word is speaking to us where we are. This is why James tells us that Elijah was a man with a nature like our own, so that we would apply the lesson to ourselves. Somehow, Christian people have convinced themselves that prayer is to be staid, calm, dispassionate. Religion that stirs people's souls is somehow seen as fanatical and not for respectable people.

Such a view would be entirely alien to biblical figures such as the Patriarchs, Moses, Joshua, David, and the rest of the prophets. New Testament men and women would be equally baffled by this approach. I look at the classic, well-known Heinrich Hofmann painting of Jesus in Gethsemane, beseeching His Father with hands clasped and face serenely upturned. Images such as this, sadly, have done more to affect our collective thinking about how Jesus actually prayed in His most desperate hour than the Scriptures themselves. Consider this passage from Hebrews:

In the days of his flesh, **Jesus offered up prayers and supplications, with loud cries and tears,** *to him who was able to save him from death, and he was heard because of his reverence.* ¯*Hebrews 5:7*

A simple internet search of "cry to the Lord" will yield copious results from Scripture. The Psalms especially reflect a culture of personal prayer that is anything but "churchy." Rather, biblical prayer is often gut-wrenching, confrontational, desperately transparent, and life changing. It is about pouring out the heart, dredging deep, expressing the inexpressible in its hunger for God and refusal to settle for less than God's promises, even (or especially) when God seems elusive.

Our *fervency* of prayer is connected to our *faith.* True, sincere fervency of this kind comes from the depths of our spirit, empowered by the Holy Spirit, and is not mere emotion. When we allow ourselves to let go and pray fervently, passionately, as the heroes of the faith did, things move. Sometimes that which moves is within me and not in the world around me, but in the end such a prayer is "powerful and effective."

Day 10

Today I would like to begin to address the nature of prayer itself. To this end, Paul tells us...

*And pray in the Spirit on all occasions with **all kinds of prayers and requests**. With this in mind, be alert and always keep on praying for all the saints. ⁻ Ephesians 6:18 (NIV84)*

This lets us know there are different kinds of prayer, and in the days to come I will touch on some of them. For several chapters, I'd like to discuss the matter of *petition*.

Petition might be considered the most basic kind of prayer, and rightly so. Even Jesus seems to acknowledge this. Petition is asking God for something, either for ourselves or for somebody else (I will discuss the prayer of *intercession* later). What is the nature of petition? We get insight from Jesus:

*And he said to them, "Which of you who has a friend will go to him at midnight and say to him, 'Friend, lend me three loaves,⁶ for a friend of mine has arrived on a journey, and I have nothing to set before him';⁷ and he will answer from within, 'Do not bother me; the door is now shut, and my children are with me in bed. I cannot get up and give you anything'?⁸ I tell you, though he will not get up and give him anything because he is his friend, **yet because of his impudence he will rise and give him whatever he needs.**⁹ And I tell you, ask, and it will be given to you; seek, and you will find; knock, and it will be opened to you.¹⁰ For everyone who asks receives, and the one who seeks finds, and to the one who knocks it will be opened.¹¹ What father among you, if his son asks for a fish, will instead of a fish give him a serpent;¹² or if he asks for an egg, will give him a scorpion?¹³ If you then, who are evil, know how to give good gifts to your children, how much more will the heavenly Father give the Holy Spirit to those who ask him!" ⁻ Luke 11:5-13*

Consider also,

And he told them a parable to the effect that they ought always to pray and not lose heart. ² *He said, "In a certain city there was a judge who neither feared God nor respected man.* ³ *And there was a widow in that city who kept coming to him and saying, 'Give me justice against my adversary.'* ⁴ *For a while he refused, but afterward he said to himself, 'Though I neither fear God nor respect man,* ⁵ **yet because this widow keeps bothering me**, *I will give her justice, so that she will not beat me down by her continual coming.'"* ⁶ *And the Lord said, "Hear what the unrighteous judge says.* ⁷ *And will not God give justice to his elect, who cry to him day and night? Will he delay long over them?* ⁸ *I tell you, he will give justice to them speedily. Nevertheless, when the Son of Man comes, will he find faith on earth?"* ˜ *Luke 18:1-8*

Leaving aside for the moment the matter of God's benevolence and willingness to answer His children—a theme in itself—a common thread between these two lessons, both of which include parables, is the matter of persistence. In both cases, Jesus tells stories about people who basically bug the daylights out of the person they are asking a favor from. They do so in ways that run counter to the acceptable norms of Jesus' day, and even our day. One simply doesn't knock on a neighbor's door after bedtime and ask for a loaf of bread to entertain an unexpected visitor. And as for the relative wisdom of irritating a judge who is weighing a case in which you are a plaintiff, well, I'll leave that up to you to determine. Jesus' choice of metaphor here is deliberate: He wants us to understand that prayer is a matter of fierce persistence— even *impudence* (a fancy word for *shameless rudeness*). *Impudent persistence*, like *fervor* (yesterday's chapter), both relate to faith and are, in fact, closely related to each other. If your child is injured and you are rushing them, bleeding, into the emergency room, you are shamelessly rude; you don't care how many people you interrupt or inconvenience in the process of getting them proper care. Your fervor makes you impudent and persistent. I think of Rocky Balboa's prayer in the 1976 movie *Rocky*, in which he promises never to bother God again if he can just "go the distance" with Apollo Creed, is the kind of prayer God *never* wants to hear (no matter how the movie turned out). God *wants* to be bothered, He *longs* to hear from us—continually. The "Gee shucks, God, I don't mean to bother You" approach is completely contrary to God's will as taught by His Son. What mortals consider an irritating pest, God considers a precious child of great faith.

Remember this as you go to ask God for what you will: If it weren't part of human nature to get discouraged and give up on prayer, Jesus wouldn't have taught this. And if humans didn't have a distorted view of God, Jesus would not have taught this. We need our minds renewed in God's Word. We must humble ourselves to God's way of thinking, we must surrender presumption, we must persist and model our prayers after the impudence of the rude neighbor and the pesky widow. God wants us to act that way. Jesus said so.

Day 11

Continuing in the theme of petition, I want to discuss the metaphor of Jesus used in both Luke 11 and Matthew 7, namely, "ask, seek, and knock." Here are the passages:

Ask, and it will be given to you; seek, and you will find; knock, and it will be opened to you. 8 For everyone who asks receives, and the one who seeks finds, and to the one who knocks it will be opened. 9 Or which one of you, if his son asks him for bread, will give him a stone? 10 Or if he asks for a fish, will give him a serpent? 11 If you then, who are evil, know how to give good gifts to your children, how much more will your Father who is in heaven give good things to those who ask him! ‐ *Matthew 7:7-11*

And I tell you, ask, and it will be given to you; seek, and you will find; knock, and it will be opened to you. 10 For everyone who asks receives, and the one who seeks finds, and to the one who knocks it will be opened. 11 What father among you, if his son asks for a fish, will instead of a fish give him a serpent; 12 or if he asks for an egg, will give him a scorpion? 13 If you then, who are evil, know how to give good gifts to your children, how much more will the heavenly Father give the Holy Spirit to those who ask him! ‐ *Luke 11:9-13*

We can see that these passages are nearly (but not quite) identical. It is highly probable that Jesus taught this lesson multiple times in different contexts, even as Matthew and Luke present them differently (Matthew as Jesus taught the Sermon on the Mount, Luke as Jesus taught His disciples privately about prayer). This means this was especially important to Him.

We can interpret Jesus' three illustrations of petitioning God differently. One way would be to see them as artful synonyms for prayer. From that angle, asking, seeking, and knocking would all be basically the *same thing* but expressed in *different ways* to drive the point home through varied metaphors. Asking, seeking, and knocking could all, therefore, be seen as the same thing: petition, no more and no less.

Another way to see them is as *successive stages* of petition, with each stage becoming more intense and effectively a more advanced stage of petition. To *ask* is one thing—we might ask a total stranger for something. To *seek* is deeper; seeking cannot be done as casually as asking might be, and usually indicates something greater is at stake. *Knocking* is greatest of all, because it requires stepping onto turf that is by definition not our own and petitioning entrance; knocking is the least casual of the three and demands the most earnest humility.

While both of these interpretations have merit, I lean towards the second. I believe Jesus was trying to drive home the matter of persistence and the (seemingly paradoxical) truth that, by nature, the more we press into God, the more is required of us as He leads us deeper. Put another way, the more we receive from God, the more He pulls out of us into Himself. He grows greater and we grow less (John 3:30), even as He stoops down to make us great (Psalm 18:35).

When we ask, seek, and knock, we move into the realm of appropriating the promises that follow. Jesus assures us by way of comparison that God the Father loves us, because even fallen, mortal fathers are good to their children. As we move from *asking* God for things to *seeking* that which is deeper, to (finally) *knocking* and even pounding on God's door for entrance, we should know that we are not on a wild goose chase. Some things require only asking, some matters seeking, and some issues knocking. But whatever we find ourselves doing, however we petition God, we should begin and end with the understanding that God loves us more than any human love can conceive, and He is working for our good. He doesn't give stones, snakes, and scorpions where bread, eggs, or fish are what we need and desire.

Day 12

Now, in respect to the prayer of petition, there is a matter that is of some confusion to some people and should be explained. Jesus tells us this in Matthew 6...

And when you pray, do not heap up empty phrases as the Gentiles do, for they think that they will be heard for their many words. Do not be like them, for your Father knows what you need before you ask him. ˜ Matthew 6:7-8

Some have taken this word from the Lord as an absolute principle, to the point that they scold others for asking the Father for something more than once. "God is not mentally challenged," I once heard a pastor chide as he preached against asking God for something more than once.

No, He most certainly is not—not even when He gives us parables like that of the persistent widow in Luke 18 and Himself prays the same thing repeatedly in the Garden of Gethsemane (Matthew 26:39-44; see also the parallels in Mark 14 and Luke 22). Praying the same thing repeatedly is not only Jesus' teaching, it is His practice. Why then does He tell us what He does in Matthew 6?

This is not a matter of contradiction, but matter of clarification, because the truth of both principles reveals the true nature of petition. Jesus does not pray the same thing over and over the night He is betrayed in order to inform the Father, as if God doesn't know, or praying thrice is going to capture God's attention more than once or twice. And He certainly isn't trying to rack up favor points with God in some way, thinking three prayers "count" three times as much as one does. That is the ignorant, pagan thinking that Jesus warns us against. Only people who do not know God think and pray that way.

No, Jesus prays multiple times—and tells us to do the same— because persistent prayer about the same request *positions us* in God's presence. It is what old time Pentecostals used to call "praying through." God is not deaf, or ignorant, or in need of arm twisting. But we are in the natural world and see through a glass darkly. Faith, the currency of prayer, is a *spiritual substance* (Hebrews 11:1). We must pray repeatedly not to engage our *need* more, or to "convince" God; we pray repeatedly to position ourselves in God's presence, to engage *God Himself in respect to our need.* It is the same principle as *waiting* upon God—which is *never* a matter of toe tapping while God finally gets on the ball and catches up with us, and *always* a matter of us deeply submitting to God's larger designs in the midst of our asking and God working in us and others. Reading between the lines, it is clear that God conquering our *need,* no matter how great it is to us, is a small thing to Him, while God conquering *us and our will* is another thing entirely. God uses our need to draw us deeper into Himself. Let us remember, Jesus died to bring us back into fellowship with the Father, and everything else He provides is effectively a by-product of that redemption (see Matthew 6:33 and Romans 8:32).

By persistent and, yes, even *repetitive* prayer, we press into God. If we do this in a detached fashion, simply repeating by wrote a prayer thinking we will "pray through," we fall into the ignorance Jesus warns us against. We won't get anywhere that way. But if we fervently pursue God, pestering Him like the widow does the unjust judge, over and over, we are promised a breakthrough. Remember, what we seek, first and last, is God's presence as we pray. By positioning ourselves there, and abiding there, petition becomes effective.

Day 13

Today, let's discuss the subject of *thanksgiving*. Paul tells us in Philippians...

Do not be anxious about anything, but in everything by prayer and supplication **with thanksgiving** *let your requests be made known to God. And the peace of God, which surpasses all understanding, will guard your hearts and your minds in Christ Jesus.* ‾ *Philippians 4:6-7*

Similarly, Paul tells us,

...Be filled with the Spirit, addressing one another in psalms and hymns and spiritual songs, singing and making melody to the Lord with your heart, giving **thanks always and for everything** *to God the Father in the name of our Lord Jesus Christ...*
                                                                    ‾ *Ephesians 5:18-20*

For my money, thanksgiving is one of the most underplayed power factors in an effective prayer life—in spite of abundant scriptural testimony regarding its importance. The prayer of thanksgiving is really a kind of prayer all its own. It is a prayer that bridges the gap between *praise and worship* on one hand and *petition* on the other. As with worship, thanksgiving refocuses our spirit on the glory and power of God, but more specifically it expresses gratitude in specific terms for what God has already done on our behalf. As such it opens our eyes in the midst of our (sometimes desperately felt) need, because as we give God thanks, we remind ourselves of how good God has been to us. Consider David's spiritual strategy in a time of great distress:

"Will the Lord spurn forever, and never again be favorable? Has his steadfast love forever ceased? Are his promises at an end for all time? Has God forgotten to be gracious? Has he in anger shut up his compassion?" Then I said, **"I will appeal to this, to the years of the right hand of the Most High. I will remember the deeds of**

the LORD; yes, I will remember your wonders of old. I will ponder all your work, and meditate on your mighty deeds."

- Psalm 77:7-12

Remembering God's goodness and giving Him thanks brings to our inner man that vital component of faith in prayer: *perspective.* When we lose perspective, our faith suffers; when we keep perspective, faith is restored.

And, of course, *faith* is the issue when we pray. A person who gives thanks as they pray—like including salt in the process of baking bread—keeps their *God* bigger than their *need.* Everyone has, at one point or another, prayed in such a way as to essentially recite all their problems, one after another, until by the end they are more discouraged than they were at the beginning. By focusing on their need rather than on the God who resolves those needs, their God became smaller than their problems, leading to spiritual defeat. God, of course, still fills the universe, but once again we are dealing with perspective and the faith that results from it—be it healthy faith or anemic faith.

This is why Paul tells us to give thanks *as we pray.* Like Jesus Himself in Mark 11:24, we are believing we receive before we see the manifestation. We walk by faith, not by sight. The ultimate expression of the Christian who sees God as more than able to meet them at the point of their need is thanking Him in advance for His response.

If you feel like your needs are gang piling upon you and beating you down, give thanks to God and let His praise flow out of your spirit. This turns the tables on your spiritual condition. It can be grueling to do this, and actually contradict how you feel. But there is great power in it. Thanksgiving in prayer, especially before we see a desperately needed answer, is a *sacrifice.* Again, David speaks to us:

The one who offers **thanksgiving as his sacrifice** *glorifies me; to one who orders his way rightly I will show* **the salvation of God!"**

⁻ Psalm 50:23

When we give thanks, *order* comes to our inner being—in the form of divine perspective and a correcting of inner matters—that leads to answered prayer, the salvation of God.

Day 14

Before moving on to intercession, I'd like to bring up one more very important item regarding petition. This is the matter of *motive.*

James tells us this,

What causes quarrels and what causes fights among you? Is it not this, that your passions are at war within you? **²** *You desire and do not have, so you murder. You covet and cannot obtain, so you fight and quarrel.* **You do not have, because you do not ask.** **³** **You ask and do not receive, because you ask wrongly, to spend it on your passions.** **⁴** *You adulterous people! Do you not know that friendship with the world is enmity with God? Therefore whoever wishes to be a friend of the world makes himself an enemy of God.*
- James 4:1-5

It is tempting to lift the latter part of verse 2 and the whole of verse 3 out of their context and deal with this issue as a kind of principle (or pair of principles) of prayer, that is, "I don't have because I don't ask. Check. And I need to make sure my motives are sound. Check #2. Got it."

Beware of reducing things to "principles to live by," especially in respect to true spiritual maturity, because only in the rarest cases can that be done without doing violence to Scripture. James is not talking about "principles" here, he is talking about *our hearts.* "You have not because you ask not" is something we've already covered, and is certainly a powerful truth. God does not respond to *need,* but to *faith expressed in prayer by a submitted disciple.* We need to ask God, and for this reason I resist the trite chiding I've heard so often from those who want to scold fellow Christians that "God is not Santa Claus" (i.e., so don't keep peppering Him with requests). They're right, He's not: Santa takes limited requests, while God wants to hear from us directly, all the time. (And God doesn't make you wait until someone else tells Him what *they* want.)

But James spends far more time addressing the matter of motive. He describes a people fraught with quarreling, covetousness, passions, and even murder (perhaps meaning murder in their hearts, or hatred, which Jesus has told us has the same spiritual effect). *In this context* he tells them that they don't have because they don't ask, and when they do ask, they do so (predictably, per his description of them) with impure motives. God will not and indeed *cannot* answer such prayers. In other words, to ask with impure motives is, for all intents and purposes, to offer an "un-prayer" to God; it is as if the prayer hadn't been offered at all.

But how can this be? Are our hearts ever truly pure in this life? Aren't our motives always mixed to some degree? Well, there's no need to debate that, because what follows strikes at the heart of the issue: The people James speaks to have made friends with the world, and that has alienated them from God. On a whole, their hearts are in a bad place. They are not abiding in Christ, they are cozying up to the world system, its values, lusts, and perspective. How can they possibly be asking for the right thing?

So our takeaway from this ought to be twofold. First, we should order our affections carefully, comprehensively repent of looking at the world as if it were our home, and do all in our power to draw near to God as our Father, Savior, and friend. Second, and by corollary, we should not think that asking for something we might enjoy falls under the category of "spending what we get on our passions." God wants us to be at peace and enjoy life. He just wants those things (and indeed can only grant them) when we are walking close to Him. If our lives bear the marks of the strife James describes, we should pause and take stock. But if we do abide in Christ, and ask God to examine our hearts as we ask Him for things, He will guide us.

Day 15

*The next day Moses said to the people, "You have sinned a great sin. And now I will go up to the LORD; perhaps I can make atonement for your sin."³¹ So Moses returned to the LORD and said, "Alas, this people has sinned a great sin. They have made for themselves gods of gold.³² **But now, if you will forgive their sin—but if not, please blot me out of your book that you have written."***

⁻ Exodus 32:30-32

*And **I sought for a man among them who should build up the wall and stand in the breach before me for the land, that I should not destroy it,** but I found none.³¹ Therefore I have poured out my indignation upon them. I have consumed them with the fire of my wrath. I have returned their way upon their heads, declares the Lord GOD." ⁻ Ezekiel 22:30-31*

Today I'd like to move on from *petition* and into *intercession*. Some might make the case that intercession is a form of petition, but as I'm not trying to quibble but rather explain, I'm treating it as a separate kind of prayer. As usual, the best way to begin is with the Scriptures, and the two I have presented might be seen as the quintessential passages on the subject.

As we can perceive, intercession has to do with *praying for someone else.* But praying for the needs of another crosses the line from petition into intercession when it takes on a certain character. In other words, I might ask the Lord to meet another person's need without it necessarily being intercession. Moses demonstrates the heart of an intercessor by *identifying* with those he is praying for to the extent that he is willing to literally surrender his eternal salvation for their sakes, so great is his compassion for them. That God (in verse 33) immediately turns down Moses' offer is beside the point; Moses has already shown what God needed to see and hear, and reprieve is granted to Israel after what Jews to this day consider the nation's vilest sin ever.

The passage from Ezekiel is probably the one most quoted in reference to intercession, and its truths are manifold. God makes clear that His will is to have mercy on Jerusalem, but *He cannot do so* unless someone "stands in the breach" of prayer for the nation's sake. Finding none, He pours out His wrath. Again, we have the idea of a person of prayer standing in the "in between"— the "mercy gap" between God's wrath and our sin; we see a sense of substitution, of taking the place of someone else who cannot (or hasn't the sense to) pray for themselves. In the case of Moses, the intercessor was found; in the passage from Ezekiel, they were not. In both, we learn that God responds to prayer from one who spiritually takes the place of the person in need of God's mercy and *prays as if he or she were them.*

Of course, the ultimate model of intercession is the Cross: Jesus is the ideal intercessor, the Great High Priest. Crucified, He stood in the breach of all breaches; He laid down His life and bore the weight of the eternal damnation that Moses refers to, but himself never could have borne because only Jesus was and is up to the task. But Jesus sets an example for us to follow, even if we follow it knowing our intercession operates in the shadow of His Cross and the power of His resurrection. For this reason, Paul speaks as he does in Romans...

I am speaking the truth in Christ—I am not lying; my conscience bears me witness in the Holy Spirit— ² *that I have great sorrow and unceasing anguish in my heart.* ³ **For I could wish that I myself were accursed and cut off from Christ for the sake of my brothers,** *my kinsmen according to the flesh.* ¯ *Romans 9:1–3*

Paul's emulation of Christ's intercession (and doubtless taking the specifics of his wording from Moses as well) teaches us a great deal about Paul's effectiveness as the early church's model missionary. Soul-winning and intercession go hand in hand.

There is a lot to say about intercession that we should cover, but beyond what I've already said, I will say this for now: Intercession, by its nature, can never be dispassionate, detached, or aloof. The intercessor not only shows concern, they *identify* with the plight of the one they are praying for in a way that grips their entire inner being. They pray for another as if the burden that person is bearing were their own. Effective intercession flows in and through a heart of compassion, a compassion born and sustained of the Holy Spirit and not of the natural man. True intercessory compassion is not to be confused with sentiment or "touchy feely" sympathy— an emotion that makes us feel good about ourselves but often leaves the person we feel for in precisely the same condition they are suffering. Rather, it is grounded in God's desire to redeem and liberate people from bondage and bring about His great purposes in their lives.

Let us pray and ask God that He use us as intercessors, because through intercession God does His greatest work.

Day 16

I would like to continue in the vein of intercession, returning to the passage from Ezekiel I touched on yesterday:

And I sought for a man among them who should build up the wall and stand in the breach before me for the land, that I should not destroy it, but I found none.[31] *Therefore I have poured out my indignation upon them. I have consumed them with the fire of my wrath. I have returned their way upon their heads, declares the Lord GOD." - Ezekiel 22:30-31*

Briefly touched upon yesterday, I will go deeper into a truth revealed in what appears to be a strong paradox in the passage.

It is clear from the whole of v. 31 that God's *desire* is to preserve Jerusalem and the land of Judah. He does not want to destroy it. But in order for His goodwill towards them to be realized, He needs an intercessor to pray for the divine will to come to pass. Mere petition is not enough; someone must "build up the wall and stand in the breach"—clearly referring to a spiritual reality and not a natural one. This means that someone must step up, fiercely and passionately identify with Judah's sinful plight, feel the weight of both God's wrath and God's mercy, and pray until the breakthrough comes. God looks for such a one, but cannot find him or her. The result (v. 32) is that God's wrath is poured out, Jerusalem and her temple are destroyed, and the people are carried into exile. The "therefore" at the beginning of v. 32 tells us that God's manifest wrath is the immediate consequence—not of His perfect will, which we understand from His description of His futile search for an intercessor—but of not being able to find such a one. (Note also that the opposite result takes place time and again in respect to Moses and the Israelites in the wilderness.)

I remember the testimony of my first pastor, Lester Sumrall. When he was a young missionary, he was traveling in China with a group of people in a remote area. Sick with severe dysentery, he was literally bleeding to death from his bowels. He had to drop out of his group and rest by the wayside, hoping to catch up later. Instead, he swooned from blood loss and lay helpless on the ground. Back in the States, the Holy Spirit woke one of Sumrall's supporters from a sound sleep, revealing to her that Lester Sumrall was dying at that very moment from Chinese dysentery. She knew all this by the Spirit, but was exhausted from her day's work and asked God to find someone else to pray. His response? *There is no one else to pray.* So she arose and prayed until the burden lifted, and when it did, the Spirit spoke to her and said, *"He will live."* Sumrall awoke from his unconscious state, completely healed. He got up and was able to continue his journey. He did not know about the intercessor back in the States until months later when he returned.

Both the Scripture and this testimony (and many others) communicate a powerful truth: God is all powerful, but He will not and indeed *cannot move* without prayer. In the big picture, God will always have His way. But in the immediate, an important principle comes into play: even if something is His will, He responds only to the prayers of His people to bring it about. Why is this?

Psalm 115:16 gives us a clue...

The heavens are the LORD's heavens, **but the earth he has given to the children of man.**

The earth belongs to the Lord (Ps 24:1-2), but He has entrusted this part of creation to humanity by covenant. The closest thing we can use from the human realm to illustrate this truth is a lease. God, in fashion similar to a human landlord, will not violate the lease and enter the "property" in question without permission from the lessee. For this reason, God partners with His people through prayer to bring about His will in the world. This teaching doesn't contradict the truth of God's omnipotence—as if God needed us in the way we need Him—because the very nature of covenant is that a strong partner chooses to limit the expression of their own

60

strength on behalf of the weaker (as does the owner of a house when he leases it out). In the end, the lease expires and the landlord enters the property whether the lessee desires it or not (this we call the Second Coming of Jesus Christ), but *until then* this is how things are. For this reason the old adage, "God does nothing except by the prayers of His people" is very true.

And so we must pray, we must intercede. God's desire to move in our midst, to convert sinners and set the captive free, is not enough in and of itself. If it were, God's desire to preserve His people as described in Ezekiel 22:30 would have sufficed, and would have been followed by a very different outcome in verse 31.

Let us be the one God finds, so He can show mercy and blessing rather than allow the consequence of sin take its terrible toll.

Day 17

Continuing in the theme of intercession, let's note a central truth that we've already implied, but is stated explicitly in Hebrews 7:25...

Consequently, [Jesus] is able to save to the uttermost those who draw near to God through him, since he always lives to make intercession for them.

This verse is one of the great verses in the New Testament that describes Jesus Christ's continual heavenly ministry on behalf of the church; fundamentally, Jesus' ministry at the right hand of the Father is a priestly one of intercession. Without launching into a full-blown discussion of Christology (the theology of Christ), let me just observe that this tells us a great deal about the heart of God. The divine motive for the Incarnation is multifaceted, and its depth will take an eternity to reveal, but this much we know: God became Man in large part so He Himself could intercede for us.

This truth should come as no surprise given what we have already read. Moses and others pleading with God is not an act of convincing God to change His mind and His will. God is already more merciful than we can imagine, more willing to do His creation good than our heart can conceive. No, for reasons we have discussed, intercession is something He longs to hear so that He can move on behalf of the children of men. Now that Old Covenant truth is confirmed explicitly through New Covenant realities in Christ.

But the ministry of intercession (Greek: *entygchano*) is not used exclusively of Christ in the New Testament. The verb occurs two more times in reference to prayer, both times in this passage from Romans...

Likewise the Spirit helps us in our weakness. For we do not know what to pray for as we ought, but the Spirit himself intercedes for us with groanings too deep for words. And he who searches hearts knows what is the mind of the Spirit, because the Spirit intercedes for the saints according to the will of God. [28] And we know that for those who love God all things work together for good, for those who are called according to his purpose. [29] For those whom he foreknew he also predestined to be conformed to the image of his Son, in order that he might be the firstborn among many brothers. [30] And those whom he predestined he also called, and those whom he called he also justified, and those whom he justified he also glorified. [31] What then shall we say to these things? If God is for us, who can be against us? [32] He who did not spare his own Son but gave him up for us all, how will he not also with him graciously give us all things? [33] Who shall bring any charge against God's elect? It is God who justifies. [34] Who is to condemn? Christ Jesus is the one who died—more than that, who was raised—who is at the right hand of God, who indeed is interceding for us. ~ Romans 8:26-34

The *second instance* (v. 34) practically echoes Hebrews 7:25 and confirms the heart of God as a Lord who longs to hear intercession so much that its activity is bound up in the mystery of the trinitarian Godhead. Of special interest to us here is the *first instance*, because it touches upon God's will for our prayer life.

The gist of Romans 8:26-27 is that the Holy Spirit carries not only the mind and will of God, but also His heart to intercede. As the Spirit indwells us, He empowers us to pray beyond the limitations of our natural human weaknesses. Paul basically describes this weakness as *ignorance*: we do not know how to pray as we ought to pray. Not knowing how to pray as we ought is not just a matter of not being aware of pertinent facts, like whether someone is sick or the specifics of their troubling family circumstances. It goes much deeper than that. It has to do with praying the perfect will of God in all its intricacies and unfathomable subtleties. One who intercedes by the power of the Spirit, beyond the capacity of their own mind to grasp, sees their weakness turn to strength *as the Holy Spirit is actually praying through them.* The intercessory

64

partnership between our devotion and discipline in prayer and the Holy Spirit's limitless power and wisdom is "powerful and effective" (James 5:16) because God Himself intercedes through us.

The deepest level of intercession is praying in the Holy Spirit. We should seek Spirit-saturated lives and ask the Lord for the anointing of intercession to empower us to pray.

Day 18

A significant aspect of intercessory prayer is the question of a *prayer burden* and what it means to pray through that burden. The idea of a "burden"—a metaphor used to describe the sense of Holy Spirit prompting that feels like an inner heaviness—can be perceived in the language of a number of key passages pertaining to intercession in the Old Testament. Men like Moses, Jeremiah, Ezekiel, and Daniel clearly exhibit the traits of men carrying a prayer burden for their people. I think about Nehemiah and his fasting and prayer, which bear all the marks of a working of the Holy Spirit laying Jerusalem upon his heart, far beyond the confines of his own sentiments. Women like Hannah and Esther also prayed and fasted with an angst driven by the Holy Spirit.

There are a couple passages in the New Testament that speak to this sense of deep pray, both written by Paul...

My little children, for whom I am again in **the anguish of childbirth** *until Christ is formed in you!* ‑ *Galatians 4:19*

Epaphras, who is one of you, a servant of Christ Jesus, greets you, **always struggling on your behalf in his prayers***, that you may stand mature and fully assured in all the will of God.*
                                        ‑ *Colossians 4:12*

Both of these passages refer to an arduous, burdensome condition of spirit. The second refers to Epaphras, the founding shepherd of the church at Colossae (see Colossians 1:7), "struggling" in prayer (the NIV translates this "wrestling") for his flock. It is battle prayer of a particular order. Paul's language does not seem to be explicitly about prayer, but it relays his spiritual inner workings towards the Galatians (which is very similar to that of Epaphras towards the Colossians), and for reasons I will now explain I believe does have to do with intercessory prayer.

Yesterday's meditation referred to *groaning.* The verbal form of the word used to describe the Holy Spirit's prayers through us is also found in Romans 8:23 and 2 Corinthians 5:2. Both of these passages refer to our future transition from this mortal existence to the resurrection body—what Paul calls "our adoption as sons." This mirrors the actions of the creation itself, as Paul says,

*For we know that the whole creation has been **groaning together in the pains of childbirth** until now.* Romans 8:22

So the groaning of the Holy Spirit is really spiritual *childbirth*— "birthing" one (better) spiritual reality out of a previous, inferior one. Paul is doing this in reference to the Galatians, his heart gripped with an intercessory burden. Epaphras' "struggling" in prayer reflects this same thing, a shepherd "birthing" spiritual maturity in his people. Note that the same verb is used of Jesus Himself in Mark 7:33-34...

*And taking him aside from the crowd privately, he put his fingers into his ears, and after spitting touched his tongue. And looking up to heaven, **he groaned** and said to him, "Ephphatha," that is, "Be opened."*

Once again, we see this particular type of "spiritual groaning" accompanying an event of profound spiritual change and deliverance, this time a miraculous healing. It is a kind of prayer that is Holy Spirit-empowered, deeply empathetic, and hard work. Not without reason is it likened to a mother giving birth.

The prompt for such prayer is often the *burden* I mentioned above—the burden being the onslaught of "spiritual labor pains." I remember one day in college—with a prayer meeting planned for that night—I felt a particular heaviness. I had never felt it before, and it felt like a cloud hanging over me, as if I were alienated from God. I spent my activities that day asking God to forgive me (for whatever I might have done), but the heaviness did not lift. The Holy Spirit was working in me but I was ignorant of His ways. That night in prayer with others I felt waves of God's sorrow and pain for the lost, and I wept and travailed in prayer, doubling over with (literally) clenching pains in my midsection. Others in our campus fellowship experienced the same thing. I did not know any of what I have shared above. But at the end of the prayer time a lightness filled my spirit and the burden lifted. In the months to follow people began to come to Christ on the campus, and were filled with the Holy Spirit and powerful manifestations took place. I am convinced none of that would have happened had we not prayed.

I believe we can draw close to God and ask that God use us to intercede; it is a choice, not an exclusive calling or "gift" in that sense, reserved for a few. Anyone who desires to be used by God to intercede, God will use. But it is a costly commitment, because it means identifying with God's own heartbreak for the lost and hurting at a whole new level.

May we be open, and follow God's leading for our lives.

Day 19

Moving on from intercession, I'd like to cover one more kind of prayer before we delve into some corollary matters. This last kind is, perhaps, a category of my own making, but it is very real to me and I believe the spirit and character of this kind of prayer is testified to in sources biblical and elsewhere. I would call it the *prayer of fellowship* or the *prayer of communion with the Lord.*

Some might argue that what I am about to present is more of a posture or an attitude, a maturity of faith that permeates all of the prayer we engage in, and not a kind of prayer all its own. I wouldn't debate the point, other than to say from experience that the *prayer of communion* can be practiced all by itself, and someone who cannot do so will not experience its fragrance in other areas of their prayer life.

Consider these words from Thomas à Kempis (*Imitation of Christ,* Book Two, Chapter 8):

> *When Jesus is near, all is well and nothing seems difficult. When He is absent, all is hard. When Jesus does not speak within, all other comfort is empty, but if He says only a word, it brings great consolation.*
>
> *Did not Mary rise at once from her weeping when Martha said to her: "The Master is come, and calls for you"? Happy is the hour when Jesus calls one from tears to joy of spirit.*
>
> *How dry and hard you are without Jesus! How foolish and vain if you desire anything but Him! Is it not a greater loss than losing the whole world? For what, without Jesus, can the world give you? Life without Him is a relentless hell, but living with Him is a sweet paradise. If Jesus be with you, no enemy can harm you.*
>
> *He who finds Jesus finds a rare treasure, indeed, a good above every good, whereas he who loses Him loses more than the whole world. The man who lives without Jesus is the poorest of the poor, whereas no one is so rich as the man who lives in His grace.*

It is a great art to know how to converse with Jesus, and great wisdom to know how to keep Him.

These are the words of someone who has come to the point where he treasures *foundationally* Jesus for who Jesus is to him, and not primarily for what Jesus can do for him. We are mortal, and needy, and weak in our virtue, and we will never get to the point where we are not dependent upon Jesus for the essentials of life. But we can grow to the point in our relationship with Him so that our prayerful intimacy with Him becomes that which we crave the most, and all other prayers are couched in that fellowship rather than our communion with Him being an afterthought.

So many Bible passages reflect this attitude of enjoying God *for His own sake.* Consider David:

...I remember you upon my bed, and meditate on you in the watches of the night; for you have been my help, and in the shadow of your wings I will sing for joy. My soul clings to you; your right hand upholds me. ~ Psalm 63:6-8

Everything about David's words reveals a heart that finds bliss in communion with God. David is dependent, but has moved past a mortal's struggles with that dependency and is now resting joyfully in it. He's glad to be in the shadow of God's wings just because. He is resting, basking, abiding there.

Or this from Psalm 73...

*Whom have I in heaven but you? And there is nothing on earth that I desire besides you. My flesh and my heart may fail, but God is the strength of my heart and my portion forever... **But for me it is good to be near God**; I have made the Lord GOD my refuge, that I may tell of all your works. ~ Psalm 73:25-26, 28*

Psalm 73 is actually a song of complaint, with the writer taking issue with God's justice early, but finding solace and resolution in the end simply by nearness to God.

Or, of course...

One thing have I asked of the LORD, that will I seek after: that I may dwell in the house of the LORD all the days of my life, to gaze upon the beauty of the LORD and to inquire in his temple. ¯ Psalm 27:4

Here the *prayer of petition* morphs into the *prayer of communion*; David's request is God Himself.

I am convinced that all our neediness—even painful crisis—is what St. Augustine calls "severe mercy" for the reason à Kempis articulates: whatever we have, whatever we receive, if we don't have Jesus, we're impoverished. God uses our need to draw us to Himself so we might know *real wealth*. When all our petitions are subsumed under our desire for God Himself, and a longing just to be with Him, those other matters order themselves and those prayers flow much more smoothly and our understanding of how they "work" deepens considerably.

Day 20

Continuing in the vein of the prayer of communion, let me offer another quote from Thomas à Kempis' *Imitation of Christ* (Book Two, Chapter 7):

> *Affection for creatures is deceitful and inconstant, but the love of Jesus is true and enduring. He who clings to a creature will fall with its frailty, but he who gives himself to Jesus will ever be strengthened.*
>
> *Love Him, then; keep Him as a friend. He will not leave you as others do, or let you suffer lasting death. Sometime, whether you will or not, you will have to part with everything. Cling, therefore, to Jesus in life and death; trust yourself to the glory of Him who alone can help you when all others fail.*
>
> *Your Beloved is such that He will not accept what belongs to another—He wants your heart for Himself alone, to be enthroned therein as King in His own right. If you but knew how to free yourself entirely from all creatures, Jesus would gladly dwell within you.*

In some cases, à Kempis clearly offers advice that is particular to a 15th century monk (such as remaining in your cell, avoiding any contact with women at all costs, and references to other particulars of abbey life). We might be tempted by his apparent severity of language to chalk this passage up to that same mindset. We would do so, however, at considerable cost to ourselves, because the lesson he offers is little different from Jesus' own words that all must be forsaken to become His disciple.

> *Now great crowds accompanied him, and he turned and said to them, "If anyone comes to me and does not hate his own father and mother and wife and children and brothers and sisters, yes, and even his own life, he cannot be my disciple.* ‾ Luke 14:25-26

Thomas à Kempis is not suggesting cold disregard for others any more than Jesus is. Rather, he is bringing perspective so that our lives might be properly ordered and our deep longing for intimacy be properly satisfied. A person who seeks fundamental satisfaction from another mortal creature rather than the Creator will always be chasing an elusive communion. Only the Creator can satisfy the creature. People—even good, Christian people—who do not truly ground themselves in intimacy and communion with Christ, but look to their marriages, friendships, even church connections, will frustrate themselves and put a stress on the very people they love, expecting those people to do for them what only Jesus can do.

For this reason, we must "seek Jesus alone." We must pursue intimacy with Him with all our hearts. In that intimate place, we find deep peace, and other kinds of prayer are enriched and make sense.

Day 21

Today we continue to ponder the theme of the prayer of communion, and intimacy with the Lord. We find the truth of this level of relationship with the Lord throughout Scripture, but not by means of some formula, or a rote prayer. Most of the time we observe the prayer of communion in the life of someone by means of their actions or a testimony after the fact by God's own word.

Of Enoch, the Bible simply says,

Enoch walked with God, and he was not, for God took him. ˉ Genesis 5:24

This short verse has birthed endless speculation, both in ancient times and at present. But what is not debated is the nature of Enoch's relationship with God; it was clearly deeply intimate to the point where God couldn't bear to be apart from His child any longer and simply took him home.

Regarding Abraham, the Lord tells us...

But you, Israel, my servant, Jacob, whom I have chosen, the offspring of Abraham, my friend... ˉ Isaiah 41:8

(See also 2 Chronicles 20:7 and James 2:23)

Abraham's interaction with the Lord in Genesis 18, where he intercedes for Sodom, is clearly undergirded by a sense of reverent familiarity and a confidence that can only come from intimate friendship. Abraham is so respected by God that the Lord feels obliged to reveal His plan to him (Genesis 18:17).

About Moses, the Lord says...

Thus the LORD used to speak to Moses face to face, as a man speaks to his friend. ˉ Exodus 33:11

(See also Number 12:8 and Deuteronomy 34:10)

For all the wonders Moses worked, the giving of the Law, and the role he played by interceding for Israel, Moses was, above all, intimate with the Lord, and God called him "friend." All of his other achievements and greatness should be couched in that friendship.

Mary of Bethany shows her heart like this...

Mary therefore took a pound of expensive ointment made from pure nard, and anointed the feet of Jesus and wiped his feet with her hair. The house was filled with the fragrance of the perfume.
                                                              ¯ John 12:3

...while Paul reveals his walk with Christ in these words:

Indeed, I count everything as loss because of the surpassing worth of knowing Christ Jesus my Lord. For his sake I have suffered the loss of all things and count them as rubbish, in order that I may gain Christ... ¯ Philippians 3:8

All of these examples of the faith—deeply flawed and mortal like we are—communed deeply with God. By the time they got done with all their prayers, those requests began to blur into a single request: *I want you, God.*

Let us consider these things as we seek God in prayer. I will end with David's words in Psalm 63:5-8:

My soul will be satisfied as with fat and rich food, and my mouth will praise you with joyful lips, when I remember you upon my bed, and meditate on you in the watches of the night; for you have been my help, and in the shadow of your wings I will sing for joy. My soul clings to you; your right hand upholds me.

The Lord is so, so good.

Day 22

In my chapters about kinds of prayer, I have thus far focused upon *solitary* prayer—the kinds of prayers we pray by ourselves. This has been implied. About these three—petition, intercession, and communion—I would contend that all of them *may* be practiced in a group setting, but usually they are private, and at very least we should be equipped and mature enough to practice them privately. In my view, petition is the easiest of the three to practice in a group, then intercession, and finally communion, which really must be practiced privately and intimately for it to be all God wants for it to be in your prayer life.

But there is some prayer that, by the same token, is practiced in a group by definition. There are powerful examples from both the Old and New Testaments of God's people coming together for prayer, and touching God in the process with the results being dramatic (2 Chronicles 20 and Acts 4:23ff come to mind right away). But I want to restrict my comments to a specific prayer that actually requires multiple believers, and what it actually means. It is found in Matthew 18, and we call it the *prayer of agreement.*

Here is the passage:

Truly, I say to you, whatever you bind on earth shall be bound in heaven, and whatever you loose on earth shall be loosed in heaven. [19] *Again I say to you,* **if two of you agree on earth about anything they ask, it will be done for them by my Father in heaven.** [20] *For where two or three are gathered in my name, there am I among them."* ~ *Matthew 18:18-20*

Why does Jesus specifically mention that He will be in the midst of "two or three"? Does He mean that if four or more are present, He'll feel crowded and make His exit? Surely not—we all know that is absurd. So why this number? Why does He say "if two agree on earth" regarding a petition, God the Father will respond and do it?

The key is found in Deuteronomy 19:15, the source passage for Jesus' teaching:

A single witness shall not suffice against a person for any crime or for any wrong in connection with any offense that he has committed. Only on the evidence of two witnesses or of three witnesses shall a charge be established.

So according to the Law of Moses, it was a legal requirement that two or three witnesses were needed to *establish* a matter. And according to the Law, God looked upon that testimony as binding—legally, something "happened" once two or three witnesses had spoken.

Now look at Jesus' teaching in this light, along with passages like Mark 11:24, which tells us to believe we have received, and it will be ours. In Matthew 18, Jesus is saying this: If two or three of you, according to the Law of Moses, join together and *agree by faith* that something is done—if you "see it as done" *before it even happens,* bearing witness by faith to its reality—then God will do it. You will call things that are not as though they were (Romans 4:17); you "establish" them in the spiritual realm and set them up for manifestation in the natural realm. Jesus uses the phrase "two or three" as a "hook" to reference that greater truth—not because He's saying this won't work with, say, four people, or seven, or whatever.

The prayer of agreement is extraordinarily powerful. But it takes real agreement. It takes two or more people coming together, believing and praying powerfully, telling the Father that they see Him doing something—*they bear witness to it beforehand,* by faith. But faith is contagious. There have been times someone said to me, "Agree with me in prayer!"—and it sparked my faith, and I could agree.

I encourage you, pray the prayer of agreement with others. Husbands and wives praying prayers of agreement is a powerful thing. Children and parents also. "A cord of three strands is not easily broken" (Ecclesiastes 4:12) is a principle and a truth that applies to prayer as much as to anything else!

Day 23

So far, we have covered some foundational issues pertaining to prayer and a strengthened relationship with Christ. These include some basics about worship, God's Word, and some fundamentals about repentance, love for each other, attitude, and pure speech. We've also obviously addressed some things about *types of prayer*. While there are certainly many more aspects of prayer to cover, I'd like to circle back to them a bit later because I want to touch on some corollary aspects that I consider vital. Let's remember: at the end of the day, *form* is precisely that. Dead religion thrives on form because empty religious form is the very substance of dead religion. Once vibrant expressions of faith in prayer have all, at one time or another, been reduced to religious form (or formula) that is entirely powerless, useless to God, and useless for touching God's throne. So learning the form of different kinds of prayer (even the prayer of communion, if that were possible) *in itself* is not some sort of silver bullet. We must learn them, but we have to keep our hearts in a place where God can move in and through us, because only by His Holy Spirit does prayer move past the realm of religion and into the realm of living faith.

For this reason I want to address the matter of what previous Christians of great devotion have called our *affections*. When we speak of our affections, we touch upon the themes of *spiritual hunger* and *appetite*. To speak of *hunger and appetite* is to use the spiritual metaphor of tasting and eating, whereas the speak of *affections* brings us into the somewhat less metaphorical realm of *relationship*. But either way, what we are speaking of is what we *want*, *desire*, or *deeply long for*. I struggle to imagine a way in which this matter could be overemphasized in the life of the Christian, because our heart is a continual battleground of desires. Much is made of the enemy's use of bad ideas—false doctrine, misinformation, factual distortions, and so forth—but a close look at the first sin in the Garden will reveal that the devil appealed to Eve's *affections*—her appetite—much more than to her intellectual processes. A bit of reflection upon our own failings will lead us to the prompt conclusion that it is far more common for us to push past clear thinking in the name of what we (wrongly) lust for, than for us to violate a heartfelt and godly desire because we are intellectually mistaken about something. In short, our fundamental life motivations have much more to do with what we *desire* than they do with different theories our mind ponders.

God wants us to desire Him. Desire for God—sincere, burning, fiery desire—is a basic ingredient of sincere worship, and from there, of successful prayer. I am convinced that faith, hope, and love, what Paul identifies as the fundamentals of the Christian life (1 Corinthians 13:13), all operate properly—indeed, can only be understood at all—in the heart of someone who *desperately wants Jesus.* Consider this passage from 1 Peter 1:6-9...

*In this you rejoice, though now for a little while, if necessary, you have been grieved by various trials, so that the tested genuineness of your **faith**—more precious than gold that perishes though it is tested by fire—may be found to result in praise and glory and honor **at the revelation of Jesus Christ.** Though you have not seen him, **you love him.** Though you do not now see him, you **believe in him and rejoice with joy that is inexpressible and filled with glory,** **obtaining the goal of your** faith, the salvation of your souls.*

Faith (believing on Jesus), hope (the expectation of seeing Jesus face to face), and love (sight unseen) all are couched in the language of come-what-may longing, joy, and the fierce drive towards a spiritual goal. Apart from that strong desire, those three things fall apart.

Jesus Himself identified the first commandment:

*And you shall love the Lord your God **with all your heart and with all your soul and with all your mind and with all your strength.**'*
                                                              ~ *Mark 12:30*

This is one of those passages that simply does not beg for explanation, because it explains itself. Any willing heart receives it for what it says. The word "all" occurs four times, applying itself to every corner of our inner man in respect to the love we should express towards God. The passage is saturated with passion, hunger, and desire. There is no way to obey the spirit of this command dispassionately, there is no way to do it in the mind alone, there is no way one can love God according to this word without truly desiring Him.

If we are in any doubt, let's see what Jesus says to some early Christians who had lost their way...

I know your works: you are neither cold nor hot. Would that you were either cold or hot! So, because you are lukewarm, and neither hot nor cold, I will spit you out of my mouth. ¯Revelation 3:15-16

This well-known word to the Laodiceans is one of the hardest Jesus ever speaks to people He also calls His disciples. But reading between the lines, there is great comfort in it, because it means that *He wants us.* God is not asking for us to pour out our hearts to Him, hunger after and pursue Him, all while He sits detachedly on His throne judging our pleas with score cards like a judge at the Olympics. He longs for His people, for their own sake, and wants us to want Him, also for His own sake.

We must order our hearts. They tend to disorder, but by the grace of God they are not beyond redemption. If we submit and seek Him with all of our hearts, great reward awaits. But if we cannot bring ourselves to stir desire for God, the source of all things good and the Author of Life, then what's the point?

Day 24

Our affections in their very essence constitute our deepest inner attachments and motivations. As I wrote yesterday, if someone's affections are bent in a particular direction, those attachments ultimately will determine the unfolding of that person's life. Affections are like a determined helmsman at the rudder of a ship, while the winds that blow the sails are the ideas and thoughts that he has to navigate; those winds are not powerless, but by and large if the helmsman chooses a particular course, that is what will transpire for the ship.

As Christians, we want to do the will of God. So we say. But there's saying that and then there's *saying* that. Jeremiah 17:9 tells us the human heart is desperately sick and wicked above all things, and beyond our own understanding. It is deeply conflicted. A pastor of mine used to say, "Lots of times people *want* the things of God, but they do not *desire* them." His semantics may have been imprecise, but the point strikes home: It's one thing to parrot that we want God, it's another thing entirely to desire Him deeply enough to make the necessary reforms in our life to make room for His Spirit to move and transform us. The same goes for churches, and almost certainly more so, because in that case God is dealing with a group of people.

Our heart—our inner man—is at war with itself. It is conflicted. Most people, even many Christians, have no sense of disciplining their own desires. Hollywood has so saturated our thinking that we actually buy this line about unbridled passions destroying entire families somehow being a romantic reality that sort of "happens." You can hear the script now: *"We didn't plan this, it's not our fault, it just came upon us—like a force of nature." ("Which is why I'm abandoning you and our children for a woman young enough to be my daughter, blah blah, blah...")* The "Christian" manifestation of this drivel is people wrestling with deeply sinful and even perverse desires, "praying God would take it away," and when "He" doesn't, well, then it must be God's will that I violate His Word, the laws of nature, and the standards of Christian truth in place for 2,000 years. These modes of thinking, whether secular or religious, fail to recognize that we are told to *command* our inner man how it is to behave, fully understanding that our inner man will push back. It is a conflict.

Paul says this:

But I say, walk by the Spirit, and you will not gratify the desires of the flesh. [17] For the desires of the flesh are against the Spirit, and the desires of the Spirit are against the flesh, for these are opposed to each other, to keep you from doing the things you want to do. [—] *Galatians 5:16-17*

Once again, I find Thomas à Kempis very enlightening on this score:

When a man desires a thing too much, he at once becomes ill at ease. A proud and avaricious man never rests, whereas he who is poor and humble of heart lives in a world of peace....[the avaricious man] can hardly abstain from earthly desires. Hence it makes him sad to forego them; he is quick to anger if reproved. Yet if he satisfies his desires, remorse of conscience overwhelms him because he followed his passions and they did not lead to the peace he sought. (Imitation of Christ, Book One, Chapter 6)

Understand that à Kempis is speaking in the context of a religious community—he is speaking of Christians. He is telling us of a deeply dissatisfied person who has in word committed to Christ, but has not tamed their affections. The attachments to worldly desires are tearing them apart from the inside out. They know they should have peace, but they cannot have it because the desires that war within them prevents any peace from taking root.

We must take charge of our own hearts. We have to repent of double-mindedness, ask God for strength, and give ourselves wholly to Him. We have to pray for the grace and the strength to move in the realm of holy affections and appetites, embrace that which we know brings life, and cultivate personal holiness. At the same time, we have to rebuke those affections and inner attachments—and the habits that coddle them—and fiercely eliminate them from our lives. They are heart-dividers and parasites that steal our peace, joy, and the best God has for us. This is what Jesus meant by cutting off the right hand or gouging out the eye—not literal self-mutilation, but "violent" steps that do not flatter our tender egos, that make no excuses for our lusts, and that accept no more postponements. In truth, and at our core, we are powerless to change our own lives. But God aids those who commit themselves to an obedient course, and we can take comfort in this promise:

For the eyes of the LORD run to and fro throughout the whole earth, to give strong support to those whose heart is blameless toward him. ˜ *2 Chronicles 16:9*

By doing this, worship, prayer, Scripture reading, and every other aspect of our life becomes *drastically transformed*, because our heart is no longer divided, but unified and determined to go in one direction—heavenward.

Day 25

When discussing our affections, and the innately distracted nature we tend to because we are fallen and undergoing a process of sanctification, it can be helpful to take a hard look at the alternative. The enemy of our souls does his best to paint his playthings as if they were truly something worth having. Certainly the devil would love for everyone to give in completely to his deceptions and fully partake, like a shipwrecked sailor drinking gulp after gulp of saltwater, until it destroys them from the inside out. But with many he'll be satisfied with blunting our edge, distracting us, keeping us from fully giving ourselves over to a driving hunger for the things of God because we can't bring ourselves to completely abandon foolish fantasies. His glittering lies, then, remain an unattainable but still somehow desirable goal for the dark places in our heart.

In her essay "The Other Six Deadly Sins" (*Letters to a Diminished Church*), Dorothy Sayers puts the question to us regarding our reaction to a pop-culture movie: do we call the fantasy of superficial people surrounded by endless wealth the drivel it really is? Or do we secretly wish that we could give up our honest labor and relationships to soak ourselves in that vapid luxury?

Now, our spiritual vanity flatters us that we aren't really pursuing those things, but by secretly admiring what we know is forbidden fruit, we reserve a part of our soul for something dark—"just in case"—rather than for God. Our yet-to-be-consecrated parts are holding on to a backup plan for a rainy day, a safety net, if by chance this whole Jesus thing doesn't work out as promised. In the end this might not cause our complete fall, but it does carry a heavy cost because we surrender potential to a lie, and it is probably others who will pay for what we fail to achieve in Christ.

Consider Jesus, and how John Bunyan in *The Pilgrim's Progress* describes His behavior in the allegorical Vanity Fair...

Yea, because he was such a person of honor, Beelzebub had him from street to street, and showed him all the kingdoms of the world in a little time, that he might, if possible, allure that blessed One to cheapen and buy some of his vanities; but he had no mind to the merchandise, and therefore left the town, **without laying out so much as one farthing upon these vanities.**

This is a deeply impactful passage to me. Jesus, in all His time in this world, didn't spend a penny of His soul on its glittering vanities. He held nothing back from His Father, held nothing in reserve for Himself. Yes, this was true heroism. But it was also wisdom and good old common sense embodied: the devil's wares are lies, and only Jesus had the sense to call them for what they were. Jesus didn't spend a cent on them because they weren't worth a cent. We need that wisdom when weighing our affections. Again, à Kempis lends his thoughts...

Perhaps you think you will completely satisfy yourself, but you cannot do so, for if you should see all existing things, **what would they be but an empty vision?** *Raise your eyes to God in heaven and pray because of your sins and shortcomings.* **Leave vanity to the vain.** *Set yourself to the things which God has commanded you to do.ˉ Imitation,* Book One, Chapter 22

Wisdom indeed. In contrast, let not Isaiah's words, speaking of those who've allowed idolatrous desires to creep into their lives like poisonous weeds in a field, be true of us:

You were wearied with the length of your way, but you did not say, "It is hopeless"; you found new life for your strength, and so you were not faint. ˉ Isaiah 57:10

It is always tempting to keep those vain things alive in the basement of our souls, even as we are pressing into God more and more. Even though we know they are useless, vain, and have never—not once—yielded joy for us, we submit to the tiresome lie that a card up the sleeve is somehow "good sense." Only the Lord

Himself can liberate us from this deception, can shine the light in our hearts, reveal our most subtle motives, and purge us from all those wicked reserves so we can be all He plans for us to be.

It's time.

Day 26

I think it fitting to write about one particular aspect of our affections and how it impacts our walk with God. That aspect is *perseverance*.

Now, perseverance or tenacity aren't typical paired with the idea of affections or desires. But a little thought will illuminate the subject and help us to realize they are deeply connected. As I've noted, a passing whim is easily and even thoughtlessly abandoned. The Lord makes this grieved remark about the devotion of His people:

What shall I do with you, O Ephraim? What shall I do with you, O Judah? Your love is like a morning cloud, like the dew that goes early away. ˉ Hosea 6:4

This frankly terrifying passage makes it quite clear that even the most important thing we could (and should) do with our lives may be treated in a light and cavalier fashion, to our own great harm. Put another way, whimsy is a condition of the heart, not a characteristic of the object of our affections. People can and do treat stupid things as important and crucial thing as trivial. We must beware. And we must take care to ascribe weight to the weighty things as we pursue God, and move out of the realm of whim and into the realm of determined desire.

Another passage from à Kempis (Imitation, Book Two, Chapter 9) is very helpful:

I have never met a man so religious and devout that he has not experienced at some time a withdrawal of grace and felt a lessening of fervor. No saint was so sublimely rapt and enlightened as not to be tempted before and after.

The lesson in this verse is powerful in the overall context of *The Imitation of Christ*, because the book is loaded with statements about keeping up our spiritual fervor. Here à Kempis doesn't merely admit something about human nature—that there is ebb and flow to it—but he is also teaching us something: true desire for Christ is more evident in our long-term actions than in our tone or feeling at any given moment.

My father used to tell me, "I'd like to believe what you are telling me, but your actions are speaking so loud I can't hear a word you are saying." Our actions speak volumes about our desires—about what we *really* want. I remember a time, halfway through my seminary education, when I had had enough. What was billed as a three-year degree was taking twice that long because of my workload and ministry work at the church, I wasn't enjoying my classes, I couldn't see where it would take me, and in general I wanted to get on with things. I felt it was a ball and chain. At the same time, I knew deep down God was requiring it of me in some way. After attempting to negotiate with my pastor a lesser degree (my church was helping pay the tuition), and he turned me down flat, I got in a full-blown wrestling match with the Lord over the issue. I've never won one of those matches yet, and that conflict was no exception. I finally felt from the Lord a very simple response: I didn't need to understand why I had to do it, I didn't need to see where it would take me, I didn't need to want it or like it, I didn't even need to feel it was worthwhile. I just had to do it as an obedience to Him. That answer gave me peace, and I dropped the issue and proceeded with my degree. I wish I could tell you at that some intervention happened, but nothing did; it took me a few more ugly years before I graduated. Now, did I want that degree? Most would say my affections weren't the slightest bit inclined towards it. But the truth is, in the end my affections were more engaged in that issue than any of the lesser ones that I "felt" more strongly about. We speak by our actions.

Perseverance and tenacity play a huge role in telling us and others what we *really* want. If we push through the tiresome aspects of a fast, if we stick with daily prayer even when the glory days are over, if we keep pressing into God on the days when it seems our prayers are bouncing off the ceiling, we show where our affections truly lie. In Greek, the language in which the New Testament was written, there is only one word used for both *faith* and *faithfulness* (*pistis*), not two; only context tells the difference. For this reason an *unfaithful* person is often called *faithless*. There's a message there. We demonstrate our *faith* to a large degree by being *faithful*, by sticking with something.

Let our love for the Lord not be like the morning mist, or the dew that quickly evaporates in the heat of the day. Let our devotion not be a season, a fad, or a whim. Let our affections for Jesus run to the bottom of our souls.

Day 27

Now, to continue briefly with the matter of perseverance-as-affection. As I noted in yesterday's chapter, our desires are truly reflected, not just in what we express a fervent desire for in a season, but in what we choose to persevere in over the long haul. There have been times when I judged a desire I had as strong, but it really turned out to be a whim, while other things I never dreamed of as a young man have become the driving motivators of my life as it has unfolded. The primary mark of lasting desire vs. whim is that true desire continues to be pursued *even when it doesn't feel like desire at all.* This is what the saints of old called *patience.*

Patience in this sense is a theme all its own but cannot adequately be addressed without also bringing up the matter of *temptation.* But to understand these words properly, we have to talk about their fuller definitions. Most see patience as something along the lines of the ability to endure an unexpected, momentary setback without losing their cool. And, of course, temptation is the allure of evil, the enemy's attempt to get us to sin. Understood these ways, patience and temptation touch each other, perhaps (as in, "Somebody cut me off on the freeway and I was *tempted* to lose my *patience*"), but do not have significant overlap. But in the older sense, and I daresay the broader biblical sense of the words, they share quite a bit of overlap. This is because true patience involves perseverance in the face of trial over the long term. Someone might be what we consider "patient" in the immediate sense, but not be patient at all with a long-term trial that tests their endurance. In the older sense, the trial that never seems to end, that puts our wits, our wisdom, and our willingness to submit to the Lord no matter what to the test, is called *temptation.*

Along this line, let's have a look at James 5...

Be patient, therefore, brothers, until the coming of the Lord. See how the farmer waits for the precious fruit of the earth, being patient about it, until it receives the early and the late rains. [8] *You* *also, be patient. Establish your hearts, for the coming of the Lord is at hand. [9] Do not grumble against one another, brothers, so that you may not be judged; behold, the Judge is standing at the door. [10] **As an example of suffering and patience, brothers, take the prophets who spoke in the name of the Lord. [11] Behold, we consider those blessed who remained steadfast.** You have heard of the* **steadfastness** *of Job, and you have seen the purpose of the Lord, how the Lord is compassionate and merciful. [12] But above all, my brothers, do not swear, either by heaven or by earth or by any other oath, but let your "yes" be yes and your "no" be no, so that you may not fall under condemnation. [13] Is anyone among you suffering? Let him pray. Is anyone cheerful? Let him sing praise. [14] Is anyone among you sick? Let him call for the elders of the church, and let them pray over him, anointing him with oil in the name of the Lord. [15] And the prayer of faith will save the one who is sick, and the Lord will raise him up. And if he has committed sins, he will be forgiven. [16] Therefore, confess your sins to one another and pray for one another, that you may be healed. The prayer of a righteous person has great power as it is working. [17] Elijah was a man with a nature like ours, and he prayed fervently that it might not rain, and for three years and six months it did not rain on the earth. [18] Then he prayed again, and heaven gave rain, and the earth bore its fruit.* ⁻ James 5:7-18

(Notice how the words on *prayer* follow immediately after the words on *patience*.) This passage is a nearly perfect example of this older sense of patience under trial, especially when paired with what James says at the outset of his letter:

Count it all joy, my brothers, when you meet trials of various kinds,[3] for you know that **the testing of your faith produces steadfastness. [4] And let steadfastness have its full effect, that you may be perfect and complete, lacking in nothing.** ⁻ James 1:2-4

So patience and trial go hand in hand, and have a winnowing effect on both individuals and groups of believers, separating the mature from the immature. It is one thing to endure a momentary setback; it takes another depth of spirit entirely to outlast the difficulties of life and the tests of our faith so as to emerge stronger than before. This longer view of what it means to be a fruit-bearing person of faith is truer to the witness of both Scripture and the centuries-old testimony of the church than pop-psychology and the "coping" tricks that riddle the thinking of so many modern Christians.

Here again I find Thomas à Kempis insightful...

*Until God ordains otherwise, a man ought to bear patiently whatever he cannot correct in himself and in others. Consider it better thus—***perhaps to try your patience and to test you, for without such patience and trial your merits are of little account.*** Nevertheless, under such difficulties you should pray that God will consent to help you bear them calmly.* (*Imitation,* Book One, Chapter 16)

...and also...

When Christ was in the world, He was despised by men; in the hour of need He was forsaken by acquaintances and left by friends to the depths of scorn. He was willing to suffer and to be despised; do you dare to complain of anything? He had enemies and defamers; do you want everyone to be your friend, your benefactor? ***How can your patience be rewarded if no adversity test it?*** (Book Two, Chapter 1)

Whereas today so many teachings and indeed entire movements consider such trials to be the mark of someone with a deficient faith or even someone under God's judgment, this view is vastly different: difficulties are part and parcel of how God forms us into the image of His Son, and all our accomplishments are worthless until they undergo the fire that purifies and proves them as true.

I'll close with this: The prayer life of a tested person, one who has demonstrated this kind of gut-level, long-term patience, is worlds different than the prayers of one who resents and resists such a purification process. **I want to be a man of prayer *as God defines that phrase*, not as mortals do.**

Day 28

As I shift gears into another (but related) theme, I'd like to touch upon an issue with a certain passage of Scripture that speaks to this matter of temptation, trial, and testing. The passage is as follows...

*No temptation has overtaken you that is not common to man. God is faithful, **and he will not let you be tempted beyond your ability**, but with the temptation he will also provide the way of escape, that you may be able to endure it.* ˜ 1 Corinthians 10:13

This passage (sometimes whether people recognize it or not) is the source passage of the oft repeated phrase, "God will never give you more than you can handle," a refrain that has taken on the character of a proverb.

The problem is, it isn't a proverb; it isn't a maxim or a "principle to live by." It's a truth that Paul states in a particular way and a particular context, with a particular application. The problem with using this as a proverb—a sort of "absolute truth" that uniformly applies no matter what—is that using it that way can actually have the *opposite effect* than Paul intended.

You see, before we complete this pilgrimage we call the Christian life, the truth is that God gives us "more than we can handle" *almost as a matter of course.* Look at what Paul says in his next letter to the same church...

*For we do not want you to be unaware, brothers, of the affliction we experienced in Asia. **For we were so utterly burdened beyond our strength that we despaired of life itself.** [9] Indeed, we felt that we had received the sentence of death. But that was to make us rely not on ourselves but on God who raises the dead.* [10] *He delivered us from such a deadly peril, and he will deliver us. On him we have set our hope that he will deliver us again.*
˜ 2 Corinthians 1:8-10

Here Paul describes the riot in Ephesus (see Acts 19), and his spiritual condition at the time. This is the same man who wrote that God "will not let you be tempted beyond your ability." (Remember, in the original Greek text "tempted" and "tested" are the same thing.) But here he says that he was "utterly burdened beyond his strength that he despaired of life." What's the difference between "ability" in 1 Corinthians 10 and "strength" in 2 Corinthians 1? Nothing, that's what. It's the same thing. At first blush this looks like a flat contradiction, with Paul saying God allowed in 2 Corinthians 1 what he thought He wouldn't in 1 Corinthians 10.

But that is simply not true, as a closer look (and really not that much closer) reveals the consistency in Paul's thought. In both passages a vital ingredient is included: *dependence on God.* The truth is, left to ourselves, and depending on our own strength, we have every reason to despair. This life is too much for us. And God regularly allows burdens to be laid upon us that are beyond our own ability to bear. In fact, that a condition is not only common, but is increasingly the rule as we mature in Christ, especially for those who are fiercely committed to Him and following His call, like Paul was. In 1 Corinthians 10, Paul makes it clear that God and God alone provides the "way of escape" from temptation; without Him, forget it—you're toast. In 2 Corinthians 1, Paul says the same thing, but emphasizes the condition of his soul during the trial, and basically appeals to the resurrection power of Christ as the only thing that brought him through.

This is how God wants us to live—utterly dependent upon Him. He allows His children, His favorites, to be so burdened so that we will depend upon Him completely so that Christ's power will rest upon them (see 2 Corinthians 12 and Paul's discussion of weakness and his "thorn"). People who do not understand this often suffer despair, a loss of faith, and even the death of their prayer life because the "proverb" approach to 1 Corinthians 10:13 leads to confusion—they think either God isn't faithful to His promises, or (more typically) that somehow they are themselves rejected concerning the faith. This resulting condition is, of course, precisely the *opposite result* of Paul's intention in writing these words. He wanted to encourage us, to help us overcome by Christ's power in us. But by reducing his words (and, incidentally, ignoring the testimony of the lives of all the patriarchs, prophets, and godly kings throughout the entire Old Testament), we expect a "formula" approach to life, and end up deeply frustrated one way or another.

As we press into maturity in prayer, let us then realize that sometimes life does indeed give us more than we ourselves can handle. But God is faithful, and *if we stay very close to Him and lean on His power,* the way out will be provided for us—even if that way out is resurrection itself.

Day 29

In my heart I would like to address the sticky matter of "unanswered" prayer. That discussion is both vital and inevitable if we are going to put any steam to the matter of a mature, long-term persevering prayer life. But I believe that before we go to that subject some other issues should be dealt with first, so that they will be behind us when we do.

Let's take a look at a renowned passage from Ephesians 6...

Put on the whole armor of God, that you may be able to stand against the schemes of the devil. [12] *For we do not wrestle against flesh and blood, but against the rulers, against the authorities, against the cosmic powers over this present darkness, against the spiritual forces of evil in the heavenly places.* [13] *Therefore take up the whole armor of God, that you may be able to withstand in the evil day, and having done all, to stand firm.* [14] *Stand therefore, having fastened on the belt of truth, and having put on the breastplate of righteousness,* [15] *and, as shoes for your feet, having put on the readiness given by the gospel of peace.* [16] *In all circumstances take up the shield of faith, with which you can extinguish all the flaming darts of the evil one;* [17] *and take the helmet of salvation, and the sword of the Spirit, which is the word of God,* [18] *praying at all times in the Spirit, with all prayer and supplication. To that end, keep alert with all perseverance, making supplication for all the saints,* [19] *and also for me, that words may be given to me in opening my mouth boldly to proclaim the mystery of the gospel,* [20] *for which I am an ambassador in chains, that I may declare it boldly, as I ought to speak.*
Ephesians 6:11–20

To say there's a lot going on in this passage is a monumental understatement, so let's go at it generally then get more specific in some follow up chapters.

First, Paul is obviously likening the Christian life to a warfare. It isn't the only metaphor he uses (his other favorite is an athletic competition), but it is a very common one—Paul uses the military/soldier/battle illustration not only here, but also in Romans, 2 Corinthians, Philippians, 1 Thessalonians, 1 & 2 Timothy. Clearly, doing battle in the spirit is a fundamental part of Paul's thought, and not coincidentally these passages also often emphasize prayer. To pray is to do battle. Put another way, to *not* pray is to *not* do battle, or perhaps better said, to not pray is to *pretend* there is no battle when there actually is a very serious battle—the most serious battle—raging around us.

Second, what Paul calls the armor of God is not something we can simply rattle off as we pray, imaging that is what "putting it on" means for Paul. To "pray on the armor" (i.e., go through this passage and name each piece in prayer to prepare for the day) can be powerful and edifying to be sure, but that's not all there is to it. Carefully read, Ephesians itself, front to back, is the life plan for "putting on the full armor of God," and this passage from Ephesians 6 is the summary of that teaching, not its introduction. The armor of God is a *consecrated lifestyle* we must live in order to be effective in prayer. You do not want to engage in battle without wearing the armor, you really, really don't.

Third, there's no avoiding the battle. There are those Christians who either live or speak as if they can live a quaint life of faith, a polite and sentimental Christianity pulled from paintings of charming churches in pastoral surroundings. They imagine a quiet, non-confrontational religion of yesteryear that comforts but does not ruffle, that blesses but does not offend. Ironically, the opposite approach—acting as if doing spiritual battle is some sort of unique calling, or somehow reserved for the "super spiritual" or even a movement or subculture within the larger Christian movement—is equally problematic. (In truth, I don't see either of those views as accurate to the past or the present.) Paul describes spiritual warfare as something that simply *is*. No Christian is exempt from it, no Christian can avoid it, no Christian can pretend it is not happening around them. To live and act as if our words, actions, and prayers—or lack of them—do not *directly impact* our battle-worthiness is to play the petrified soldier in a foxhole, hands over eyes in the midst of pitched battle, whispering desperately to himself, "They'll never find me in here."

The battle is met. We have been born into it. How we live our lives affects how we perform as Christ's soldiers. Let's take courage that we serve a Commander in Chief who has already defeated death and can never be struck down, has won the battle, and goes before us.

Day 30

Continuing with the theme of spiritual warfare, and the Ephesians 6 passage about the armor of God more specifically, let's talk about what the phrase "armor of God" really means.

For starters, there's the obvious: Paul is describing the protective equipment and weaponry that a soldier of his day would have worn, and that would have been readily recognized by his readers. It has been romanticized, but at the time there was nothing particularly romantic about it, at least not any more than a modern soldier's helmet, rifle, and Kevlar would be. It was the uniform of a warrior, and brutally practical for fighting in every respect. None of it was optional; none of it was for show. We should keep that in mind as we consider it and pray about its application to our own lives in preparation for spiritual warfare.

The next question regards Paul's intent: what does *armor of God* mean? Does this mean *godly armor? Armor from God*—as a gift to us? Or does it literally mean *God's* (own) *armor?* Which it might be actually does matter for how we go to battle, and unfortunately the Greek grammar doesn't help us—any of those readings is grammatically possible.

The answer is found in a series of Old Testament passages, and the resulting truth is more powerful than most realize. When we search the Scriptures, we find a number of passages that Paul is clearly using:

Righteousness shall be the belt of his waist, and **faithfulness the belt of his loins.** ⁻ Isaiah 11:5

While this would slip by most of us, a simple check of the Greek Old Testament rendering for this verse—which Paul was certainly using—reveals the word used to describe the belt of the Messiah in Isaiah 11:5 is *aletheia... truth*. So Paul is not creating the idea of the **belt of truth** in Ephesians 6:14, he's drawing it from Isaiah 11:5 and the armor described there.

He put on righteousness as a breastplate, and a helmet of salvation on his head; he put on garments of vengeance for clothing, and wrapped himself in zeal as a cloak. ¯ Isaiah 59:17

This passage doesn't need much description; Isaiah 59:17 is obviously the source for the **breastplate of righteousness** and the **helmet of salvation** found in Ephesians 6:14 and 6:17, respectively.

*He will cover you with his pinions, and under his wings you will find refuge; his **faithfulness is a shield and buckler**.* You will not fear the terror of the night, nor the arrow that flies by day...
¯ Psalm 91:4-5

Keep in mind that *faith* and *faithfulness* are nearly *identical ideas* in the mind of the New Testament writers because of the way their language worked. Recognizing this, we can see that God's *faithfulness* is the ground for our *faith*, and the basis for not fearing the *darts* or *arrows* (Greek *belos*, used to describe the enemies attacks in both Psalm 91:5 and Ephesians 6:16). So Psalm 91 is the source for the **shield of faith**.

The source for the **sword of the Spirit** is likely multiple because the idea of God's word being as a deadly weapon He wields is found in many places. The clearest seem to be...

*...he shall strike the earth with the **rod of his mouth, and with the breath of his lips he shall kill the wicked**.* ¯ Isaiah 11:4

This is almost certainly Paul's source passage (as we have seen, Paul uses the same passage for the *belt of truth*), and although for us a "rod" and a "sword" don't seem the same thing, see Revelation 19:15 for how the Hebrew mind processes a verse like this. The thought is echoed elsewhere in Isaiah...

*He made **my mouth like a sharp sword**; in the shadow of his hand he hid me...¯* Isaiah 49:2

...and in Hosea...

*Therefore I have hewn them by the prophets; **I have slain them by the words of my mouth**, and my judgment goes forth as the light.*
¯ Hosea 6:5

The holy **footwear of peace** (Ephesians 6:15) is likely a combination of Jesus' own commissioning of His disciples and His command that they impart peace to receptive households (Mark 6:8ff, and parallels in Matthew and Luke), and Isaiah 52:7...

*How beautiful upon the mountains are the feet of him who **brings good news, who publishes peace, who brings good news of happiness**, who publishes salvation, who says to Zion, "Your God reigns."*

So now we see that "armor of God" actually means *God's own armor that* He has given over to us, that we might wear it into battle. This is a stunning thought all by itself. But when we locate this idea in the larger picture of Old Testament covenant making and practice, it becomes clearer. Let's look at 1 Samuel 18:3-5...

*Then **Jonathan made a covenant with David**, because he loved him as his own soul. ⁴ **And Jonathan stripped himself of the robe that was on him and gave it to David, and his armor, and even his sword and his bow and his belt.** ⁵ **And David went out and was successful wherever Saul sent him**, so that Saul set him over the men of war. And this was good in the sight of all the people and also in the sight of Saul's servants.*

In ancient times, covenants were made by means of *exchange*. Two people entering into covenant with each other would exchange things of value and identity with each other, forming a life-long alliance that basically said something along the lines of,

"For purposes of mutual help and protection, I will henceforth treat you as if you were me, and you will look upon me as if I were you." There were all sorts of covenants, but they had this character pretty much in common, even between the great and the small. Vestiges of this practice are still found in modern wedding ceremonies, with an exchange of vows, rings (as symbols of wealth), the changing of names, and even bride and groom feeding each other cake. In 1 Samuel 18, as far as Jonathan was concerned, *David became him.* David now wore Jonathan's armor, carried his weapons, and held his rank (as symbolized by the belt). For all intents and purposes, David was now the crown prince (which explains, incidentally, Saul's fear and jealousy of David in the following passages). What is most powerful, however, is that both God and the enemies of Israel also recognized David's new identity—in the case of the enemies whether they liked it or not.

So here's the punch line: God has given us *His armor* just like Jonathan gave David his. And as far as our opponents are concerned, they no more face us than Israel's enemies faced a lowly shepherd boy in David—they faced the crown prince, mighty in battle. The principalities and forces of spiritual wickedness are facing the Lord Himself when we go into battle wearing His armor. Consider this: the One who wore the armor we are now commanded to wear has never lost a battle. Never.

We have been equipped, and God is with us in covenant faithfulness. Let us take courage, and fight.

Day 31

Let's begin to break down the armor of God, piece by piece. As we do so, we must never lose sight of the context it is drawn from, namely, *prayer as spiritual warfare*. Let's have another look at it to keep everything in front of us...

Finally, be strong in the Lord and in the strength of his might. [11] *Put on the whole armor of God, that you may be able to stand against the schemes of the devil.* [12] *For we do not wrestle against flesh and blood, but against the rulers, against the authorities, against the cosmic powers over this present darkness, against the spiritual forces of evil in the heavenly places.* [13] *Therefore take up the whole armor of God, that you may be able to withstand in the evil day, and having done all, to stand firm.* [14] *Stand therefore, having fastened on the belt of truth, and having put on the breastplate of righteousness,* [15] *and, as shoes for your feet, having put on the readiness given by the gospel of peace.* [16] *In all circumstances take up the shield of faith, with which you can extinguish all the flaming darts of the evil one;* [17] *and take the helmet of salvation, and the sword of the Spirit, which is the word of God,* [18] *praying at all times in the Spirit, with all prayer and supplication. To that end, keep alert with all perseverance, making supplication for all the saints,* [19] *and also for me, that words may be given to me in opening my mouth boldly to proclaim the mystery of the gospel,* [20] *for which I am an ambassador in chains, that I may declare it boldly, as I ought to speak.*

~ Ephesians 6:10-20

We've already discussed the Old Testament sources for this passage, and the covenantal meaning of an invincible God giving us His own, personal armor. We will discuss our spiritual foes later on. For now let's look at the armor, beginning with the **belt of truth**.

Although the ESV translates v. 14 in such a way as to make us think the noun "belt" is present, a closer rendering would be, "Stand therefore, your waist girded about with truth." In other words, it isn't so much a "belt of truth" (in the sense that the belt is somehow merely associated with truthfulness), as it is that (for Paul) *truth itself functions as a belt does.* The belt we wear *is* truth.

What does a belt do? Well, it holds our guts in—it keeps us upright and consolidates our strength. Think of people who wear belts to do heavy lifting; the belt helps them focus their core strength on the task. For a soldier, the belt is important because he is wearing heavy armor, and the entire uniform is, in a way, "built" or assembled around that belt—it is located at his center of gravity, so to speak. Biblically, the belt was a sign of rank—we're describing an officer, someone of status (which makes sense, given that we are describing the armor of our Commander in Chief). These are good insights, the last being (in my view) the best. But we should stay close to the text and not try to get too "cute" in our application, because Paul is up to something when he speaks of being "girded with truth."

As I noted before, the armor of God in Ephesians 6 in many ways serves as a summary for the entire book. And Paul has already spoken extensively about truth-telling in Ephesians:

*Therefore, having **put away falsehood**, let each one of you **speak the truth with his neighbor**, for we are members one of another.* [26] *Be angry and do not sin; do not let the sun go down on your anger,* [27] *and give no opportunity to the devil.* [28] *Let the thief no longer steal, but rather let him labor, **doing honest work with his own hands**, so that he may have something to share with anyone in need.* [29] ***Let no corrupting talk come out of your mouths**, but only such as is good for building up, as fits the occasion, that it may give grace to those who hear.* [30] *And do not grieve the Holy Spirit of God, by whom you were sealed for the day of redemption.* [31] *Let all bitterness and wrath and anger and clamor and slander be put away from you, along with all malice.* [32] *Be kind to one another, tenderhearted, forgiving one another, as God in Christ forgave you.* ˜ Ephesians 4:25-32

The implication of this passage is obvious: as children *born of truth* (see Ephesians 4:21), we must *speak truth*. And not only must we *speak truth*, we must *live the truth*. And living the truth hasn't only to do with things like not stealing (v. 28), but also with a pattern of speech that is comprehensively consistent with the *gospel of truth*. For Paul, lying, stealing, and "corrupting talk" *are all forms of lying, and all grieve the Holy Spirit.* If we congratulate ourselves that we are not thieves, but we deliberately mislead our brothers and sisters in Christ through exaggeration or selective retelling, we are still dishonest. And if we are sticklers for precision in our retelling but are mean-spirited gossips, critics, and slanderers, then we are liars just the same—our speech is not consistent with the truth. When the Holy Spirit is grieved, then we've just cut off our nose to spite our face when it comes to prayer, because *all prayer works by the power of the Holy Spirit, or it doesn't work at all.*

Let's consider this again: we wear the armor of God *in order to pray effectively,* in order to defeat our spiritual foe, the devil, whom Jesus called the "father of lies" (John 8:44). Prayer is speaking with God for communion, petition, intercession, and more. It is, in its pure, God-intended form, the ultimate in human truth telling, for what mortal thinks he or she can lie to God and expect God to answer that prayer? Paul is observing something basic here: we must walk in truth comprehensively across the panorama of our lives in order for God to hear us when we pray. If we lie, or live a lie, God cannot answer us because we are acting like the children of another father—we are playing into the devil's hands, and doing so, we can never defeat him.

This is why God says, "gird yourself with truth." With that belt on, we disown the devil and his ways, we conform to God's nature, and we position ourselves for success in prayer. By speaking and living the truth when we are not praying, God recognizes us when we do—our life and our prayers are a continuum and not at odds with each other. Lord of truth, purify us in your truth today!

Day 32

Moving on to the next piece of holy armament from Ephesians 6, we look to the **breastplate of righteous** (v.14). We've already discovered Paul pulls this from Isaiah 59:17. We should also note Paul artfully recasts the breastplate as "faith and love" in 1 Thessalonians 5:8, while 2 Corinthians 6:7 speaks of the "weapons of righteousness for the right hand and the left." Generally speaking, he speaks of the "armor of light" in Romans 13:12. The lesson is that Paul uses his metaphors rather freely depending on context, and becoming dogmatic about this virtue being exclusively associated with *only this piece* of armor (and what it provided the contemporary soldier of Paul's day) is a bit risky when it comes to living the truth out. Still, Paul grounds Ephesians 6:14 and the breastplate pretty clearly in a source passage from Isaiah, ascribes covenantal meaning to it, and sends us on our way. So with these other passages in mind, let's consider the breastplate.

In terms of the armor, the *breastplate* quite nearly speaks for itself. For many, (along with a helmet) wearing armor *means* wearing a breastplate. This is a cast metal, form fitting body plate that protects the heart, lungs, and vital organs of the abdomen. It is by nature thicker and more impervious in the front and sides compared to the back, where straps and buckles hold it in place. It is worn by someone expecting to face an enemy who desires to do serious harm to those parts of our body that keep us alive. It isn't a stretch to suggest Paul is thinking these things when he speaks of righteousness. Without it, our most important inner spiritual parts are exposed (and incidentally, to the ancient mind, the *intestines* and the *kidneys* were seen as every bit the seat of emotion and spirituality as the *heart*).

As for *righteousness* itself, for how commonly the Scriptures refer to it, it can be a fairly sticky term to define. Righteousness in one sense is a *status*, a *standing* that God grants to us as a free gift; the words "justify" and "righteous" are from the very same root in Greek—only English translations make them different (one of the reasons this can be so tricky). So righteousness is a *gift* to us, by *faith* (Romans 3:24, etc.). Essentially, God is counting us as having conformed to His nature and image, even though we haven't.

On the other hand, for all of Paul's treatises on justification (i.e., being counted as righteous) as a free gift by faith, he doesn't let us off the hook for a minute when it comes to *living out* that freely given status. Even in Paul's own day, people accused him of teaching that righteousness had nothing to do with changed behavior (see Romans 3:8, 6:1), and he fiercely rejects that idea. A glance at Ephesians lets us know why: Paul wants us to live as righteous, not as unrighteous...

But sexual immorality and all impurity or covetousness must not even be named among you, as is proper among saints. ⁴ Let there be no filthiness nor foolish talk nor crude joking, which are out of place, but instead let there be thanksgiving. ⁵ For you may be sure of this, that everyone who is sexually immoral or impure, or who is covetous (that is, an idolater), has no inheritance in the kingdom of Christ and God. ⁶ Let no one deceive you with empty words, for because of these things the wrath of God comes upon the sons of disobedience. ⁷ Therefore do not become partners with them; ⁸ for at one time you were darkness, but now you are light in the Lord. Walk as children of light⁹ (for the fruit of light is found in all that is good and right and true), ¹⁰ and try to discern what is pleasing to the Lord. ¹¹ Take no part in the unfruitful works of darkness, but instead expose them. ¹² For it is shameful even to speak of the things that they do in secret. ¹³ But when anything is exposed by the light, it becomes visible, ¹⁴ for anything that becomes visible is light. Therefore it says, "Awake, O sleeper, and arise from the dead, and Christ will shine on you."¹⁵ Look carefully then how you walk, not as unwise but as wise, ¹⁶ making the best use of the time, because the days are evil. ¹⁷ Therefore do not be foolish, but understand what the will of the Lord is. ¹⁸ And do not get drunk with wine, for that is debauchery, but be filled with the Spirit, ¹⁹ addressing one another in psalms and hymns and spiritual songs, singing and making melody to the Lord with your heart, ²⁰ giving thanks always and for everything to God the Father in the name of our Lord Jesus Christ, ²¹ submitting to one another out of reverence for Christ. ⁻ Ephesians 5:3-21

That's a pretty lengthy quote, but it cannot be subdivided if we are to stay true to Paul's intent. *Unrighteousness* for Paul is a spiritual condition that plays itself out through a person's lifestyle, and can exhibit itself in a variety of ways. This passage lays out sexual impurity, covetousness (greed), crude or filthy talk or joking, deception, drunkenness, and all the secret sins the devil loves, which, all together, can rightly be classified as "darkness." Instead, Paul says, we should be giving thanks and practicing goodness, truth, wisdom, worship, and Spirit-filled living that is conversely called "light"—this is *righteousness* in action, lived out. (Let's remember again that in Romans 13:12 Paul refers to the "armor of light.")

No one on their own can live righteously. But if we abide in Christ and trust His grace and forgiveness, righteousness is *imputed* to us—granted to us as a gift by faith. I don't know how that works, I just know that it does. Abiding in that grace, we are empowered to live according to the status we have been granted. As our faith is imperfect, and needs to grow, we fall down a lot, but God is patient. By practice and persistence our actions more and more conform to God's righteousness, and we overcome.

A Christian who doesn't have the victory over sin always feels vulnerable in prayer, and when facing challenges from the enemy. Any adversity can knock them over because secretly they know they are wrong inside, and dread the enemy—even though Jesus has defeated him! But a person who actually walks out the holy standard of the faith they profess has tremendous confidence in spiritual battle; God hears them and the devil fears them. As Thomas à Kempis says, *"If inwardly you were good and pure, you would see all things clearly and understand them rightly, **for a pure heart penetrates heaven and hell.**"* (*Imitation*, Book Two, Chapter

4) Let us strive for holiness, for a pure and upright heart and intention, and for spotless living before God. Let's move on from the baby Christian standard of merely avoiding the worst sins, and move on to maturity in Christ, seeking to please and follow hard after Him. When we begin to thirst for righteousness, and delight in the confidence that comes with right living, then the enemy begins to shake in his boots, and we gain ground in prayer.

Day 33

Our next item in the armor of God is our **footwear** (v.15), which the ESV renders *as shoes for your feet, having put on the readiness given by the gospel of peace.* "But as with the belt of truth, the Greek here doesn't really contain the noun "shoes" (or even "sandals" as some people like to say); instead, it simply says something like, "wrap your feet with the readiness of the gospel of peace." So just as truth itself is our belt, the readiness to share the gospel *itself* is our footwear.

Here's where I need to bring in the reminder, once again, that this passage is about *prayer as spiritual warfare*, front to finish. But this piece of the armor drives home the great truth that wearing the armor is not just about *praying* these things, but about *living them*. As we live well, so our prayers will have tremendous effect.

Look at this passage from Ephesians 3, which (again) is lengthy but needs to be taken as a whole to understand Paul's thought...

*For this reason I, Paul, a prisoner of Christ Jesus on behalf of you Gentiles— ² assuming that you have heard of the stewardship of God's grace that was given to me for you, ³ how the mystery was made known to me by revelation, as I have written briefly. ⁴ When you read this, you can perceive my insight into the mystery of Christ, ⁵ which was not made known to the sons of men in other generations as it has now been revealed to his holy apostles and prophets by the Spirit. ⁶ This mystery is that the Gentiles are fellow heirs, members of the same body, and partakers of the promise in Christ Jesus **through the gospel. ⁷ Of this gospel I was made a minister according to the gift of God's grace, which was given me by the working of his power.** ⁸ To me, though I am the very least of all the saints, **this grace was given, to preach to the Gentiles the unsearchable riches of Christ,** ⁹ and to bring to light for everyone what is the plan of the mystery hidden for ages in God, who created all things, ¹⁰ so that through the church the manifold wisdom of God might now be made known to the rulers and authorities in the heavenly places. ¹¹ This was according to the* *eternal purpose that he has realized in Christ Jesus our Lord,*[12] *in whom we have boldness and access with confidence through our faith in him.*[13] *So I ask you not to lose heart over what I am suffering for you, which is your glory.* ¯ Ephesians 3:1–13

Let me break this down so you don't feel like you're having to swallow an elephant: In vv. 1-8, Paul is testifying about his calling, and how God revealed to him—a Jew—that all the promises and spiritual inheritance he once thought only belonged to Israel, he now understands by revelation belong to all Gentiles who believe in Christ. The call is to "preach the gospel," which in English is a whole phrase, but in Greek is a single verb ("gospel" and "preach" are sister words, with "gospel" being the noun and "preach" being the verb, both with the identical root—*evangel*). In vv.9-12, Paul explains God's divine purposes for His grace towards the Gentiles, then in v. 13 Paul tells the Ephesians not to take his imprisonment as somehow contrary to those purposes, but only as a confirmation of their great truth and importance. Overall, the passage teaches about the nature of being called to preach the good news, what the power of the gospel is in God's plan, and how the whole effort is well worth it.

In my mind, Ephesians 3 is the passage to which Paul refers back when he refers to the Ephesians "shodding their feet with readiness" to preach the gospel; they were given spiritual birth through someone sharing the truth with them, now he expects them to *follow his example and share with others.* The "punch line" of all this comes in Ephesians 3:14-21—one of Paul's most powerful written prayers. For Paul, *evangelism and prayer are deeply linked.* Not surprisingly, this follows in Ephesians 6 itself:

...praying at all times in the Spirit, with all prayer and supplication. To that end, keep alert with all perseverance, making supplication for all the saints, [19] *and also for me, that words may be given to me in opening my mouth boldly to proclaim the mystery of the gospel,* [20] *for which I am an ambassador in chains, that I may declare it boldly, as I ought to speak.* ¯ Ephesians 6:18-20

The Apostle Paul, now an old man, having founded churches all throughout Asia Minor and Greece, and also having written books like 1 & 2 Thessalonians, 1 & 2 Corinthians, Romans, and Galatians, *still asks for prayer to share the good news boldly*. One would think that if anyone should have it down by now, he would. But he is still dependent on prayer as the power that drives him and helps him overcome his natural timidity, and therefore he asks his spiritual children to support him. This attitude is not isolated here; he says the very same thing in Philippians 1:18-20, which would have been written around the same time as Ephesians. Paul understands that proclaiming the good news to another is far more than merely sharing information, it is an invasive assault on the devil's turf, and that takes a "working of God's power" and "grace" (Ephesians 3:7-8).

So here's the deal: if we are going to share the gospel effectively as individuals and a community, we have to *saturate* ourselves in prayer—prayer for ourselves as witnesses, and prayer for each other. If we do not pray, Jesus and His Holy Spirit will not be a present reality to us and we will have nothing to share anyway. On the flipside, people who are compelled to share Christ—like Paul, whom we are urged to imitate—are always deeply prayerful. This two-way relationship between prayer and witnessing is why Paul includes the "readiness of the gospel" as part of the armor. It was inconceivable to him that a praying soldier of Christ *wouldn't* want to be ready to share.

I read a story about the early church as background study for this chapter. In the generation just after the writing of the last books of the New Testament, there lived a brilliant young man. He sought truth, and studied with the brightest philosophers in his desire to find peace and fulfillment. But these things always left him empty, no matter which way he turned. One day he walked alone to an open field overlooking the sea, seeking solitude to sort his thoughts and take stock of his life. By chance, he came across an old man there, a fisherman. He and the rustic old man began to chat, and soon the young man was enraptured by the simple witness of the man, who was a Christian. What was a simple, low-key conversation set a fire in the heart of the younger man, and quite literally changed the world. We'll never know that old man's name, but the young man who turned to Christ as a result was named **Justin Martyr**, and he is considered the father of all Christian apologists.

Today, evangelism is often seen as a task for the pastor, a church program, or a televised event. But the earliest Christians simply talked to other people every chance they got. They walked close to Jesus, and so they walked in a way to get close to others and share Jesus with them. Let's pray and pray and pray that God does in us what He needs to. Let's give the devil reason to fear the church, "terrible as an army with banners" (Song of Songs 6:10).

Day 34

Continuing with the armor of God, let's consider the **shield of faith** (v.16). As we've noted, this piece of armor finds its roots in Psalm 91:4-5, and Paul's readers would likely have made the connection. In that passage, God's *faithfulness* (meaning, the basis for our *faith*) becomes to us a *shield* and *buckler*—two different terms that here describe pretty much the same thing: a handheld defensive barrier that the soldier can use to block his enemy's thrusts and projectiles. To be absolutely precise, a shield is usually bigger than a buckler, but what a buckler sacrifices in size it gains in mobility, but here there's no question poetry is in play, and again we shouldn't worry about that kind of precision; a Roman shield was typically pretty large. In any case, Psalm 91 goes on to point out the enemy's threat: *arrows*, aka *darts*, that the enemy hurls at us.

There are a couple things we might observe about Paul's use of the metaphor of *faith* as a *shield*. Unlike other defensive armor, the soldier of God actually *wields faith actively*. A shield is not a "set it and forget it" item. The soldier must *"take up"* the shield— he must intentionally move it to and fro to *"extinguish the flaming darts of the evil one."* Paul is telling us something about the nature of faith. We may *have* faith, but we need to actually *apply it*. We must *stir our faith* to combat the missiles of the enemy. How does one do that?

I am convinced that our faith operates in concert with the Word of God; after all, *"faith comes from hearing, and hearing by the word"* (Romans 10:17). But you might say, isn't that the **sword of the Spirit** mentioned in the next verse? It is indeed. Have you ever seen film of a soldier using his sword and shield in tandem? Just as a soldier wields a shield on one arm and a sword with the other— one his primary active *defense* and the other his active weapon of *offense*—so faith is the defensive aspect of God's word in this context, while the quoted Word works as an offensive weapon in the next. Defensively, we combat the enemy's attacks by recalling

God's faithfulness, and resting in our faith that He will continue to be faithful. Look at Psalm 77:9-10...

"Has God forgotten to be gracious? Has he in anger shut up his compassion?" **Then I said, "I will appeal to this, to the years of the right hand of the Most High."**

Notice how the psalmist moves from his distress of soul to an active recollection of God's past faithfulness. His inner distress is caused by a flaming dart of the enemy, questioning God's goodness; the shield of faith comes up when he chooses to remember how good God has been.

...or this, in Psalm 91:2...

I will say to the LORD, "My refuge and my fortress, my God, in whom I trust."

"I will **say** *of the Lord..."* Say it. Call on the Scripture. Apply the shield of your faith when the enemy attacks.

Once again, permit me to remind you of the devil's tactics. Of course he'd love to take you down, to eliminate you from battle altogether. But he'll settle for being a strength-sapper, a constant drag on your strength and focus. He wants you constantly wrapped up in pesky, fruitless skirmishes. So he hurls those flaming arrows, one here, there another. If our faith isn't ready, if we aren't willing to fight and put them out, we are constantly burned and pierced, and we cannot make any headway. *It's by using your* **shield** *that you'll be able to get in a position to use your* **sword**—*what the enemy fears the most.*

I appreciate this passage from John Bunyan's Christian classic *The Pilgrim's Progress:*

But now, in this Valley of Humiliation, poor Christian was hard put to it; for he had gone but a little way, before he espied a foul *fiend coming over the field to meet with him; his name was Apollyon. Then did Christian begin to be afraid, and to cast in his mind whether to go back or to stand his ground. **But he considered again, that he had no armour for his back, and therefore thought that to turn the back to him might give him greater advantage with ease to pierce him with his darts; therefore he resolved to venture, and stand his ground.** For, thought he, had I no more in mine eye than the saving of my life, it would be the best way to stand.*

Astutely, Bunyan observes that we bear our armor on the front; we cannot defeat the enemy by turning tail, we cannot defeat the enemy by bobbing and weaving or any other trick. The enemy is too wily for that. We must face him straightaway, stir our faith, and put out his lying darts as they come at us.

Lord, help our faith!

Day 35

Today we want to look at the **helmet of salvation**. (Ephesians 6:17) Once again, this piece of armor is pulled directly with no modification from Isaiah 59—it is armor that the Lord Himself wears into battle against His enemy for the sake of our redemption. Now He has bestowed that same helm upon us in covenant relationship. What was the marquis armament in His battle for our salvation now becomes what we wear as the ultimate badge of His approval, and therefore protection, as we march against the devil.

A helmet doesn't need much explanation. For Paul's readers it would have been an imposing thing, a piece of armor forged of hammered metal and formed in such a way as to cover the skull, back and sides of the neck, cheeks, and nose. It would protect the soldier from deadly blows to the head. It cannot be coincidence that salvation is our helmet—arguably the most vital piece of armor we have (some gladiators, in fact, wore the helmet as their only protective armor).

As far as *salvation* being a *helmet*, what does that mean, exactly? If I am already in the Lord, why am I instructed to *put on* the helmet? How can I even take it off if I am truly a Christian? Without getting into the debate about "losing" our salvation— falling away—I'll simply say that I think Paul's intent is otherwise. For his purposes, I believe the helmet of salvation is much like the shield of faith in the sense that we can have something from God but not know how to apply it. For someone who is already a Christian, putting on the helmet is not "making sure we're saved" or the like, but rather understanding how to take the benefits of our salvation into battle with us.

If you have confessed Jesus in faith, you have been saved. But if you do not mature in your understanding of that salvation, if you do not have its assurances deeply settled in your inner person, the enemy can score blows upon you in the heat of battle—even though you have been granted the power to avoid those blows.

Growing in this knowledge is a lifelong question—indeed, a pilgrimage called the *Christian life*. This is especially true considering that "salvation" encompasses all that Jesus has done for us—redemption and forgiveness from sin, healing, provision, reconciliation, and more. Frankly, by worldly standards, the gospel is just too good to be true—*except it is true*. Our naturally cynical and unbelieving mind, affected by sin, resists these truths. We also know we are unworthy. Only the power of the Holy Spirit can renew our minds and quicken these truths to us.

Obviously, I cannot cover the whole of this process in one reflection—or in a lifetime of writing. But I will say this, and focus upon it: *You have been forgiven*. You have been purchased, redeemed, cleansed, sanctified, purified, translated, lifted, adopted, sealed, and reconciled. Entirely on God's own initiative, He loved you and raised you up, and called you by His name. Read Ephesians 1-2, and you will understand the substance of the helmet of salvation. The faith soldier who knows they are forgiven— knows that they are forgiven to the bottom of who they are— strides confidently into battle. Such a soldier does not arrogantly saunter, because their confidence and strength has a source in Another. Nor does the soldier sheepishly creep forward, as if they were still guilty and could only think of how their unworthiness will be exposed. No, the soldier walks forward, head held high, knowing that not only guilt but also shame has been wiped away, that the purchase is complete, that the devil's claims are nullified and are only empty lies, and that no darkness find a foothold any longer.

Know that you have been forgiven. Know it. Know that He loves you, not tenuously, not half-heartedly, not entertaining buyers regret. You were costly to the Father, the priciest of purchases that exacted from His purse no less than the life of His only Son. But He looks on you and brags to the angels around His throne about His purchase; you were worth it, and if He had to, He'd do it again. *That knowing in your "knower" is the putting on of the helmet of salvation.*

I love these lyrics:

Oh happy day
Oh happy day
When Jesus washed
When Jesus washed
When Jesus washed
Washed my sins away

He taught me how
To watch, and fight, and pray...

If you spend your time praying—indeed, your life—always dealing with that opening issue—whether the Lord accepts you, whether He hears you, even whether He even wants you, *how can you fight and pray?* How can you look the devil in the eye when he comes after you and those you love? But if you know how deeply the Lord loves you, and how completely He has redeemed you, oh, yes, then you'll watch, and fight, and pray. And thus submitted to God, you will resist the devil, and he will flee from you.

Day 36

In our review of the armor of God, we finally come to the **sword of the Spirit**—the Word of God (Ephesians 6:17). As we've seen, the Old Testament passages that refer to God's Word as His weapon are many. The same follows in the New Testament, as 2 Thessalonians 2:8 and Revelation 1:16 and 19:10, 21 reflect. Here Paul tells us that God is giving that sword into our keeping, just as Jonathan gave David *his* sword in covenant love. When we swing God's sword, our foes no longer face us and our cheap threats, but God's own might.

As far as the natural aspects of the *sword* metaphor are concerned, the Greek word used in v. 17 (*machaira*, the "ch" being pronounced like "Christ") mirrors the word used in Isaiah 49:2 (i.e., in the Greek Old Testament), and in keeping with the image of a Roman soldier is almost certainly meant to be the Greek equivalent of the Roman *gladius*. The *gladius* was the standard issue short sword given to common infantrymen, and the root behind the word *gladiator*. For those who might be disappointed that this is not a two-handed "dragon slayer" of some sort, stay your concern for a moment. The *gladius* conquered the known world of Paul's day. A soldier could not only fight much longer with the lighter short sword than his top-heavy opponents, but the sword in the hands of a skilled warrior was lighting quick, striking two or three times for every single blow of his enemy. It was a weapon therefore not only meant for speed and agility, but also for long combat. I should also note that a unified troop of *gladius*-wielding soldiers was especially deadly in battle. I believe a lesson is to be drawn from this image of the sword of the Spirit—a weapon that is thin on liabilities but heavy on advantages for the soldier who carries it.

As far as the spiritual truths implied in the passage, there's a great deal about this metaphor that isn't mysterious in the slightest. First, while our defensive armor is multiple, our offensive weaponry is *singular:* we aren't given any options when it comes to our attack—it's the Word, or nothing at all. Only our footwear comes close in its role (taking us into battle). Second, it is the sword of the *Spirit.* The Holy Spirit inspired the Word of God, and the Holy Spirit empowers us in the Word today as we apply it. Remember, the Word is far more than just information. It is *alive:*

For the word of God is living and active, sharper than any two-edged sword, piercing to the division of soul and of spirit, of joints and of marrow, and discerning the thoughts and intentions of the heart.¯ Hebrews 4:12

This passage from Hebrews is very enlightening. If it seems like the sword of the Spirit is something that first cuts *us,* you haven't read it wrong. Those who wield God's Word must first *submit to it,* and that means pain to our flesh. As I noted with the helmet of salvation, we are *forgiven,* and have every reason to be confident. But to reach our full potential, we must also be *sanctified.* Areas not surrendered to the Lord will be judged, winnowed, and purified. The result will be a soldier more battleworthy than ever before. There is nothing the devil fears in you more than a meek and submitted spirit, one that meditates on the Word then softly and sincerely prays, *"Not my will, but Thine be done, O Lord..."* Call it "boot camp" for your soul to be so trained by the Master Swordsman, who in His severe mercy has nothing but your best in mind, knowing what kind of fight you are going to face.

For me, the definitive passage on the use of the sword of the Spirit by a Christian foot soldier can be found in the temptation passages of the Gospels (Mark 1, Matthew 4, and Luke 4). In these passages, Jesus parries the thrusts of the devil's temptations not with superior wit, or scornful replies, or the glory of His person— all of which would have been legitimate, considering who He was and whom he faced. No, Jesus stuck with the Word, and the Word prevailed. The power of God's Word is that it *disheartens* the enemy even as it *encourages* us. Unlike natural swords which weary their wielder, the sword of the Spirit makes us *stronger and more agile* as we swing it; it edifies us as we wear down the enemy.

As far as I am concerned, it doesn't matter if you open the Bible and read it or quote from memory, as Jesus did. The Word is equally deadly to the devil so long as we quote in faith. There is no prize for eloquence here; the issue is our conviction and consistency in applying it. Naturally, the more we commit to memory, the greater agility in prayer we will have—spontaneously *praying the Word* is extraordinarily powerful. But sometimes, when our faith is challenged and we find ourselves at a loss, it would be better just to read the Scriptures in prayer form than to "pray our problems" and end up more discouraged than we were when we started! But, however you do it, the enemy hates it. For this reason he will distract you from God's Word if ever you allow it. So read the Word, meditate on the Word, memorize the Word, listen to the Word, and talk the Word with other believers. The Word is our deadly weapon!

Day 37

We have examined each element of the armor of God—six pieces in all—one after the other. But before I summarize and tie them together in regard to action, I'd like to point something out by highlighting some things in the overall text:

Finally, be strong in the Lord and in the strength of his might. [11] *Put on the **whole armor** of God, that you may be able to stand against the schemes of the devil.* [12] *For we do not wrestle against flesh and blood, but against the rulers, against the authorities, against the cosmic powers over this present darkness, against the spiritual forces of evil in the heavenly places.* [13] *Therefore take up the **whole armor** of God, that you may be able to withstand in the evil day, and having **done all**, to stand firm.* [14] *Stand therefore, having fastened on the belt of truth, and having put on the breastplate of righteousness,* [15] *and, as shoes for your feet, having put on the readiness given by the gospel of peace.* [16] *In **all circumstances** take up the shield of faith, with which you can **extinguish all** the flaming darts of the evil one;* [17] *and take the helmet of salvation, and the sword of the Spirit, which is the word of God,* [18] *praying at **all times** in the Spirit, with **all prayer and supplication**. To that end, keep alert with **all perseverance**, making supplication for **all the saints**,* [19] *and **also for me**, that words may be given to me in opening my mouth boldly to proclaim the mystery of the gospel,* [20] *for which I am an ambassador in chains, that I may declare it boldly, as I ought to speak.* ~ Ephesians 6:10-20

Notice the pattern... *whole, whole, all, all, all, all, all, all, all, also...*

We are to put on the *whole* armor of God—not part of the armor, not most of it, not our personal favorites, not those pieces with which we are comfortable—*all* of it. The element we leave out becomes the gap our enemy will exploit. The Ten Commandments are not the Ten Suggestions, the Sermon on the Mount is not the Op-Ed Article in the Galilee Times, and the Whole Armor of God is not the Mix-and-Match Office Wear

Ensemble of God. We need to consider *all* the elements, and pray that God refine in us that armor.

The result of putting on the whole armor is a constancy in spiritual battle. Remember, the armor of God is a *spiritual metaphor for a way of life* that puts us on solid inner footing so we can walk in victory. There is essentially no seam between the five expressions of "whole" and "all" in verses 10-17 and the five expressions of "all" and "also" (i.e., Paul's final inclusion of himself in verse 19) in the rest of the passage. There is no putting on the armor of God for a photo op, there is no glamor contest for who fills it out best on the catwalk. We put on the armor because we are in a war; we are under attack, and we are commanded to attack the kingdom of darkness. The gates of hell will not prevail against the church.

How is this actually done? Being a spiritual warrior includes a larger picture I will address in coming chapters, but for now let's stick with this passage. Take a look at vv.17-20. This is one of Paul's famous run-on sentences, which shows that he is linking the subject matter of the beginning to the subject matter throughout, all the way to the end. In other words, at the very least he connects taking the helmet of salvation and the sword of the Spirit with the thoughts found in vv. 18-20—which are (literally), "praying at all times in the Spirit," "all prayer," "supplication," "keep(ing) alert with all perseverance," "making supplication for all the saints," and prayer for Paul. Closer to the mark, as I've stated, is that the *entirety* of the armor is linked to those prayerful actions in the latter part of the passage. The armor of God is about *constant prayer*, all the time, in the Spirit, for all the saints, and for those servants who proclaim the Word to others.

I am convinced that the whole armor of God, in practice, stirs and provokes prayer in us. Why? A couple of reasons at least. First, there is no way to walk in truth, righteousness, evangelistic zeal, faith, revelation of God's salvation in you, and a love for God's Word and not be a praying person. Those virtues can only function by means of prayer, and to walk in them means you are walking close to God and communing with Him. Second, victory begets battle-waging. Soldiers who win in battle develop a thirst for battle—they *want* to take it to the enemy. Spiritual battle will never parallel natural battle in this way, nor should it. But my point is simply that as we feel traction and walk in victory, we are drawn to continue in that which *gives* us that victory. This pull to prayer is the often-referred to and much-coveted "prayer groove"— that rhythm that mature people of prayer develop, a stride they hit so that day by day they develop consistency and gain ground, sensitivity, and strength, going from "glory to glory."

I've never met a victorious Christian who wasn't also a person of prayer. I've met wealthy ones, clever ones, charismatic ones, eloquent ones, even brilliant ones. But I've never met a true soldier of Christ who remained true to the Lord and true to the Word who was not also true to prayer. They go hand in hand.

Let's be soldiers, as the Lord tells us we must, and let's be people of prayer. It isn't a season, it isn't a fad, it isn't for a time. It's our life, and it means life to those around us.

Day 38

Before I turn to a discussion of who our enemy is (and is not), I'd like to broaden the lens a bit on Ephesians 6 and take a look at the other passages Paul writes regarding the armor of God. These are enlightening for a fuller picture of his thought as prompted by the Holy Spirit, and will "flesh out" Ephesians 6. Let's remember, although Ephesians 6 is the *best known* passage about spiritual armor, it is not the *only* one, and by far it is not the only passage addressing the subject of prayer as spiritual warfare. Below we have three famous Pauline passages, listed here in the order in which they were written: 1 Thessalonians in AD 50, 2 Corinthians in AD 57, Romans later in AD 57 (Ephesians was written last of all, in about AD 60)...

So then let us not sleep, as others do, but let us keep awake and be sober. ⁷ *For those who sleep, sleep at night, and those who get drunk, are drunk at night.* ⁸ *But since we belong to the day, let us be sober, having put on the* **breastplate of faith and love, and for a helmet the hope of salvation.** ⁻ 1 Thessalonians 5:6-8

We put no obstacle in anyone's way, so that no fault may be found with our ministry, ⁴ *but as servants of God we commend ourselves in every way: by great endurance, in afflictions, hardships, calamities,* ⁵ *beatings, imprisonments, riots, labors, sleepless nights, hunger;* ⁶ *by purity, knowledge, patience, kindness, the Holy Spirit, genuine love;* ⁷ *by truthful speech, and the power of God;* **with the weapons of righteousness for the right hand and for the left;** ⁸ *through honor and dishonor, through slander and praise.* ⁻ 2 Corinthians 6:3-8

The night is far gone; the day is at hand. So then let us cast off the works of darkness and **put on the armor of light.** ¹³ *Let us walk properly as in the daytime, not in orgies and drunkenness, not in sexual immorality and sensuality, not in quarreling and jealousy.* ¹⁴ *But* **put on the Lord Jesus Christ,** *and make no provision for the flesh, to gratify its desires.* ⁻ Romans 13:12-14

In all of these passages we find common ground with Ephesians 6 in that the spiritual armor we are to wear is framed in terms of *our walk*—how we behave, our way of life from the heart. We actually wage war *by how we live.* There is a subtle but important nuance here, because if we aren't careful we will think that living right is something we do *in order to fight.* While there is some truth to that, the broader truth is that we wage battle *by the act of right living itself.* In all of these passages, and especially in 1 Thessalonians and Romans, the contrast to the armor of light is not the demonic opposition described in Ephesians 6, but *ungodliness itself.* Furthermore, Romans simply tells us to "put on the Lord Jesus Christ"—*Jesus Himself is our armor!*

This is very telling in many ways. I've run into some folks over the years (not many, but some) who are all gung-ho about "spiritual warfare"—books, braggadocious prayers, big talk, and spiritual experiences—but they were also terrible gossips, they were eaten up with pettiness, they were divisive and formed cliques in the church, and some were subversive to godly authority as if they had a special "inside track" with the Holy Spirit. But Jesus has no use for such "warriors." He exalted a child in the midst of His disciples and said the greatest among them would have the mildness of that child. By the world's standards, the Kingdom of God is upside down: servants are kings, the meek inherit the earth, and those who weep and mourn will be comforted. In keeping with that spirit, let's keep some things in mind: if you really want to whip the devil in spiritual combat, give thanks in all circumstances, raise your hands in worship when you don't feel like it, turn the other cheek, bless and do not curse, forgive and pray for those who despitefully use you, bear with each other's faults without grumbling, consider others better than yourself, spend yourself for the weak, choose righteousness when it feels like a mouth full of gravel, flee immorality when it bats its eyes at you, repent your sins daily. That kind of a person is the one the devil cannot get a foothold in. I repeat, living with your eyes on Jesus and *seeking to be exactly like Him is warfare.*

Paul makes his statement about the weapons of righteousness in both hands in the midst of a passage that hardly paints him as a warrior: he basically recounts how he's lived his life for Jesus getting the stuffings beaten out of him, and with very little to show for it by human standards. But he persists in right living, and carries the day. Those who gave Paul such a hard time are forgotten at best and named as villains at worst, while he has served as a spiritual template and hero to billions of people.

Walking holy, walking in love, walking in perseverance for the upward call of God in Christ Jesus...these things are armor to us, these things are warfare to us, these things are victory to us. When you break and weep in God's presence for the sheer beauty of it, when you choose to spend a bit more time in the Bible rather than watching another rerun on TV, when you shake the sleep from your bones to rise and pray because you know that it is the only time you can realistically make it happen, well, that's war. That's real war.

Walk in victory today!

Day 39

The Chinese war strategist Sun Tzu (who lived around four centuries before Paul but whose work was not published in the West until the 1500s) famously said, *"Know yourself; know your enemy."* Some truth belongs so absolutely to the realm of common sense that it achieves universal application, and this maxim strikes me as one of those. I say this because Paul is essentially demonstrating the very same idea in Ephesians 6.

Here, again, is our passage:

Finally, be strong in the Lord and in the strength of his might. [11] *Put on the whole armor of God, that you may be able to stand against* **the schemes of the devil.** [12] **For we do not wrestle against flesh and blood, but against the rulers, against the authorities, against the cosmic powers over this present darkness, against the spiritual forces of evil in the heavenly places.** [13] *Therefore take up the whole armor of God, that you may be able to withstand in the evil day, and having done all, to stand firm.* [14] *Stand therefore, having fastened on the belt of truth, and having put on the breastplate of righteousness,* [15] *and, as shoes for your feet, having put on the readiness given by the gospel of peace.* [16] *In all circumstances take up the shield of faith, with which you can extinguish all the flaming darts of the evil one;* [17] *and take the helmet of salvation, and the sword of the Spirit, which is the word of God,* [18] *praying at all times in the Spirit, with all prayer and supplication. To that end, keep alert with all perseverance, making supplication for all the saints,* [19] *and also for me, that words may be given to me in opening my mouth boldly to proclaim the mystery of the gospel,* [20] *for which I am an ambassador in chains, that I may declare it boldly, as I ought to speak.* ⁻ Ephesians 6:10-20

In terms of the order of this passage, I chose to begin with the armor of God (i.e., knowing ourselves) before grappling with knowing the nature of our enemy—in other words, I've reversed it. But I've done so because I believe the Book of Ephesians overall emphasizes the salvation we have in Christ and how that salvation has transformed us, over against the nature of the enemy and how we are to deal with him. But that doesn't mean the enemy is incidental to Paul, nor even that here in chapter 6 is the only place Paul mentions our enemy, as we will see.

Paul introduces the armor of God by stating That the very reason for putting on this armor that we've come to know is to *"be able to stand against the schemes of the devil."* Then Paul gets more specific: he makes it clear that our battle is not a natural one—at the heart of the issue, we do not battle against flesh and blood (meaning, people), "but against *the rulers, against the authorities, against the cosmic powers over this present darkness, against the spiritual forces of evil in the heavenly places."*

What is Paul talking about here? Generally speaking, Paul is talking about the same thing other New Testament writers talk about. He and others talk point-blank about *understanding the enemy's wiles* as part of the strategy to defeat them. It isn't to glorify the devil, or be fascinated with him, or find him mysteriously alluring. All that is foolishness. As C.S. Lewis famously remarked in his book *The Screwtape Letters* that we can easily fall into one of two extremes when it comes to how we see the devil—either to disbelieve in him and his minions, or to become excessively interested by them. We should avoid these extremes. Rather, we are to understand what may be known and should be known about the enemy of our souls. Paul tells us that we are to live and act *"...so that we would not be outwitted by Satan; for we are not ignorant of his designs."* (2 Corinthians 2:11). Similarly, the Risen Lord refers to the *"so-called deep secrets of Satan"* (Revelation 2:24). Both Paul and Jesus Himself *demystify* Satan's designs and tactics. The enemy loves mystery, hiddenness, and mystique, but the Lord scorns those ideas, and Paul says his designs are laid bare before the discerning believer. What falls to us is not *decoding* the devil—that has already been done—but rather *having understood* his tactics, being watchful, and *resisting him* steadfastly.

Consider Peter...

Be sober-minded; be watchful. Your adversary the devil prowls around like a roaring lion, seeking someone to devour. [9] **Resist him**, *firm in your faith, knowing that the same kinds of suffering are being experienced by your brotherhood throughout the world.* ¯ 1 Peter 5:8-9

...and James...

Submit yourselves therefore to God. Resist the devil, and he will flee from you. ¯ James 4:7

These truths lie at the heart of what Ephesians 6 and all spiritual combat is about. In days to come I will flesh out the language Paul uses, but for now, let's allow the simplicity of these truths hit home: we are not to find the devil and his minions mesmerizing, we are not to find them bewildering, we are not to wonder what secrets they hold, and (above all) we are not to be afraid of the devil. What we must know about him we can know about him, and that is enough. Now it falls to us to rest in the fact that he has been unmasked and defeated (more on that later), and we are to resist him and collect on the defeat Jesus has already won for us.

Day 40

Yesterday I wrote about knowing our enemy, the devil, or more precisely, knowing his tactics and schemes. We know him and use the knowledge we have of him for a one-dimensional reason: to defeat him and emerge victorious in spiritual warfare. We are to be aware, but not fascinated; guarded, but not jittery; wary but not fearful. Due to his former exalted angelic nature, there is a certain respect we must maintain when dealing with the devil (see Jude v. 9), but that is what might be called a "reflected respect"— *God* made him glorious, and though fallen, he is still beyond us in many ways due to the nature God originally gave him. On the other hand, he is to command *none* of the awe that is God's alone, and (most importantly for this reflection and the subject of spiritual battle), he is to be seen and treated as a *defeated enemy.*

Many Christians have heard this said, but do not really understand what it means, particularly for the question of spiritual warfare. But Satan's defeat is a present and powerful reality, and for all the vast study that could be applied to make that clear, I will limit myself to a few verses.

In Hebrews 2:14-15 it says this...

*Since therefore the children share in flesh and blood, he himself likewise partook of the same things, **that through death he might destroy the one who has the power of death**, that is, the devil,* [15] *and deliver all those who through fear of death were subject to lifelong slavery.*

Before Jesus came, the devil held the power of death, and with it, held all humanity captive. Death is the ultimate trump card, the whip hand, the final word. By it, the devil enslaved humanity. By dying and rising from the dead, Jesus "destroyed" the devil— meaning, he broke his power over humanity. Read Revelation 1:17-18...

When I saw him, I fell at his feet as though dead. But he laid his right hand on me, saying, "Fear not, I am the first and the last, ¹⁸ *and the living one. I died, and behold I am alive forevermore, and* **I have the keys of Death and Hades.**

Jesus now holds the keys. Before the Crucifixion and Resurrection, the devil held the keys. Now his power is broken, and he is defeated.

We now live in the "already and the not yet"—the age between the Resurrection and the Second Coming, wherein the devil is defeated, but humanity is still in the "Valley of Decision"...people may choose redemption and be saved, or may reject and stay in the darkness. This period of time is confusing and frustrating to many Christians. If the Lord has whooped the devil, how come there's so much of the devil's works in play? Why does the world continue in its self-destructive tailspin? Well, the Lord could end it all in a snap, but that would mean no more chance for people to turn of their own accord. Personally, I'm glad the Lord was patient, and waited for me!

But the Lord's patience needs to become our own. And we need to understand our role while we live in this dark age. The devil can still deceive, even though he has been defeated and lost the power of death and the grave. These truths should direct our prayers. We can pray victoriously, assured that the outcome is already decided. But the enemy is still a formidable foe. The threat he poses, though, is not because he holds real "legal" power in the courts of heaven because of our sin (Jesus has defeated him in that respect), or because he can threaten us with eternal death; he's done in respect to those things, though he may pretend otherwise. No, his power is in deception, temptation, smoke screens, and threats. And those things are serious enough—not only towards us as believers, but against others who might come to know Jesus through our prayers. Is it any wonder the word of truth is the answer to defeat him?

Know yourself, know your enemy. The more you meditate on the Word, the better you know who God is and who you are in God, the better you will be able to stand against the devil's schemes. Likewise, if you cast aside stereotypes of the devil, throw out superstitions and fears and absurd caricatures of him, and understand who he really is in the Scriptures, what he can do and what he cannot do, the better you will be able to fight him.

We do not taunt the devil. We quote the Scriptures and soberly rebuke him in the name of Jesus, recalling the devil's defeat at the hands of the Lord. That is enough, and that is all that is required of us.

Day 41

So far in our discussion of prayer as spiritual warfare, mostly drawn from Ephesians 6, we have expounded upon the subtheme of "know your enemy" in terms of Ephesians 6:11. That verse simply speaks about taking our "stand against the devil's schemes." As we've seen, multiple writers in the New Testament, and even the Lord Himself, speak in terms of battling and vanquishing the devil. As Luke 10 describes the Lord's word to those who returned victoriously in His name...

The seventy-two returned with joy, saying, "Lord, even the demons are subject to us in your name!"[18] And he said to them, "I saw Satan fall like lightning from heaven.[19] Behold, I have given you authority to tread on serpents and scorpions, and over all the power of the enemy, and nothing shall hurt you."~ Luke 10:17-19

So Jesus Himself connects the disciples' casting out of demons with Satan's downfall. This squares with Ephesians 6, which frames "standing against the devil's schemes" more specifically as a larger conflict with the devil's minions in the following verse:

*Put on the whole armor of God, that you may be able to **stand against the schemes of the devil**.[12] For we do not wrestle against flesh and blood, **but against the rulers, against the authorities, against the cosmic powers over this present darkness, against the spiritual forces of evil in the heavenly places**.~* Ephesians 6:11-12

In this verse Paul is clearly speaking in terms that his readers understood, but that we might not. So this requires a bit of explanation.

First of all, it seems clear that when Jesus and Paul refer to Satan/the devil, at least *sometimes* they are making a general reference to demonic forces under his sway. In other words, to "cast out the devil" doesn't necessarily mean (and probably usually doesn't mean) dealing with *the* devil—Satan himself. Unlike God, the devil is not omnipresent, omniscient, or omnipotent. When we call on the Lord, we are aware that He is all those things, and more. But rebuking, binding, and otherwise resisting the devil is not any sort of "opposite" of the Lord, because the Lord is incomparable—He has no opposite. So *the* devil is not everywhere—not by a long shot. On the other hand, demonic forces are numerous and indeed prevalent, even if they do not compare in power to the Lord. These forces are those Paul refers to in Ephesians 6:12, and the defeat of which Jesus connected with the devil's downfall. Just as Paul calls the devil *"the prince of the power of the air"*(Ephesians 2:2), these demon princes are located in *"heavenly places"*—not meaning the Lord's heaven, but the earth's atmosphere.

People have asked me in the past if the demons can be "numbered"—almost as if a "biblical census" of demons could give us some sort of a handle on how to whip them in spiritual conflict. Simply put, there's no way of knowing. Revelation 12:4 refers to the devil sweeping a third of the stars from the sky with his fall, and stars are commonly used to illustrate angels. This is where people get the idea that a third of the angels fell with Satan. But that doesn't help much, because there are *billions* of angels (Revelation 5:11). Where does this put us? Back to the simple truths we've already covered: the devil and his minions are (collectively) a defeated enemy. Although we may not be able to see them, number them, or otherwise have a sensory awareness of them as if they were a natural enemy, we know that we have been given *"authority to tread on serpents and scorpions, and over all the power of the enemy, and nothing shall hurt [us]."*

But a general knowledge of what Paul is talking about is helpful. He refers to these selfsame "rulers, etc." in various places—here in Ephesians and elsewhere. Consider...

He disarmed the rulers and authorities and put them to open shame, by triumphing over them by it [the cross]. – Colossians 2:15

...and...

None of the rulers of this age understood this [wisdom], for if they had, they would not have crucified the Lord of glory.
~ 1 Corinthians 2:8

...also...

...through the church the manifold wisdom of God might now be made known to the rulers and authorities in the heavenly places.
~ Ephesians 3:10

The Colossians passage tells us Jesus overcame and shamed the demonic rulers and authorities by the cross; the 1 Corinthians passage tells us that if they had understood God's wisdom, they would never have crucified the Lord at all; the Ephesians 3 passage tells us that their shame continues through the church, which God has chosen to exalt as His means for their final defeat. In all of these passages we get a picture of a cosmic battle into which we were born, whether we desire it or not. We are reminded of Daniel's battle with angelic forces in Daniel 10. There, he fasted and prayed, and Gabriel finally came, but explained that his delay was for battle with the "prince of Persia" (v. 13) That is not a natural prince, but a demonic spirit that desires to resist God's will.

Paul tells us that our conflict is with such forces. When we refer to "the devil," in practical terms we are really dealing with these minions. They are defeated, so we have confidence as we pray. The substance of our battle is to resist their attacks, oppressions, and temptations in our own lives as we journey forward in the Lord, and also to seek to set others free through our prayers and testimony. Remember, we have authority over them. They are snakes and scorpions we tread down, and nothing will harm us at all. We are to be sober, vigilant, but fervent, of good hope, and confident in the Lord and the power of His might.

Day 42

We've been discussing the nature of spiritual warfare and, lately and more specifically, the nature of our enemy. The devil and his minions are described in Scripture as much as we need them described, whatever unhealthy curiosity some might have for more, or even pretend to know. It's incumbent upon us to pay attention to what is said, and have a sort of "no more, no less" approach to the matter.

Along those lines, I'd like to return to the nature of prayer and that particular form of prayer that might properly be called "rebuking" or "casting out the devil." Jesus commissioned His disciples in His lifetime to cast out demons (Luke 10:19), and predicted that those who believed in His name would cast out demons (Mark 16:17). The Book of Acts contains examples of this (Acts 16:18; 19:12). Whether you ever have such a power encounter with a demonized person, or just engage in spiritual warfare in prayer, some truths may be garnered from these passages.

All deliverance prayer, all breaking of spiritual strongholds, is really an imitation of the Lord Jesus and His power—not merely by means of playacting, like a boy pretends to be his soldier father by dressing in his uniform, but in truth. Jesus has commissioned us and clothed us *for real* in His armor, and we operate in His name. (I will expound more on the authority of the believer and what it means to pray and speak in His name in the near future, but for now let's just go with it for the sake of this lesson.) Whenever we see Jesus rebuking the devil, we should emulate Him, not in pretense of equal standing, but in submission and dependence upon Him as we fight in His name and at His bidding. Now note how Jesus speaks and acts:

...there was in their synagogue a man with an unclean spirit. And he cried out, ²⁴ *"What have you to do with us, Jesus of Nazareth? Have you come to destroy us? I know who you are—the Holy One of God."* ²⁵ *But Jesus rebuked him, saying, "Be silent, and come out of him!"* ̄ Mark 1:23-25

And when Jesus saw that a crowd came running together, he rebuked the unclean spirit, saying to it, "You mute and deaf spirit, I command you, come out of him and never enter him again."
~ Mark 9:25

Note that Jesus *rebukes* and *commands*. He is stern, He is forceful and direct, He speaks with absolute authority. It is no coincidence that Paul speaks the same way....

And this she kept doing for many days. Paul, having become greatly annoyed, turned and said to the spirit, "I command you in the name of Jesus Christ to come out of her." And it came out that very hour. ~ Acts 16:18

The tenor of spiritual battle—on our end—should be one of fierce spiritual fervor. It will of course not do any good to be angry in the flesh. But if to stir our spirit and speak forcefully is something Jesus and Paul did, it's good enough for me. Paul's "annoyance" in Acts 16:18 is more precisely a grieving of his spirit unto action—it is a spiritual state of being, not a natural and mental irritation. When we pray against strongholds, let us pray like we mean it, in Jesus' name.

I like this passage from *The Pilgrim's Progress* (Book One, Stage 2):

*Then the Interpreter took him, and led him up towards the door of the palace; and behold, **at the door stood a great company of men, as desirous to go in, but durst not.** There also sat a man at a little distance from the door, at a table-side, with a book and his inkhorn before him, to take the names of them that should enter therein; he saw also that in the doorway stood many men in armor to keep it, being resolved to do to the men that would enter, what hurt and mischief they could. Now was Christian somewhat in amaze. At last, when every man started back for fear of the armed men, Christian saw a man of a very stout countenance come up to*

the man that sat there to write, saying, "Set down my name, sir;"
the which when he had done, he saw the man draw his sword, and
put a helmet on his head, **and rush towards the door upon the**
armed men, who laid upon him with deadly force; but the man,
not at all discouraged, fell to cutting and hacking most fiercely. *So*
after he had received and given many wounds to those that
attempted to keep him out, he cut his way through them all, and
pressed forward into the palace; *at which there was a pleasant*
voice heard from those that were within, even of those that walked
upon the top of the palace, saying,

> *"Come in, come in,*
> *Eternal glory thou shalt win."*

So he went in, and was clothed with such garments as they. Then
Christian smiled, and said, **I think verily I know the meaning of**
this.

The "meaning" Christian gained was that the victory is not so much a matter of cleverness but of simple and direct courage, and the determination to go at the enemy with all we have. When others hang back, we forge ahead. Look at David's determination when facing his enemies:

I pursued my enemies and overtook them, and did not turn back
till they were consumed. [38] *I thrust them through, so that they*
were not able to rise; they fell under my feet. [39] *For you equipped*
me with strength for the battle; you made those who rise against
me sink under me. [40] *You made my enemies turn their backs to me,*
and those who hated me I destroyed. [41] *They cried for help, but*
there was none to save; they cried to the LORD, but he did not
answer them. [42] *I beat them fine as dust before the wind; I cast*
them out like the mire of the streets. ~ Psalm 18:37-42

Be fierce in spiritual warfare, be determined. "Be strong in the Lord and in the power of His might." There is a time for soft, contemplative prayers of surrender. And there is a time to rise up in your spirit and claim what you know is yours in the Lord, and what the devil has stolen or is trying to steal.

Day 43

Again using Ephesians 6 as a starting point, I'd like to make another observation about the nature of the battle we are engaged in. Here's our passage again:

Finally, be strong in the Lord and in the strength of his might. ¹¹ Put on the whole armor of God, that you may be able to stand against the schemes of the devil. ¹² For we do not wrestle against flesh and blood, but against the rulers, against the authorities, against the cosmic powers over this present darkness, against the spiritual forces of evil in the heavenly places. ¹³ Therefore take up the whole armor of God, that you may be able to withstand in the evil day, and having done all, to stand firm. ¹⁴ Stand therefore, having fastened on the belt of truth, and having put on the breastplate of righteousness, ¹⁵ and, as shoes for your feet, having put on the readiness given by the gospel of peace. ¹⁶ In all circumstances take up the shield of faith, with which you can extinguish all the flaming darts of the evil one; ¹⁷ and take the helmet of salvation, and the sword of the Spirit, which is the word of God, ¹⁸ praying at all times in the Spirit, with all prayer and supplication. To that end, keep alert with all perseverance, making supplication for all the saints, ¹⁹ and also for me, that words may be given to me in opening my mouth boldly to proclaim the mystery of the gospel, ²⁰ for which I am an ambassador in chains, that I may declare it boldly, as I ought to speak.
Ephesians 6:10-20

We've already been through the pieces of the armor, one by one, and we've unpacked what Paul means when he refers to *"rulers...authorities...cosmic powers over this present darkness...[and] spiritual forces of evil in the heavenly realms."* I've also touched upon the inner posture we are to adopt, namely, one of holy aggression. I'd like to continue in that last vein but with a specific eye towards the structure of this passage and what might be called the DNA of Ephesians itself from the very beginning of the letter.

163

If you look carefully at the passage above, you'll notice that Paul begins his discussion of the armor speaking about our *defensive* needs. His exhortations in vv. 11-14 are all about *standing against* and *withstanding*, and the armor (as we've seen) is almost exclusively defensive, meant to turn aside the blows of the enemy and/or extinguish them (as with the shield of faith). But in v. 17 there is a decided shift: upon taking up the sword of the Spirit, the soldier of Christ goes on the *offensive*, and that offensive takes the form of *prayer*. Whereas various Greek verbs for *stand* occur four times in vv. 11-14, words for *prayer* occur four times in v. 18 alone. In other words, Paul shifts from *standing defensively* to *moving forward offensively* through prayer as the passage comes to its conclusion.

But—now knowing our enemy better than before—how do we go on the offensive against an enemy described as a *"[a] ruler...[an] authority...[a] cosmic power over this present darkness*? If Michael the Archangel dared not be flippant with the devil (Jude 9), where does that put little old me?

The answer is actually found in that obscure little passage, believe it or not. Michael doesn't let the devil get away with anything, but rather says, *"The Lord rebuke you."* In ourselves, we do not have the authority to defeat the devil. But Jesus is strong enough. As we've seen, He has stripped the devil of the keys of death and hell (Revelation 1:18). But this message is present from the beginning of Ephesians, and Paul intends for us to have it in mind as we read about the armor of God:

[God] raised [Christ] from the dead and seated him at his right hand in the heavenly places, [21] **far above all rule and authority and power and dominion, and above every name that is named,** *not only in this age but also in the one to come. [22]* **And he put all things under his feet and gave him as head over all things to the church,** *[23] which is his body, the fullness of him who fills all in all.* Ephesians 1:20-23

Jesus is Lord. He reigns over all powers and authorities, and His name is above every other name. And God the Father exalted Him this way for a purpose: Paul says Jesus was placed as head over all *to the church.* Other translations like the NIV and the NRSV render this verse as *"for the church."* In other words, Jesus' authority is *available to us* in the spiritual warfare we wage. So the issue isn't whether we have to deal with demonic "authorities," but whether there is a *greater authority* working on our behalf. And there is.

Day 44

We must face the facts: we are not powerful enough, clever enough, virtuous enough, or brave enough in ourselves to triumph in spiritual warfare. Even defeated, in this dark age before the Second Coming of Jesus our enemy is still too strong. But for this reason we are told to *be strong in the Lord and the power of His might.* What does that mean in practical terms?

To be strong in the Lord is really a comprehensive lifestyle, and even though I am going somewhere with this we can never lose track of that. There is no "trick," or "silver bullet" to defeating the enemy. It's about how we live, how we develop dependency on the Lord. This is especially true on the defensive end of things. But there are specific prayer weapons we can and should use when fighting the devil, and particularly in reference to the *authority of Christ for the church* which I wrote of yesterday.

Consider these passages:

The seventy-two returned with joy, saying, "Lord, even the demons are subject to us in your name!" ~ Luke 10:17

While Jesus yet walked among them, His disciples invoked His name to vanquish demons.

And these signs will accompany those who believe: in my name they will cast out demons... ~ Mark 16:17

The Risen Lord foretold and commissioned His future disciples (us!) to cast out demons in His name.

But Peter said, "I have no silver and gold, but what I do have I give to you. In the name of Jesus Christ of Nazareth, rise up and walk!" ~ Acts 3:6

Sickness is overcome in Jesus' name.

Paul, having become greatly annoyed, turned and said to the spirit, "I command you in the name of Jesus Christ to come out of her." And it came out that very hour. ˉ Acts 16:18

Demons are driven out in Jesus' name.

Then some of the itinerant Jewish exorcists undertook to invoke the name of the Lord Jesus over those who had evil spirits, saying, "I adjure you by the Jesus whom Paul proclaims." [14] Seven sons of a Jewish high priest named Sceva were doing this. [15] But the evil spirit answered them, "Jesus I know, and Paul I recognize, but who are you?" [16] And the man in whom was the evil spirit leaped on them, mastered all of them and overpowered them, so that they fled out of that house naked and wounded. ˉ Acts 19:13–16

This passage about the sons of Sceva is one of the more important ones we have because it demonstrates that the name of Jesus cannot be used like a magic password. Jesus said that *those who believe* would cast out demons in His name.

What we have in these passages and others is a demonstration of how Christ's authority is passed on to the individual Christian believer. As Paul tells us, *"whatever you do, in word or deed, do everything in the name of the Lord Jesus, giving thanks to God the Father through him."* (Colossians 3:17) We live and breathe and worship and wage war *in the name of the Lord Jesus.* We are even called by that name— *Christian* (1 Peter 4:16). In the name of Jesus we have been given what is commonly called today the *power of attorney.* When we are carrying out the Lord's commission, we invoke the name to release His authority. The Archangel Michael told Satan, *"The Lord rebuke you."* (Jude 9) But as Jesus became human like us, we are actually given more direct access to His authority through His name. Paul did not tell the demon in Philippi *"The Lord rebuke you"*; he said, *"I command you in the name of Jesus Christ to come out of her."*

In ourselves, we are nothing. In ourselves, we command no respect before the throne of heaven or the demons of hell. But when we live and pray and speak in the name of Jesus, as we've been told we should, God the Father hears us through Jesus' intercession, and the devil and his minions quail because of Jesus' cross and resurrection. Let's remember this and apply these truths when we pray, and let us fearlessly rebuke the devil in Jesus' name.

Day 45

We've discussed the armor of God, defensive and offensive spiritual warfare, the nature of our enemy, and the authority of the believer in Jesus' name. Now I'd like to touch on a particular way we should be applying that authority and "wrestling" with those foes.

Let's look at this passage, which also is found in similar form in Mark 3 and Matthew 12. It is a powerful an important text for understanding spiritual warfare through prayer:

Now he was casting out a demon that was mute. When the demon had gone out, the mute man spoke, and the people marveled. [15] But some of them said, "He casts out demons by Beelzebul, the prince of demons,"[16] while others, to test him, kept seeking from him a sign from heaven. [17] But he, knowing their thoughts, said to them, "Every kingdom divided against itself is laid waste, and a divided household falls. [18] And if Satan also is divided against himself, how will his kingdom stand? For you say that I cast out demons by Beelzebul. [19] And if I cast out demons by Beelzebul, by whom do your sons cast them out? Therefore they will be your judges. [20] But if it is by the finger of God that I cast out demons, then the kingdom of God has come upon you. [21] When a strong man, fully armed, guards his own palace, his goods are safe; [22] but when one stronger than he attacks him and overcomes him, he takes away his armor in which he trusted and divides his spoil." ~ Luke 11:14-22

The context is fairly straightforward: Jesus casts out a demon, as He often did. In this case, however, His religious adversaries accuse Him of being demonized Himself—in league with the devil, and therefore empowered to cast out demons. Jesus, of course, promptly shreds their argument. But it is how He sums things up that is so telling: He tells us that casting out demons is akin to attacking and overcoming a strong man who is guarding his house (Jesus refers to Satan's kingdom as his "house" in verse 17). Once he is overcome (the same story in Mark and Matthew uses the verb "bind" to describe how the strong man is vanquished), the attackers can plunder the house at will.

As He often does, Jesus is using *role reversal* in His parable to make it "pop" in the minds of His hearers. One would think in a story Jesus tells that the innocent party would be the homeowner, and the devil the one breaking in. But Jesus casts the devil as the one guarding the house, and Jesus (*or those operating in Jesus' name*—see yesterday's reflection) as the attacker or attackers. It is *we* who must "bind the strong man" by taking authority over the devil, so that we may plunder his "house."

But what is the plunder? In the passage from Luke, the "plunder" Jesus claims is both the mute man who is delivered, and the people who saw the miracle and marveled (verse 14). **People** are the plunder. The devil holds people captive, but we, in Jesus' name, are coming to "rob" the devil of those souls. And why not? He's the real thief who has stolen them in the first place! Jesus bought and paid for those souls with His own blood! We are plundering the greatest thief in history!

I want to encourage you to **pray for souls**. Rebuke the forces of the devil that have *"blinded the minds of the unbelievers, to keep them from seeing the light of the gospel of the glory of Christ, who is the image of God"* (2 Corinthians 4:4) Keep in mind that this can be done by means of "power encounter" (like Jesus has in this passage), or long intercession, persisting in prayer for a church in a community. Either way, praying for souls is the epitome of spiritual warfare!

The Lord has laid a verse upon my heart, and has confirmed it through others:

Thus says the Lord GOD: This also I will let the house of Israel ask me to do for them: **to increase their people like a flock.**
                                                              ˜ Ezekiel 36:37

I want to encourage you to bind the devil, to rebuke him in Jesus' name, to do it zealously, fiercely, and authoritatively in the name of the Lord Jesus Christ. I want to encourage you to break his deceptive power off of the minds of unbelievers. Pray against strongholds of fear that hold back God's people from sharing Christ. Pray for a spirit of evangelism, for divine appointments, for lost lambs to come across your path—people who know the Lord but are wandering without a church. Pray for all kinds of people, in all kinds of ways. But pray, pray, pray that souls be redeemed, and that God's church "increase like a flock." *God is specifically granting us permission to ask Him for that, so ask, ask, ask!*

Day 46

In the same vein of yesterday's study, I'd like to take a look at another famous Scripture passage that deals with the subject of "binding" and "loosing"—Matthew 16...

And I tell you, you are Peter, and on this rock I will build my church, and the gates of hell shall not prevail against it. [19] I will give you the keys of the kingdom of heaven, and whatever you bind on earth shall be bound in heaven, and whatever you loose on earth shall be loosed in heaven." Matthew 16:18-19

Now, there's a lot of distraction about this passage since it has been used from ancient times by the Roman Catholic Church to justify the primacy of Peter as the first leader—or Pope—of the Church. To delve into that debate would take me far afield from my intended discussion here, but there's no avoiding touching on a couple of things: 1) Jesus is clearly making a play on words when he tells Simon that he is "Peter" (Greek: *petros,* a small rock you could hold in the palm of your hand), and that upon this "rock" (Greek: *petra,* bedrock, or mountain crag) Jesus will build His Church, and 2) while the phonetic connection between these terms is obvious, the distinction between the words is equally as evident. Catholics and Protestants have wrestled over this question for centuries and I won't attempt to resolve it here; I only define these words to point out another truth more central to my purpose.

As with the passage about "binding the strong man" in Luke 11 (also Mark 3 and Matthew 12), Jesus associates the authority He is giving His people to "bind and loose" with power over the forces of darkness. (Note that while Jesus speaks in the *singular*—to Peter—in this passage, two chapters later in Matthew 18:18 He says the same thing while speaking in the *plural,* meaning, to all His people.) In other words, as He tells Peter he has the power to bind and loose, He also declares that the Gates of Hell (Greek: *Hades*) will not prevail against the Church.

175

What of this "binding and loosing"? I won't pretend this is easy pickings, but I will offer my read on the passage: Jesus is saying that your prayers on earth have a direct effect in the spiritual realm—in heaven. Even as you are on earth, in the flesh, in this *natural realm*, you have been given authority (references to "keys" are always references to authority) that extends into the *spiritual realm*. Jesus has empowered you and given you the power of attorney in His name. It is a stunning passage. But lest we run away with it, as some have in their presumption, see what He says the authority is for: *it is for building His Church*. It is for taking authority over the forces of the devil—the Gates of Hell. It's about taking the battle to the enemy. That battle can only be waged by the fear of God, humility, brokenness, and sincere faith. It would do us well to remember as we pray that Jesus won the battle by being crucified, so let's spare Him any bravado. We pray with authority, but we pray knowing the price paid for that authority. Christians win their battles against the devil by imitating the Crucified and Risen Lord; when we live and act and pray that way, the devil trembles.

Now, what of these "Gates of Hell"? Here is where *context* is so important for a passage. Matthew tells us this encounter happened in *Caesarea Philippi* (also Mark 8). This city was far to the north of the mostly Jewish area of Galilee where Jesus lived, and was in truth a pagan, Gentile city. It was famous for a shrine to the Roman god pan, which was located in a massive natural cave found in an even more imposing rocky cliff face (a *petra*). A natural spring issued from the cave, and from even more ancient times it was used for pagan sacrifice—even perhaps human sacrifice. Pagans would kill the sacrifice and hurl it into the spring, and how the blood boiled up the surface told them whether they had the god's favor. In Jesus' day the cave was very much a center of pagan worship and dark blood sacrifice; *most importantly for understanding this passage, the cave itself was considered a portal to the underworld—Hades itself.*

Now we have a clearer picture of what Jesus was saying. He didn't provoke the discussion about His identity ("*Who do you say that I am?*") in His hometown, outside of a synagogue. He provoked it in a pagan Gentile town outside of a shrine known at the Gate of Hades. He didn't talk about Peter and the rest of the Church "binding and loosing" in Jerusalem, but in a center of unclean idol worship. It was on decidedly unsafe, foreign turf that Jesus first confirmed and declared that he was, indeed, the Christ, and that He was investing His authority in His disciples (us!), and that he would build His Church, and that the Gates of Hell (yes, those ones right there behind Him, in all their imposing grandeur) would NOT prevail against that Church. The whole discussion was about *mission.*

Why would we even talk about the Gates of Hell prevailing (or not) against the Church? Because we are attacking those gates with a battering ram, that's why. We are coming to get the goods. We are binding the strong man, we are praying like crazy and calling down the power of heaven because Jesus commanded us to, and we are seeking to fulfill the Great Commission and see the captive set free. We aren't picking a fight; the fight has already been picked, long before we were born. As incredible as Jesus' words must have sounded to His disciples (although without a doubt they were used to it by then!), what's more incredible is that by the time the Gospel of Matthew was written, the Church of Jesus Christ was flourishing in the strongholds of pagandom all over the Roman world. Ephesus, Athens, Corinth, Rome herself—all these cities were strongholds of pagandom, and all of them had local churches that were storming the Gates of Hell within living memory of the Lord Jesus. *This prophecy of the Lord was fulfilled within the disciples' lifetime.*

If it happened for them, it can happen for us. Let us bind the strong man, and loose the power of the Holy Spirit. Let us pray that the Lord Jesus build up His church, and pray that through us He take down the Gates of Hell in the community around us.

People are bound by chemical addictions, porn, deceptions, hatred, and just plain old worldliness. God wants to set them free.

Pray!

Day 47

We've been studying about plunder, and plundering the enemy. In respect to this, I'd like to touch upon something I mentioned at the outset of our journey: worship. This theme is fitting not only because there are passages that connect worship and plunder, but also because to return to worship at this point in the discussion about spiritual warfare is strategic.

The Apostle Paul says this:

For though we walk in the flesh, we are not waging war according to the flesh. 4 *For the weapons of our warfare are not of the flesh but have divine power to destroy strongholds.*
~ 2 Corinthians 10:3-4

We repent, we seek holiness, we read the Word, we pray, we fast, we bind the devil and cast him out, we are deadly serious about fighting him and his minions so that we might set the captive free. All this is true. But let us remember that what we do is not just a spiritualized version of what earthly battle is like—the grimness, the gloom, the fear. No, Paul is telling us *the way we fight is fundamentally different.* Worship is one of the great ways we walk in this difference and demonstrate it.

Isaiah says,

You shall have a song as in the night when a holy feast is kept, and gladness of heart, as when one sets out to the sound of the flute to go to the mountain of the LORD, to the Rock of Israel. 30 *And the LORD will cause his majestic voice to be heard and the descending blow of his arm to be seen, in furious anger and a flame of devouring fire, with a cloudburst and storm and hailstones.* 31 *The Assyrians will be terror-stricken at the voice of the LORD, when he strikes with his rod.* 32 *And every stroke of the appointed staff that the LORD lays on them will be to the sound of tambourines and lyres. Battling with brandished arm, he will fight with them.* ~ Isaiah 30:29-32

Translation: when the battle is joined, it falls to the devil and his bunch to be terrified. It falls to us to sing, and be glad, and play the flute, tambourine, and lyre. Our God fights for us. We fight differently—our weapons are not natural weapons.

Read 2 Chronicles 20, and the story of Jehoshaphat and the enemy army marching on Jerusalem. After praying and fasting, God prophetically gave them direction on how to win the battle. And this is what they did:

And when he had taken counsel with the people, he appointed those who were to sing to the LORD and praise him in holy attire, as they went before the army, and say, "Give thanks to the LORD, for his steadfast love endures forever."²² And when they began to sing and praise, the LORD set an ambush against the men of Ammon, Moab, and Mount Seir, who had come against Judah, so that they were routed. ⁻ 2 Chronicles 20:21-22

After all you've read about spiritual warfare in the past days, remember this: praise the Lord! Rejoice and be glad! Be of good cheer in Him! And as you glorify the Lord, His blows will fall upon the forces of darkness, and they will flee.

Rejoice in the Lord this day.

Day 48

Continuing in this line of thinking, but painting with broader brush strokes, I'd like to call attention to a particular truth that we can observe through the Gospels and Acts, but I find articulated lucidly in Revelation 12:10-12...

*And I heard a loud voice in heaven, saying, "Now the salvation and the power and the kingdom of our God and the authority of his Christ have come, for the accuser of our brothers has been thrown down, who accuses them day and night before our God." And they have conquered him by the blood of the Lamb and by the word of their testimony, for they loved not their lives even unto death. ¹² Therefore, rejoice, O heavens and you who dwell in them! But woe to you, O earth and sea, **for the devil has come down to you in great wrath, because he knows that his time is short!"~***
Revelation 12:10-12

I could spill an ocean of ink over this passage alone, which is the thematic and mathematical center to the Book of Revelation; the intersection of themes and truths in this passage, converging from the beginning of the book to the end, is literally mind-boggling, but to quote someone much greater, *"of these things we cannot now speak in detail"* (Hebrews 9:5). I'd like to focus on 12:12, which refers to the *rage of the devil.*

If you read Revelation 12 from the beginning of the chapter, you'll read about the downfall of Satan. The chapter is enigmatic for many, but basically it comes down to this: through the "Christ event"—Jesus' incarnation, death, resurrection, and ascension, the devil has been utterly defeated (as we've noted in previous chapters), and the "standing" he had stolen from Adam has been reclaimed by Jesus, who is the "Second Adam" (see Romans 5). What ensues in Revelation 12 is the battle between the devil and his angels and Michael the Archangel and the angels of heaven. Many have misinterpreted and misapplied the reference to Michael, but seeing it in the context of the rest of the Bible and the New Testament, basically what is happening here is that

Michael is taking out the trash—he is God's "bouncer"; the real defeat of the devil was something Jesus had already accomplished.

Now follow the sequence: *After* Satan is defeated by Christ and cast out of heaven is when the fireworks begin. Read the rest of the chapter, and into Revelation 13. The very nature of God's redemptive plan and timing, together with the nature of our enemy, creates an arena—a platform and an opportunity—for the devil to thrash around and cause us problems. What is often called the "already and the not yet" is heavily in play— Jesus "already" sits at the right hand of the Father, we are "already" redeemed by the blood of Christ, and the devil has "already" been cast down, but Jesus has "not yet" come, we do "not yet" have our new glorified bodies, and the devil is "not yet" cast into the lake of fire. This is the Age of the Church—the season in which we paradoxically must do battle with a defeated enemy who is like a mortally wounded tiger who can still do serious damage.

For me, this is one of the most difficult truths to follow, because it seems so at odds with human experience. The rage and danger posed by a human enemy is typically greatest *before* the question of victory is decided; once they are defeated the fighting stops. But Revelation reveals that with the defeat of the devil and his being cast down, that's when things become the most intense.

But it isn't just Revelation that says so. Look at case after case of encounters with demonic forces in the rest of the New Testament. To choose a couple: As Jesus casts out the demon from the deaf and mute boy (Mark 9), the demon shakes the lad so hard he appears as dead; the devil fought hardest and seemed to achieve success in his lifelong attempts on his victim's life *upon being defeated. After* Paul cast the demon out of the soothsaying slave girl, he was wrongly convicted, beaten, and jailed (Acts 16). Then we have big picture things: both Paul and Jesus suffered what appeared to be ultimate defeat after they had spent years of ministry beating the daylights out of the devil.

Grasping this truth calls for wisdom and maturity, discernment and perseverance. In this respect the devil is very much like many wild animals that make a big show, puff themselves up, thrash about, and essentially go for broke when they know the game is up. The devil will seek to blindside you, catch you defenseless when your guard is down (a very common inner response after you've won a victory), use sneak attacks to undermine you just when you've made significant headway, throw up a smoke screen to pretend that you haven't really gained ground on him. He may go all-in to tempt you into a sin you have a weakness for, to break your morale and "remind you" that you are "still his" after all that.

We are not unaware of the devil's schemes. He does these things because he knows his time is short. His time is short in the big picture, and his time is short in your life and your striving against him. He's mad. But his rage is a symptom of his defeat. Keep praising the Lord, keep pressing into prayer, keep your guard up. Stand, stand, and stand some more.

Day 49

Permit me now to synthesize some things from the last two days, namely the subject of *worship of God* in relation to the *defeat and thrashings of the devil.*

Once again, the Book of Revelation is instructive. No book in the New Testament is so graphic about the devil's downfall and associated demonic activity. In fact, many Christians are hesitant to read the book for this reason, and avoid it because they are frightened of its strong imagery. But that is a terrible shame, because by the same token, no book in the New Testament is so worshipful of God as Revelation; it is filled with songs and scenes of worship from beginning to end. Some of the best songs of the Church throughout history are inspired by Revelation.

But allow me to go deeper, and into what I believe to be the heart of the matter: Revelation is, among other things, a story of *spiritual warfare* for the hearts of humankind—or rather, the culmination of that story which began in the Garden of Eden. No book describes open rebellion against God in more flagrant manifestation than Revelation, where a mortal man (the Beast, or Antichrist) seeks to make himself God, and basically convinces the world that they should worship him. But at the same time, no book in the New Testament reveals God as sovereign so lucidly, and presents the glory of a Church submitted to that lordship like Revelation does. Revelation is a study in stark contrasts.

So what does this have to do with our prayer life? In a word, it has to do with the Christian's superweapon: **submission**. Once again, we do not wage war as the world does. Hollywood has filled our heads with the romantic imagery and rhetoric of rebels, tough guys and gals who saunter around, talk tough, and wear it as a badge of honor that they break all the rules to hit quicker and harder than their adversaries. That's the world. But the people of God—the *real* people of God—win by mildness, by submission, by yielding to God the Father. *We carry the day by laying down our lives.*

Consider Samuel's words to Saul:

*And Samuel said, "Has the LORD as great delight in burnt offerings and sacrifices, as in **obeying the voice of the LORD**? Behold, to obey is better than sacrifice, and to listen than the fat of rams. ²³ **For rebellion is as the sin of divination**, and presumption is as iniquity and idolatry. Because you have rejected the word of the LORD, he has also rejected you from being king."˜* 1 Samuel 15:22–23

Saul was tall and strong and a powerful, charismatic military leader. Of note, he knew the *forms* of worship; Saul was offering a sacrifice. **But his heart was not submitted.** Because of this, Samuel compared his behavior to *divination* (aka *witchcraft*). Was this simply because Samuel picked a particularly bad sin to compare Saul's rebellion to? I do not think so. Witchcraft is when a human being dabbles in the demonic in an attempt to manipulate God's natural order and get what they want. Witchcraft might rightly be called the ultimate counterfeit of prayer. Witchcraft comes at a terrible price, because it removes the covering of divine protection that keeps us safe in "this present darkness." Even unbelievers have some protection, granted by what has long been called "common grace"—God's goodness and mercy extended to all humankind. But Saul's rebellion was likened to witchcraft because what it did was remove the covering of God's favor from his life—it amounted to walking out from under the umbrella of God's protection into demonic acid rain. In the end, Saul couldn't let go of his self-determination; he died by suicide after actually consulting a witch.

The contrast to Saul, of course, is *David.* David wasn't perfect, not by a long shot. But he was *submitted.* Paul describes David in Acts 13:22...

'I have found in David the son of Jesse a man after my heart, who will do all my will.'

Should any of us be surprised that David is also the consummate worshipper of the Old Testament, and perhaps even the entire Bible? To worship—not just in form, like Saul, but from the heart, like David—*this is submission*. We cannot simply meditate a bit on submission, or tell ourselves we will be submitted, or (worst of all) simply imagine we are submitted. *Submission is an act* that takes place as we worship, and it isn't automatic. Like yeast being kneaded through dough, we have to allow wave after wave of surrender take us. Worship on our terms is not submission, and I would argue that it isn't even really worship. Saul called what he was doing submitted worship; God called it no better than witchcraft. Saul lost his kingdom and his life; David's throne lasts forever.

Consider again Revelation: it is a book that paints in spectacular fashion the final thrashings and ultimate implosion of demonic power in the world. But in the midst of those demonic ragings, we also see persistent worship. Look at this from Revelation 19…

*And the twenty-four elders and the four living creatures fell down and **worshiped** God who was seated on the throne, saying, "Amen. Hallelujah!"* [5] *And from the throne came a voice saying, "Praise our God, all you his servants, you who fear him, small and great."* [6] *Then I heard what seemed to be the voice of a great multitude, like the roar of many waters and like the sound of mighty peals of thunder, crying out, "Hallelujah! For the Lord our God the Almighty reigns.* [7] *Let us rejoice and exult and give him the glory, for the marriage of the Lamb has come, and his Bride has made herself ready;* [8] *it was granted her to clothe herself with fine linen, bright and pure"*—for the fine linen is the righteous deeds of the saints.* ~ Revelation 19:4–8

Now look at the armor that the warriors in the Last Battle, who follow Jesus against the forces of the Antichrist, are wearing:

And the armies of heaven, arrayed in fine linen, white and pure, were following him on white horses. ~ Revelation 19:14

You see, just as witchcraft lifts the umbrella of protection, *deep submission through authentic worship actually armors us.* The devil might be raging around us, the demons going nuts, upheaval left and right—it might seem like Armageddon in your life—but as you worship, worship, worship the Lord, and place yourself through worship in a posture of deep submission, you live in the Shadow of the Almighty, and under His wings you find refuge. Submission through worship is your superweapon.

Day 50

As aspiring people of prayer, as people who seek fluency in the biblical language of spiritual warfare, we have a problem. There's no use denying it, and there's plenty to be gained by confessing it: *we are by nature rebels.* In ourselves, surrender and submission is the last thing we would incline ourselves towards. I'm in my 40th year of serving Jesus and I am astounded (and ashamed) at how rare true and ongoing submission is in me. I am especially aware of this as I come out of a time of prayer and fasting. It is during these times, when I actually do experience "submission encounters," that I realize how little I have been yielded the *rest* of the time.

We are selfish and self-centered. We want our own way, and more often than not we work out a way to get it. Those attitudes make a successful and consistent prayer life *impossible*, because submission is the very life blood of prayer. Look at this famous passage from Luke 18...

"Two men went up into the temple to pray, one a Pharisee and the other a tax collector. 11 The Pharisee, standing by himself, prayed thus: 'God, I thank you that I am not like other men, extortioners, unjust, adulterers, or even like this tax collector. 12 I fast twice a week; I give tithes of all that I get.' 13 But the tax collector, standing far off, would not even lift up his eyes to heaven, but beat his breast, saying, 'God, be merciful to me, a sinner!' 14 I tell you, this man went down to his house justified, rather than the other. For everyone who exalts himself will be humbled, but the one who humbles himself will be exalted."(vv. 10-14)

Jesus focuses on humility, but in context that might as well be a synonym for submission. There is what might be called an "elliptical" relationship between prayer and submission to God's will. Successful prayer is not possible without submission, but true submission cannot remain in the prayerless heart. We must submit to pray—unrepentant rebels *never* pray—but we must stay close to God in prayer in order to even have a *chance* at cultivating a submitted heart. No one ever "decided" to be surrendered and accomplished it on their own; it is a work of the Holy Spirit, without whom it wouldn't even occur to us to submit. Similarly, we can be submitted at one point but then "unsurrender," and go back to a fleshly, self-determining way of living (often while still being very religious in the eyes of all outsiders).

These are sobering thoughts. When I consider the dilemma of the absolute necessity of submission combined with our inability to do so, then consider that God has also commanded us to be prayerful, deeply submitted people, I look around desperately for the tie breaker He has provided, because I know it cannot be found in me.

Thankfully, He's made a way, but in our redeemed nature and by means of a method.

Day 51

There is so much to be said about submission and prayer, both in terms of spiritual warfare and also our relationship with God in general. As I've noted from Paul in 2 Corinthians 10, *we do not wage war as the world does.* If we submit deeply and intimately to Jesus, *that* is spiritual warfare. Sweetly singing His praises, bowing in worship before Him, glorifying Him and tearfully repenting of our sins in His presence, testifying of His goodness with a broken voice to a lost soul—all these are frontal assaults on the fortresses of darkness.

But how do we truly submit? As we've seen and must recognize, we are by our fallen nature rebels. God's Holy Spirit is working in us through the new birth and the ongoing work of sanctification, but we aren't there yet and to be perfectly candid we relapse quite a bit and even on good days we are spotty in how authentically and consistently we submit to the Lord. We need to understand the Lord's ways and what He has afforded us to draw close to Him in submission.

Let me draw your attention to James 1:22-25...

But be doers of the word, and not hearers only, deceiving yourselves. [23] *For if anyone is a hearer of the word and not a doer,* **he is like a man who looks intently at his natural face in a mirror.** [24] *For he looks at himself and goes away and at once forgets what he was like.* [25] **But the one who looks into the perfect law,** *the law of liberty, and perseveres, being no hearer who forgets but a doer who acts, he will be blessed in his doing.*

There are several aspects to this passage, but my angle here is that of submission. *Submission to Christ* is essentially *conformity to Christ*—we are exchanging *our* self-determination for active agreement (i.e., word, thought, deed, etc.) with *Christ's* determination for our lives. James tells us that when we look at the Word, we are looking at a mirror. The Word shows us who we are in comparison with who Christ is—it's about whether our image conforms to His image, which (of course) goes back to the goal of every true Christian: to be like Jesus in every detail. By "doing the Word" we submit and conform to Christ, being transformed by a process, day by day, into His image.

Now, the printed Word for the Christian is a practical discipline by which the Holy Spirit speaks and moves. But the truth is, the ultimate expression of God's Word for the Christian is not the Bible, as vital as that book is to us. The ultimate expression of the Word of God is *Jesus Himself.*

John 1:1 tells us,

*In the beginning was the **Word**, and the **Word** was with God, and the **Word was God.***

...and Revelation 19:13 says...

*He is clothed in a robe dipped in blood, and the name by which he is called is **The Word of God**.*

So Jesus *is* the Word, *the Word made flesh* (John 1:14). He came for us, among other reasons, to *model submission* and show us how to live successfully. As Jesus Himself says,

Truly, truly, I say to you, the Son can do nothing of his own accord, but only what he sees the Father doing. For whatever the Father does, that the Son does likewise. ˜ John 5:19

...and...

For I have not spoken on my own authority, but the Father who sent me has himself given me a commandment—what to say and what to speak. ˜ John 12:49

...and...

...I do as the Father has commanded me, so that the world may know that I love the Father. Rise, let us go from here. ⁻ John 14:31

So as we look at Jesus, we are not looking at a cocky, self-determinant and arrogant figure that leads as one of the kings of His day. Rather, we have a Lord that issues commands from a place of submission to His Father–from a position of personal brokenness. Would we ever think of Pontius Pilate apart from his role in Christ's crucifixion? And yet he was the power broker of the day when Jesus gave his life. Pilate is (rightly) seen as a petty bully who cracked under political pressure, while Jesus the Crucified is worshipped; guilty Pilate washed his own hands in cowardice from a throne, while sinless Jesus washed the world of its sins from a cross.

We worship Jesus and become like Him. We submit and conform by fixing our worshipful gaze upon Him:

And we all, with unveiled face, beholding the glory of the Lord, are being transformed into the same image from one degree of glory to another. For this comes from the Lord who is the Spirit.
⁻ 2 Corinthians 3:18

Let us fix our eyes upon Jesus, and deeply submit to Him as we look into His Word, as we worship, and as we pray.

Day 52

By adoring Jesus—the only way to really "see" Him—we are transformed into His image. Here the line between the Word, worship, and prayer become blurred, and we hit a sweet spot in what it means to be spiritually effective.

This passage has been impactful for me:

And I will pour out on the house of David and the inhabitants of Jerusalem a spirit of grace and supplication. They will look on me, the one they have pierced, and they will mourn for him as one mourns for an only child, and grieve bitterly for him as one grieves for a firstborn son. ¯ Zechariah 12:10 (NIV84)

Lots is going on in this passage, most of it simultaneous, even though it is described sequentially. People look upon Jesus, the "one they have pierced," and this causes a spiritual chain reaction. What does this mean to "look upon the one they have pierced"? The passage is quoted in John 19:37 and Revelation 1:7. It seems pretty clear that by the end all will "look upon" Jesus as crucified whether they wish to or not, and depending on their inner posture, it will be a moment of redemption or a moment of despair. The original context describes it as a heartbreaking but ultimately salvific moment for God's people; Revelation 1:7 describes it as final judgment for those who reject the Lord; in both cases there is great weeping that cannot be escaped. Lord, grant that our weeping be on favorable terms!

Assuming the redemptive end of things, as we look upon the Crucified Lord, we are smitten simultaneously by His innocence and glory, even as we take in His suffering for our sins. This Holy Spirit conviction leads to the "godly sorrow" Paul describes in 2 Corinthians. Such sorrow redeems because it breaks the rebellion in us and opens the way for the "Spirit of grace and supplication" in our lives. We cannot experience that grace and that Spirit of supplication without brokenness, and that brokenness cannot be conjured or otherwise drummed up—it can only be birthed as

Jesus the Crucified reveals Himself to us. But once we do see Him, and are cut to the quick by how our sin (not just another's— OURS) put Him there until He died, then that Holy Spirit of repentance and prayer can come. In this flow, submission begets submission, and we step towards being like the One we worship. We worship at the foot of the Cross.

We must seek the Spirit of grace and supplication. We must realize we are the walking dead without that broken, mild spirit inside of us. We must allow repentance to clean house. I know I've spoken of repentance before, but I'm returning to it from a different angle in light of spiritual warfare. Consider the priests of Jesus' day: they did not have this Spirit, they could not realize that the one they mocked as He hung dying was their awaited Messiah. They "looked upon the one they had pierced" but not as God had intended, and therefore doomed themselves to the word of Revelation 1:7 which turns that prophecy from Zechariah 12 into a word of judgment. Ironically, a Roman centurion there experienced a different outcome that day.

Seek the Spirit of grace and supplication. Ask for Jesus to reveal Himself as crucified to you. And as you do, prepare to *clean house.*

Once while praying in the sanctuary of our church I felt a strong urging about cleansing the house—purifying ourselves. I urge you, in your quest for submission to Christ and conformity to His image, to consider anything in your life, home, relationships, or habits. What is there that could be grieving the Holy Spirit? I would rather be offended than offend. I would rather be inconvenienced than hinder the Holy Spirit's flow. I would rather weep over Jesus than make Him weep over me.

Consider again this quote from à Kempis (*Imitation of Christ*, Book Two, Chapter 8):

Choose the opposition of the whole world rather than offend Jesus.

What was the end result for God's people in Zechariah's day, as he foresaw things?

On that day a fountain will be opened to the house of David and the inhabitants of Jerusalem, to cleanse them from sin and impurity. ~ Zechariah 13:1 (NIV84)

Let it be so for us. Let us be deeply cleansed, drawn in by deep love for Jesus our Lord, and may our submission come through a divinely outpoured Spirit of grace and supplication. May our prayers, worship, and obedience to God's living word draw us closer to Him and, through Him, to each other. God grant us revival and rejuvenation, restoration and rebuilding, sprouting and growth and fruit, a loosing of blessings even as hindrances are bound, cast out, and the door locked forever against them.

Day 53

As I began the discussion of submission as a kind of "superweapon" in spiritual warfare, I addressed the dilemma we have as fallen human beings: of ourselves, we are rebels.

The Apostle Paul addresses this dilemma in Romans 7...

For I do not understand my own actions. For I do not do what I want, but I do the very thing I hate. [16] Now if I do what I do not want, I agree with the law, that it is good. [17] So now it is no longer I who do it, but sin that dwells within me. [18] **For I know that nothing good dwells in me, that is, in my flesh.** *For I have the desire to do what is right, but not the ability to carry it out. [19] For I do not do the good I want, but the evil I do not want is what I keep on doing. [20] Now if I do what I do not want, it is no longer I who do it, but sin that dwells within me. ~* Romans 7:15-20

This is a difficult passage to read, but simultaneously a relief—if Paul knew this frustration, maybe there's hope for me in my pilgrimage of submission!

There is hope. Paul ends the passage with this declaration:

Wretched man that I am! Who will deliver me from this body of death? [25] **Thanks be to God through Jesus Christ our Lord!** *~* Romans 7:24-25

How does He help us, though? How does this tiebreaker actually take effect in us?

Consider these two powerful Old Testament passages foretelling the New Covenant...

For this is the covenant that I will make with the house of Israel after those days, declares the LORD: I will put my law within them, and I will write it on their hearts. And I will be their God, and they shall be my people. [34] And no longer shall each one teach his neighbor and each his brother, saying, 'Know the LORD,' for they shall all know me, from the least of them to the greatest, declares the LORD. For I will forgive their iniquity, and I will remember their sin no more.' ˉ Jeremiah 31:33-34

...and...

I will sprinkle clean water on you, and you shall be clean from all your uncleannesses, and from all your idols I will cleanse you. ²⁶ And I will give you a new heart, and a new spirit I will put within you. And I will remove the heart of stone from your flesh and give you a heart of flesh. ²⁷ And I will put my Spirit within you, and cause you to walk in my statutes and be careful to obey my rules. ˉ Ezekiel 36:25-27

Here is your tiebreaker: Jesus forgave you and redeemed you when there was nothing good in you. He bought your redemption apart from any virtue in you, because there wasn't any to be had. Notably, the two primary and competing Protestant theological "systems" for understanding redemption—Calvinism and Arminianism—actually *agree* on their first point: *Total Depravity.* (As a sidebar, I am of the opinion that, though they hold great truths, neither of these "systems" is all-sufficient in itself, and a middle view based in the biblical text is the proper route.) So when we had nothing did nothing, and were nothing, God stepped in through Jesus and forgave and adopted us as His firstborn. The small strength we had to whisper "amen" to this incredible gift was *itself* a gift from God, because in our death and blindness we didn't even have the sense or power to do that.

Now here's my point: how we *came into the faith* is how we *stay in the faith,* and how we *function in the faith.* Grace was not just how we began, it is how we live and pray every day. No matter how advanced we get, how mature, how sensitive, and how used of God—think of the great saints of old, and even modern ones—no one ever outgrows the need for God's grace. Forty years in the faith, and 35 years of ministry, and I need the Cross as badly as I ever did.

When we know—*know*—that we are forgiven, we will have traction. When it penetrates to the depth of our inner self that Jesus has accepted us, redeemed us, freed us, cleansed us, purified us, and qualified us to share in the inheritance of the saints in the kingdom of light, then the impasse is broken and we have spiritual wind in our sails. The paradox of successful submission comes to this: we are able to submit when, and only when, we know that God graciously forgave us and made us a new creature in Christ by His grace before we had a submitted bone in our body. We become what Jesus intends us to be—and what we need to be to overcome the devil—*when we believe that He has already done it.* **Other religions tell us we become righteous as we do what is right; *Jesus tells us we are able to do what is right because we understand He has already made us righteous.***

My prayer for you is this:

I do not cease to give thanks for you, remembering you in my prayers, [17] *that the God of our Lord Jesus Christ, the Father of glory, may give you the Spirit of wisdom and of revelation in the knowledge of him,* [18] *having the eyes of your hearts enlightened, that you may know what is the hope to which he has called you, what are the riches of his glorious inheritance in the saints,* [19] *and what is the immeasurable greatness of his power toward us who believe, according to the working of his great might* [20] *that he worked in Christ when he raised him from the dead and seated him at his right hand in the heavenly places...* ˜ Ephesians 1:16-20

Day 54

I have been meditating on the subject of submission, both the power that comes with walking in it and the liability for failing to do so. Inevitably, the way we grapple with the question in our own lives will end up being something of a tightrope between the truth of the gospel we believe (on one end) and the way we practically apply it (on the other). I could go on and on about those biblical underpinnings, but I think it would take us far afield from the general thrust of this writing, which is mostly about putting feet to things. But I move on but reluctantly, because of all the transformative messages I have heard, none has had such a lasting impact upon my ability to submit than the truth that Jesus loved and forgave me when I was a rebel dead in my sin. His kindness led me to repentance. Bathed in His love, I *then wanted* to submit. For this reason I call myself a "grace preacher," because by grace we know Him and are able to walk in those works and purposes He has planned beforehand that we walk in them.

But allow me to turn to prayer. In Luke 11, we read that Jesus was praying, and as He finished, His disciples asked Him to teach them how to pray. In other words, Jesus was communing with the Father, again imitating and following close after Him. *The disciples wanted to imitate His imitation;* already we have a context of submission happening. Then Jesus launched into the Lord's Prayer...

And he said to them, "When you pray, say: "Father, hallowed be your name. Your kingdom come. ˉ Luke 11:2

Matthew's version is fuller...

Pray then like this: "Our Father in heaven, hallowed be your name. *¹⁰ Your kingdom come, your will be done, on earth as it is in heaven..."* ˜ Matthew 6:9-10

I want to look at the prayer specifically in the light of submission and surrender, and how we "weaponize" our yielded, broken spirit in terms of spiritual warfare.

First, God is recognized as Father. This is crucial considering what I've already said, namely, that God's decision to adopt us as His sons precedes any ability of ours to actually submit. This always puzzled me before I got a better handle on grace. Why shouldn't I ask for forgiveness first (something Jesus places a little further down in the prayer)? Well, pray how you must if your conscience is bothering you about something; the Lord's Prayer is a guide, not a straightjacket law. But under ordinary circumstances, the structure of the prayer teaches us something: God's adoption of us by His sovereign choice paves the way for everything else in the prayer—including the prayers of surrender that immediately follow our recognition of God as Father. Along these lines, Read Ephesians chapter 1 through 2:10; this is powerful stuff. The oft-quoted Ephesians 2:10 has a powerful and lengthy lead up that extends 32 verses. We love because He first loved us, we submit to Christ because Christ submitted to the Cross.

Next comes the substance of the prayer, the very DNA of which is submission.

Day 55

To continue with my discussion of submission, allow me to begin with some observations from a spiritual classic—R.A. Torrey's *The Power of A Surrendered Will*:

"Power belongeth unto God" (Psa. 62:11), *but there is one condition upon which that power is bestowed upon us - that is absolute surrender to Him.*

Torrey later continues...

Nothing so blinds the spiritual vision as self-will or sin. I have seen questions which bothered men for years solved in a very short time when those men simply surrendered to God. What was dark as night before has become light as day.

These truths approach being *truisms* when we consider the broader picture of us as fallen-but-redeemed human beings made in the image of an all-good sovereign God. It isn't difficult from that perspective to understand why Jesus structures the prayer He taught His disciples the way He did. As we've seen, He begins by establishing the context for the prayer in God's adoptive love for us (*Our Father in Heaven, hallowed be Your name...*). This is Jesus teaching us to pray as He saw things—His intimate walk with His Father. But after this Jesus launches us into the imitative aspect of that relationship, **submission**: *Your Kingdom come* (Luke 11:2). Matthew expands Luke's briefer version into *Your Kingdom come, Your will be done* (Matthew 6:10), but that is indeed an expansion that helps us get a handle on the issue. In the end we're still talking submission.

The doorway to answered prayer is surrender. The doorway to a deeper understanding of God's plan is also surrender. The doorway to having God's power rest upon us is surrender, and therefore the doorway to being used of God at all. Jesus tells us to surrender to the father, to yield, to wave the white flag, to submit. There are layers of submission, deeper levels of submission we can reach. Pleasing submission for me when I first came to Christ might have been occasional Bible reading, considering what God might want or not want me to do in a circumstance I never included Him in before, or being mildly charitable. But now that I am mature, the submission required of me is more. So what is the yardstick?

It's best just to go right at this. Daniel interprets the fearsome vision of Nebuchadnezzar's statue, and concludes his interpretation of its demise with these words...

As you looked, a stone was cut out by no human hand, and it struck the image on its feet of iron and clay, and broke them in pieces. Then the iron, the clay, the bronze, the silver, and the gold, all together were broken in pieces, and became like the chaff of the summer threshing floors; and the wind carried them away, so that not a trace of them could be found. But the stone that struck the image became a great mountain and filled the whole earth... And in the days of those kings the God of heaven will set up a kingdom that shall never be destroyed, nor shall the kingdom be left to another people. **It shall break in pieces all these kingdoms and bring them to an end, and it shall stand forever...**

~ Daniel 2:34-35, 44

Every last earthly and human kingdom will fall. The only kingdom that will endure—that *can* endure—is Jesus' Kingdom...the Kingdom of God. He is the Rock Not Cut by Human Hands. The Rock is difficult, no matter who we are. He is costly to all who come upon Him; there is no way around Him, no easy way forward once He confronts us. But that cost can either result in redemption through submission or doom through rebellion; there is no middle ground.

Our kingdoms, whether outward or inward, are doomed. They are coming down. Now is the accepted time, the day of salvation. Now is the time we can submit and get favorable terms from the Fiery Messiah. *If we submit,* He will *not* have mercy on our petty kingdoms, but He will have mercy aplenty upon us; if we stubbornly refuse, or even passively go astray and try to play Him, the cost will be even higher—for both us and for those we might have blessed in this short life.

Let's be deeply submissive. Let's go at it, and invite Him to take down our sandcastles. Once they are down, their illusion is broken, and we can focus on our true King and His true Kingdom. Here is the practical end of the tiebreaker I referred to earlier: we submit by praying, and the more we abide in the Lord by praying, the deeper our submission will go, and the more powerfully God will be able to use us.

Day 56

Now that we've looked at the opening of the Lord's Prayer, let's take a look at the doxology in Matthew 6:13...

For yours is the kingdom and the power and the glory, forever. Amen

At the risk of getting technical, there are very good reasons why this part of Matthew 6:13 is relegated to a footnote in most modern English versions. Only few, and very late Greek manuscripts contain it. But I'd like to address it here because there is a strong tradition around it, and most Christians include it when they pray the Lord's Prayer. It also has a lot to do with how the prayer begins, namely, with the matter of God's sovereignty and the issue of submission.

For my part, the debate over whether to include this (meaning, the question of whether the doxology is "legitimate") is a red herring. The doxology is Scripture already, drawn from David's prayer in 1 Chronicles 29...

Therefore David blessed the LORD in the presence of all the assembly. And David said: "Blessed are you, O LORD, the God of Israel our father, forever and ever. [11] **Yours, O LORD, is the greatness and the power and the glory and the victory and the majesty, for all that is in the heavens and in the earth is yours. Yours is the kingdom, O LORD, and you are exalted as head above all.** [12] *Both riches and honor come from you, and you rule over all. In your hand are power and might, and in your hand it is to make great and to give strength to all.* [13] *And now we thank you, our God, and praise your glorious name.*

- 1 Chronicles 29:10-13

Note the structure of David's prayer for a moment. He begins and ends with God's glory (v. 10, v. 13). As we give ourselves to the Lord and aspire to be used by Him, the #1 ingredient in our devotion must be the priority we place on God's glory. Many ministry efforts—even entire movements—have been rendered fruitless and withered away because they compromised on this issue. It doesn't matter what we do, whatever charitable outreach, well-intentioned community involvement, even church growth— if we do not make the glory of God on His terms Number One, the whole thing will fail. Why? Because to glorify God is to submit. Can we pursue those things without submitting? People do it all the time.

Verse 11 is essentially the source verse for the doxology we have come to know as Matthew 6:13. The Lord is glorified in special terms: His is the power and the glory, the victory and the majesty, and the kingdom. Most Christians will recognize David's words in the prayer we read in Matthew 6.

But I want to focus on verse 12. Here David speaks of God's blessing that is bestowed upon those who enjoy His favor. Riches, honor, greatness, and strength all come from Him. These are those heavenly blessings that come in so handy on earth, and are so necessary for effective ministry before the Lord. But how do they come? They come to us as we submit. Here we return to the "Saul vs. David" idea, made even more powerful when we consider Daniel's vision, which I touched on yesterday.

All human kingdoms fall. But David's throne endures forever. How? David came into *submitted covenant relationship* with God. Like a twig tied to a pillar, David's line took on the strength of God Himself, and ultimately David's submission led to the birth of Jesus in his dynasty. When we submit—really, truly, sincerely surrender—God imparts to us the attributes of His kingdom. This doesn't mean that our kingdoms don't fall, of course. What it means is that our kingdoms become His as they are transformed according to His purposes.

We are to pray fervently, from the heart, **come** *Your Kingdom,* **be done** *Your will.* We are to literally invite the steamroller of God's will, God's kingdom, the Rock Cut Not by Human Hands, to come and wipe out our vision of things and supplant it with His. This can be traumatic. But it is also the only way to experience the true joy of being entirely submitted to the Father.

Day 57

I'd like to continue in the matter of submission to the Lord's will for one more important aspect, the question of *unity among believers.*

Perhaps oddly, I begin by looking at a famous story of unity from the Old Testament—the Tower of Babel.

Then they said, "Come, let us build ourselves a city and a tower with its top in the heavens, and let us make a name for ourselves, lest we be dispersed over the face of the whole earth." ⁵ And the LORD came down to see the city and the tower, which the children of man had built. ⁶ And the LORD said, "Behold, they are one people, and they have all one language, and this is only the beginning of what they will do. And nothing that they propose to do will now be impossible for them." ˜ Genesis 11:4-6

Of course, the rest of the story is how God brought a confusion of languages and dispersed the people over the earth. Why did this project end the way it did, after such a promising beginning in a show of human unity? **Because the entire thing was grounded in rebellion.** God had made clear He wanted humanity to "fill the earth and subdue it" (Genesis 1:28), and they were bound and determined to stay put and glorify their own name rather than God's name. Jewish tradition also strongly attributes the Babel episode as the birth of both *dictatorship* and *slavery.* The unity they showed was *strong-armed* unity achieved by fear, not the kind of unity God wants.

The other kind of situation birthed by rebellion is found in Proverbs 28:2...

When a land transgresses, it has many rulers, but with a man of understanding and knowledge, its stability will long continue.

Solomon begins this proverb describing the other end of the rebellion stick from Babel: The "many rulers" are individual people, each following their own wills and purposes, and each defending their own "kingdom." The people can be in the same "land"—apparently the same realm—but each is trying to be their own ruler, and the result is chaos.

Obviously, neither the Babel situation (oppressive, false unity) nor the "land with many rulers" (spiritual anarchy) are desirable to God or redemptive to people. The Book of Judges tells us that "in those days there was no king, and each did what was right in his own eyes"—meaning they didn't do right at all. Again, chaos. But Solomon's "man of understanding and knowledge" has arrived, and His name is JESUS, and He taught us the way. When people of faith pray as Jesus taught us, "Your Kingdom come, Your will be done" from a sincere heart, then we all tune the instruments of our hearts to the same tuning fork. We all submit to God's plan. At Babel, people submitted to the strongman's will out of fear; in the Kingdom of God, we willingly, by faith, submit to the Father's will out of love with one voice. It is not without reason that we begin the prayer with "Our father…"

What is the result?

Behold, how good and pleasant it is when brothers dwell in unity![2] It is like the precious oil on the head, running down on the beard, on the beard of Aaron, running down on the collar of his robes![3] It is like the dew of Hermon, which falls on the mountains of Zion! For there the LORD has commanded the blessing, life forevermore. ˜ Psalm 133

When we submit, each on our own, from the heart surrendering to Christ through prayer and obedience, we conform to Him. And when a congregation of such submitted people come together for worship and labor in the Lord, they find the foundation for dwelling in unity has been laid beforehand. *This is when the anointing comes.*

Allow me to be perfectly clear: People going to church, in itself, is right next to powerless. It is the anointing that rests upon a congregation that gives it power to achieve the mission Jesus has given to it. And it's that anointing, that precious, powerful, chain-breaking anointing, that makes the difference. This alone should make any act or word that compromises Christian unity a fearful thing to us. Unity is one of the great results of submission to Christ, and the power of the Holy Spirit in our midst rests upon that unity. We should pray for unity, but the first step towards achieving it is by each one of us submitting to Christ from the heart through prayer and obedience to God's word.

Now look at Acts 2...

When the day of Pentecost arrived, they were all together in one place. *²And suddenly there came from heaven a sound like a mighty rushing wind, and it filled the entire house where they were sitting.* *³And divided tongues as of fire appeared to them and rested on each one of them.* *⁴And they were all filled with the Holy Spirit and began to speak in other tongues as the Spirit gave them utterance.* *˜* Acts 2:1-4

As the early believers prayed, unified in one place and deeply submitted to God's purposes (see also Acts 1:14), *then* the Holy Spirit is poured out upon them. *The result is Babel in reverse*—an outpouring of languages that doesn't confuse but clarifies, enlightens, and saves.

Day 58

While I could go on and on about the subject of submission, I believe we've covered that sufficiently for us all to understand how vital it is for a successful prayer life and for the power of the Holy Spirit to rest upon us, both individually and corporately. That quest is never over, but reading and meditating upon it is helpful for us to grow in that area. Still, let's move on to another major aspect of prayer, and for me right now that is the theme of *God's promises.*

The Apostle Peter tells us this...

*His divine power has granted to us all things that pertain to life and godliness, through the knowledge of him who called us to **his own glory and excellence, 4 by which he has granted to us his precious and very great promises**, so that through them you may become partakers of the divine nature, having escaped from the corruption that is in the world because of sinful desire. ˉ* 2 Peter 1:3-4

I have seen over the years what might be called "promise books"— selections from the Scriptures—printed and marketed as somewhat sentimental gift items. The editions I've seen are often pretty, of small print, and seem formatted to be taken in small doses as sort of supplementary "boosts" to our faith. It sounds like I'm knocking such books; I'm not—any way we can get the Word into us I'm all for it. But the delivery medium seems part of the message to me. What Peter tells us is very different: *Promises are the fundamental essence of how we relate to God.* Promises proceed from His very nature ("his own glory and excellence"), are "precious and very great" (not a small or "supplementary" thing at all), and through them we are eternally redeemed ("partakers of the divine nature, having escaped from...corruption"). So for the Christian in relationship with God, His promises are central. Parsing them out from the rest of Scripture as if they are *an aspect* of God's truth for us can (paradoxically) distort that truth.

I'd like to spend some days on the matter of God's promises—His overarching, general promises as well as specific promises we might feel we've received from Him. How we view God's promises is essential to our prayer life. We will be exploring different Scriptures that speak to God's promises in our lives.

For now, though, I'd like to share from *The Pilgrim's Progress*. (By the way, the entire book can be had for pennies on an e-reader like Kindle, or even found in the public domain online.)

In the story, the pilgrim, Christian, and his friend, Hopeful, attempt an ill-advised shortcut and end up in the dungeon of Doubting Castle, a terrible place ruled by the Giant of Despair. They suffer long at the Giant's hands, and are at the point of self-destruction when suddenly the situation breaks...

*Well, on Saturday, about midnight, **they began to pray**, and continued in prayer till almost break of day. Now a little before it was day, good Christian, as one half amazed, brake out in passionate speech: What a fool, quoth he, am I, thus to lie in a stinking Dungeon, when I may as well walk at liberty. **I have a Key in my bosom called Promise**, that will, I am persuaded, open any Lock in Doubting Castle. Then said Hopeful, That's good news; good Brother pluck it out of thy bosom and try. Then Christian pulled it out of his bosom, and began to try at the Dungeon door, whose bolt (as he turned the Key) gave back, **and the door flew open with ease**, and Christian and Hopeful both came out. Then he went to the **outward door that leads into the Castle-yard, and with his Key opened that door also**. After he went to the **iron Gate**, for that must be opened too, **but that Lock went very hard, yet the Key did open it.***

John Bunyan was a man of great insight. I will contextualize this allegory for us, especially in light of the recent discussion of submission.

God requires submission from us; He commands it. But God is merciful, and He is good. Facing the darkness is not something that He leaves us to handle alone: *He gives us His promises.* Everyone, sooner or later, finds themselves confronting the Giant of Despair and locked in his terrible dungeon. But God has given us a key with which to escape, and that key is **Promise.**

Jesus faced Gethsemane. He prayed that the Father's will, and not His own, be done. But in Jesus' heart burned the promise of the resurrection, of which He had already spoken repeatedly to His disciples. Hebrews 12:2 tells us that Jesus was able to endure the Cross *"for the joy set before Him."* Even in Jesus' darkest hour, the promises of the Father lit the way.

There is a reason why Gethsemane is seen as the stepping off point for the crucifixion, and at its core it's the same reason Bunyan's characters are able to remember the Key called Promise—*promise and prayer are deeply linked as the way forward from where we are to the blessed place God has for us.*

Believe God's promises for you today.

Day 59

There are many different aspects we could discuss when addressing the theme of God's promises. But for the sake of a strong transition from our treatment of the power of *submission*, I'd like to begin with the issue of God's commands as they relate to His *promises*.

One of the basics of understanding God's promises is that many of them are conditional: God promises to do such-and-such if we do such-and-such as a prior or (in most cases) an ongoing condition we must meet. One might argue that all of God's promises, for all intents and purposes, are conditional, because ultimately even the most-mentioned "unconditional" promises (God's manifest love and goodness, His willingness to accept repentance, etc.) have a time limit to them—our lifespan at most. But however we see it, we should understand that to take a promise out of context and apply it carte blanche is not the nature of promise because it is not the nature of God. As we read in the quote from 2 Peter 1 yesterday, God gives us His promises not merely as a grab bag of goodies, but as part of His redemptive purposes for us. The conditions He lays on promises are part of that redemption, just as a loving earthly parent lays conditions on their promises to their children so that the good things they want to give them do not end up doing them more harm than good.

These truths are well and good, and should provide enough motivation in themselves for us to walk in submission. Hypothetically, someone who memorizes promises but refuses to obey the fundamentals of the faith will not see those promises, while someone who might be ignorant of this or that Scripture will end up seeing God manifest those promises to them whether they understand or not.

But I'd like to address a different aspect regarding the relationship between God's promises and His commands, and that is the truth of God's commands *as* promises.

When God commands something, *there is always a promise implicit in that command.* In other words, just as promise fulfillment on God's part is conditional upon obedience on our part, the inverse is also true: if we obey God's commands, a promise connected with that obedience is implied by the command itself.

Consider the Great Commission:

And Jesus came and said to them, "All authority in heaven and on earth has been given to me. [19] **Go therefore and make disciples of all nations, baptizing them in the name of the Father and of the Son and of the Holy Spirit, [20] teaching them to observe all that I have commanded you.** *And behold, I am with you always, to the end of the age."* Matthew 28:18-20

This is a command from Jesus if ever there was one. Placing ourselves in the shoes of the disciples—even those who first read the Gospel of Matthew a few decades later—this command is a lulu: *"Hey there brothers, I know you are not numerous, well-educated, not politically powerful, and not wealthy. But go preach to the entire world and convert them to faith in me."* It sounds crazy, even today. But the Great Commission has been one of the greatest successes in history, and it has been for one reason: obedience to the command came with a promise— *"I'll be with you."* In this case the promise is explicit; Jesus states it directly. But my point is that whenever God commands something, a promise is always at least *implicit*—that God will provide, guide, and comfort to the degree we will need to fulfill the command. Submission paves the way for God to bring to us what we need.

When my family and I answered the missionary call, it was really a journey—a season of steps—that led us to a place where we were serving on foreign soil and carrying out the ministry God had called us to. The *general command* of the Great Commission became a *specific command* to us to go. But in the same way, the *general promise* that God would bend His power on our behalf and be with us took on *specific manifestation* in our lives. We had faith in God's Word that He would be with us; we burned with excitement and anticipation as our sense of desire became a confirmed sense of leading, and the doors began to open. Even now, the dread some have vocalized that God might call them to missionary service is incomprehensible to us. Do you realize what that command means? It means Jesus Christ has His hand on you! It means He will be with you! It means miracles are going to happen and great deeds will be accomplished! The greater the command, the greater the cost of obedience, the greater the promise that is implicit in the giving of the command.

The upshot of all of this discussion comes down to this: Embrace God's commands as promises in and of themselves. If He tells you to go someplace, it means He has something good for you in it. If He tells you to do something, there's blessing that will come from it. If He tells you to give something up, it means He has something better for you than what you're holding on to. Whether general or specific, whether based in the reading of Scripture or a specific prompting of the Holy Spirit, God's commands are not burdensome because not only have we overcome the world, there's always something wonderful waiting on the other side.

God is good!

Day 60

Continuing in the promises of God, I want to move into the theme of actually *praying God's promises to pass*. This is an audacious statement all of itself, but what we are really talking about is a prayer relationship with God, couched in faith in His promises, guided by their truths, seeing things through unto fulfillment.

We have hundreds of promises in God's Word that are the blessing for every believer. Additionally, we have words that God has "quickened" to us by the working of His Holy Spirit—promises that we have become convinced are especially for us. To effectively pray these promises through to fulfillment we must walk in faith, because as hard as it is to hear, the promise alone is not sufficient:

*Therefore, since the **promise of entering his rest** still stands, let us be careful that none of you be found to have fallen short of it. ² For we also have had the gospel preached to us, just as they did; **but the message they heard was of no value to them, because those who heard did not combine it with faith.*** ¯ Hebrews 4:1-2 (NIV84)

This in my estimation is one of the most powerful Scriptures about the nature of promise in the New Testament and indeed the entire Bible. The example given, drawn from Israel's desert wanderings, is used throughout the Old Testament (by the prophets) and here in the New Testament as well. It is a negative example—i.e., look at what this bunch did and *don't do it yourselves.* Here the author of Hebrews makes a pointed and economical observation: a promise was delivered to them by the Supreme Promise Keeper—but it availed them not at all because *they did not mix the promise with faith.*

What we are talking about here is *prayer in light of promise.* We've already seen that faith is the currency of *prayer;* now we see it is also the currency of *promise.* The way these are brought together is by reminding God of His promises. Isaiah tells us...

On your walls, O Jerusalem, I have set watchmen; all the day and all the night they shall never be silent. **You who put the LORD in remembrance,** *take no rest,⁷ and give him no rest until he establishes Jerusalem and makes it a praise in the earth.*

˜ Isaiah 62:6–7

God tells us to "put Him in remembrance." It is our very duty to tirelessly remind Him of His promises. What does this mean? Does God forget His promises? Is He a mortal who needs to be reminded like a forgetful man? Obviously not. But the action on our part of "reminding God" in the context of meditation on Scripture and prayer keeps the substance of the promise a "front burner" faith matters in our walk with Him. That act of "reminding" God actually reminds *us*, but in a particular way—it stirs our faith to believe, to hold on, to keep the eyes of our heart open for the fulfillment that will surely come. Reminding God of His promise mixes faith in with our reception of the promise, so that we do not fall into the trap the Israelites fell prey to.

Look again at the passage in Isaiah 62. God tells us to *"put Him in remembrance"*and *"give Him no rest until He establishes Jerusalem and makes it a praise in the earth."* So what was the promise?

Take a look at the previous verses:

For Zion's sake I will not keep silent, and for Jerusalem's sake I will not be quiet, until her righteousness goes forth as brightness, and her salvation as a burning torch. ² The nations shall see your righteousness, and all the kings your glory, and you shall be called by a new name that the mouth of the LORD will give. ³ You shall be a crown of beauty in the hand of the LORD, and a royal diadem in the hand of your God. ⁴ You shall no more be termed Forsaken, and your land shall no more be termed Desolate, but you shall be called My Delight Is in Her, and your land Married; for the LORD delights in you, and your land shall be married. ⁵ For as a young man marries a young woman, so shall your sons marry you, and as the bridegroom rejoices over the bride, so shall your God rejoice over you. ˜ Isaiah 62:1-5

In this case, Isaiah 62:7 (see above) *matches* Isaiah 62:2-5. This is the pattern for all of God's promises, and how we are to "reclaim" them before God's throne: He makes sweeping, wonderfully, heart-swelling and inspiring "too good to be true" promises. It is our part to store them in our heart, to mix them with faith, to allow them to reach into our being and allow ourselves to dare to hope for the day when they manifest before our eyes. Our hearts on fire with the joy of the promise, we are to cry out to God, and fervently and faithfully, if not impertinently, "remind Him" of those promises. Write down the promises, underline your Bible, write them on note cards and plaster them around the house, do whatever it takes. But stir them up by putting God in remembrance. Give Him no rest and give yourself no rest until you see it with your eyes.

Father, You have promised. Our eyes are fixed upon You.

Day 61

Let's continue with the question of faith and promise. To this end, I'd like to direct our attention to the Book of Galatians, in which the word "promise" (Greek: *epangelia*) occurs 10 times as a central truth for Paul's argument. It is probably best to simply read that book, especially chapters 3-4, but I'll give a rundown of Paul's thesis here.

The Galatians are Gentile "baby Christians" whom Paul has evangelized and initiated into the faith, planting churches and establishing local leaders. But some time after Paul's visit to their region, the Galatians fall prey to false teachers ("Judaizers") who tell them they need to follow the Law of Moses as full-fledged converts to Judaism in order to receive the blessings of Abraham through a Jewish Messiah in the Lord Jesus. Paul's counterattack (found in this epistle) is that all of Abraham's greatness was determined by his *faith* in God's *promise* to him—not by keeping the Law. Galatians is considered a cornerstone of New Testament thought for Paul's lucid presentation of the core truths of the gospel.

Today, we might not be facing false teachers of the kind the Galatians dealt with. But the lessons from that crisis surely remain. While Law is something we understand had a limited role for a specific time—to point us to Christ—*promise is foundational:* it predates the Law and its power extends into the New Covenant and will carry us through until we see Jesus face to face. Promise is the very DNA of the New Covenant.

Now, there are promises and there are promises. The promise that all people of faith—Jew or Gentile—will receive the inheritance of Abraham, the promise of the Holy Spirit, the promise of eternal life in Christ, these are covenant level "umbrella promises" that define who we are in the Lord (in truth, these three I have named are really different aspects of one and the same promise). There are also *lesser promises* that speak to God's care for us, or His plan for our lives under the shadow of that umbrella/covenantal promise. From my experience, mostly due to the nature of our walk with the Lord and perhaps our immaturity, I find that many Christians (myself included) take those covenant promises for granted as sort of "givens;" we often concern ourselves more with the "lesser" promises because they seem more personal or speak more immediately to our situation. It is a larger discussion about the nature of promise and covenant to realize that the lesser promises are corollaries to the greater ones (see Romans 8:31-32), but we'll not pursue that right now. My point is that in the midst of his discussion, Paul tips his hand about *the nature of promise in general*—truths that we can apply as we seek the Lord in prayer for the things He has spoken and that encourage us.

Christ redeemed us from the curse of the law by becoming a curse for us—for it is written, "Cursed is everyone who is hanged on a tree"— [14] *so that in Christ Jesus the blessing of Abraham might come to the Gentiles, so that we might receive the promised Spirit through faith.* ¯ Galatians 3:13-14

But the Scripture imprisoned everything under sin, so that the promise by faith in Jesus Christ might be given to those who believe. ¯ Galatians 3:22

These passages point out what ultimately becomes obvious to anyone who studies the Word in depth—and the reason for Paul's exasperation with the Galatians: *the very purpose of a promise is to provoke faith in the heart of the recipient of that promise.* If faith wasn't the goal, then God would inform, not make a promise. Likewise, if action alone were the goal, then instruction and not promise would have been His chosen method of communication. Even between people, one person promises something to another in order to raise the hearer's sense of confidence in the words being spoken; "confidence" is just a natural word for *faith.* This is the point of Hebrews 6:17-18...

So when God desired to show more convincingly to the heirs of the promise the unchangeable character of his purpose, he guaranteed it with an oath, [18] so that by two unchangeable things, in which it is impossible for God to lie, we who have fled for refuge might have strong encouragement to hold fast to the hope set before us.

Everything we receive through Jesus is because God *promised* it. And in Jesus all those promises come true, as Paul tells us, *"For all the promises of God find their Yes in him"*(2 Corinthians 1:20). Like Abraham did, we need to let our hearts go and believe the promises God has given us. That's the reason He gave them. The demonized boy's father said to Jesus, *"I do believe! Help my unbelief!"*(Mark 9:24). God helps our unbelief with promises so that we might pray more effectively. Again, this is the DNA of the New Covenant; the very fabric of how we relate to the Father in Jesus' name.

I encourage you, as you pray, to think and process matters of faith and unbelief in terms of promise. It is a process; it isn't automatic. God is promising us because what He has to say typically runs counter to the evidence around us. People don't wrangle in prayer over the question of tomorrow's sunrise; they wrestle with God providing in the face of a financial crisis, or God's healing power in the face of disease, or even God providing the grace for a family crisis. Promises are made to help us conquer a hill that otherwise we wouldn't be able to climb, and sometimes we need to work through that issue. Abram heard the promise three times before he *"believed and it was credited to him as righteousness"* (see Genesis 12:7, 13:15, and finally 15:6). For this reason we must meditate on those promises so they get deep into our spirit and become a part of us. It is then that they become like expecting the sunrise to us.

Day 62

As I have been writing, we must let God's promises stir faith in us so that we might see their fulfillment, and God might fulfill His blessed purposes in us and through us. Promise begets faith, and faith in turn begets the fulfillment of the promise.

But I would tender a qualifying word on expectation before we go on. We must embrace God's promises and believe them, but we must do so with great humility and (once again) *submission*—submission to the *terms* of the promise and submission in the broad sense by considering the *Source* of the promise. Our God is a consuming fire, He is not a short order cook. Our expectation of fulfillment should not involve dictating terms to God regarding how He plans on fulfilling His word. The promise, after all, is His.

Mixing our preconceptions into our expectation of fulfillment is an entirely natural thing to do. As we apprehend the promise, we tend to visualize how it will come to pass. If, for example, we meditate on a promise for provision, we might imagine how that provision will come. But we need to be very careful in that process, because faith-filled expectation can quickly become nothing better than presumption. And God is beholden only to His promise; He is not the slightest bit obligated to the assumptions we mix with our faith. Consider the promise of all promises throughout the Old Testament—the coming of the Messiah. From the first verses of the Book of Genesis, messianic prophecies heralded the incarnation of a savior both indirectly and explicitly. But what happened when Jesus came?

And the Father who sent me has himself borne witness about me. His voice you have never heard, his form you have never seen, [38] *and you do not have his word abiding in you, for you do not believe the one whom he has sent.* [39] **You search the Scriptures because you think that in them you have eternal life; and it is they that bear witness about me,** [40] **yet you refuse to come to me that you may have life.** ¯ John 5:37-40

This passage gives us in a nutshell a summation of the entire narrative of the Gospels: the nation of Israel in Jesus' time, and in particular the priestly leadership, did not receive the fulfillment of the messianic promise. God in the flesh stood there, looking them in the face, and they did not, could not receive Him. And why not? Because they had assumptions that arose from within them that they allowed to be greater than the evidences God provided for them. They wanted their messiah to fit those assumptions—to conform to their own presuppositions and expectations. So when God (surprise, surprise!) chose to do things His own way, they missed the boat. For this reason Jesus wept over Jerusalem; the city did not recognize the day of her visitation, the window closed, and it was then hidden from her eyes. This is a powerful warning, perhaps one of the greatest warnings we can take in respect to promise.

The Apostle Paul, himself one who began his encounter with the gospel with distorted expectations (to the point of persecuting the church), ended up saying a similar thing about his own people:

For I bear them witness that they have a zeal for God, but not according to knowledge.[3] For, being ignorant of the righteousness of God, and seeking to establish their own, they did not submit to God's righteousness. ¯ Romans 10:2-3

Again, the assessment is that the people on a whole had allowed their own interpretation of God's word to so completely take hold of them that they could not accept God's fresh, new plan when it came. That it was a better plan was beside the point to them— *they could not let go of their preconceptions and receive the good thing God had planned.*

Let us take warning. God's promises are His. He sees what we cannot, and almost certainly the manifestation of His promise will unfold in a fashion we do not expect. God's "non-conformity" to human expectation touches on pretty much everything: timing, means, place, and scope: in short, the comprehensive nature of the manifestation rarely if ever conforms to how we think it might happen. The religious leaders in Jesus' day did not expect Him when He came, they couldn't grasp that He would be a peaceful carpenter from Galilee, and (most of all) they never envisioned that one day literally billions from all nations would be bowing down to Him as Son of David, Son of Man, and Son of God.

Thankfully—and this must be said—not everyone in Jesus' day suffered this blindness. The earliest church was entirely Jewish for its first generation, which means it would be incorrect to make too sweeping a statement about "Jewish blindness" at the time of Jesus. Not to put too fine a point on it, everyone has misconceptions about Messiah. For example, Peter had to be rebuked because he couldn't imagine Jesus' suffering like He kept predicting He would (Matthew 16); Peter simply couldn't conceive of a suffering Savior, and all the evidence indicates the rest of the disciples felt the same way. The difference between Jesus' disciples (eleven of them, anyway) and the Jewish religious elite was that they chose to let go of their preconceptions when God's plan manifested; those who crucified Jesus, in contrast, held onto their blindness, and suffered irreparable loss. Again, let's not get too cocky here; these are reactions that are not a Jewish issue, but a human issue. Every single person is forced into the choice between what they expect and what God really wants to do with them.

Having preconceptions is human. Refusing to accept God's unanticipated good when it comes, remarks C.S. Lewis, is the very definition of evil. Let's keep these things in mind as we pray, as we meditate, and as we embrace the promises. Let us discern in our own hearts the difference between faith and arrogant presumption, from humbly receiving God's promises and dictating terms to Him.

Day 63

I've written about position before, but I want to give it another look specifically from the angle of repentance unto promise fulfillment. The Scriptures are full of examples of how we must position ourselves for promise fulfillment. This is a broader, fuller, and more accurate understanding of the conditionality of God's promises to us.

Look at what Paul says about one of the Ten Commandments:

"Honor your father and mother" (this is the first commandment with a promise), "that it may go well with you and that you may live long in the land." Ephesians 6:2-3

Paul is telling us that, in this case, Moses actually explicitly weaves the matter of positioning into the commandment itself. We place ourselves advantageously in relation to God's promise that "things would go well with us and we might live long in the land" by doing something—"honoring our father and mother." Obedience is the step we take to get under the outpouring of God's blessings.

Now let's look at another passage from Paul...

...As God said, "I will make my dwelling among them and walk among them, and I will be their God, and they shall be my people. [17] Therefore go out from their midst, and be separate from them, says the Lord, and touch no unclean thing; then I will welcome you, [18] and I will be a father to you, and you shall be sons and daughters to me, says the Lord Almighty." Since we have these promises, beloved, let us cleanse ourselves from every defilement of body and spirit, bringing holiness to completion in the fear of God. 2 Corinthians 6:16–7:1

The passage begins with a catena of incredible (but conditional) promises about God being with His people. Paul sums these up by inviting us to *position ourselves* for fulfillment of those promises *through repentance.* By cleansing ourselves of all "defilement of body and spirit" we position ourselves for God to fulfill His promises to us. In fact, the broad testimony of God's Word and the experience of God's people (myself included) bears out that God uses hardship—sometimes severe hardship—to pull, push, coax, lure, or otherwise force us into the position where His promises can be fulfilled. It can be a most unpleasant process, but the end result is tremendous blessing.

By way of personal testimony, I remember a season as missionaries where we were serving in a city we loved (Cuenca, Ecuador). We never wanted to leave. But God had other plans, and when we voiced our opposition to His gentle indications that we should consider service in another, larger (and much needier, in relation to our calling) city (Guayaquil), that's when the gloves came off. Our idyllic existence in our beloved adopted hometown became difficult, then seriously troubled, then complicated to the point of downright misery. We did not feel blessed. But God permitted that temporary misery to bring us to a place of brokenness so we would yield to His will. Honestly, we didn't realize what He wanted, because we had blinded ourselves to that option through stubbornness. But through the process, things made themselves clear. When we repented, and opened ourselves to the possibility we had ruled out the previous year, everything changed. We got into the position we needed to be in, and God fulfilled His promises, and truth be told we are still reaping blessing from that decision over 20 years later.

Yesterday we studied about the confusion between faith in the promise and anti-faith human expectations that can actually prevent us from receiving the promise. That anti-faith is essentially *negative positioning.* But even if our faith is pure and we are yielded for whatever God wants to bring, *fulfillment is always a surprise.* God doing His work is always such a blessing, and how He manifests His power so remarkable, there is always a sense of freshness and amazement over the fruit of our faith. But that is the very nature of things in God's kingdom.

When we repent, and when we humble ourselves and yield to Him, the effect is like soft rain in springtime. Freshness cannot help but come. A Christian who is highly religious but not by character repentant and contrite becomes deeply cliché in their practice of the faith. There is nothing new, they become tired, and they tend to look back on an ideal past and subsist on memories of past blessings. But the repentant heart is continually positioning itself for the new thing God is doing. Through it and in it, God can create continually. I am convinced that a genuine person of prayer is also a person of repentance; a person who does not walk in heartfelt repentance (what saints in previous times called "compunction") is only praying superficially and religiously.

Let's weave repentance into our prayer life. Let's be people of prayer.

Day 64

Even when we position ourselves through repentance, the timing is always up to the Lord. This can be most difficult for us. David writes this:

My soul longs for your salvation; I hope in your word. [82] *My eyes long for your promise; I ask, "When will you comfort me?"* [83] *For I have become like a wineskin in the smoke, yet I have not forgotten your statutes.* [84] *How long must your servant endure?*
— Psalm 119:81-84

Another version puts it this way: *My eyes fail, looking for your promise.* (NIV84) All of us have felt this way before.

Some simply observations need to be made in respect to God's timing for His promises. I didn't say "easy," but I did say "simple," because these truths are fairly straightforward.

1) *God's greatest saints received God's promises in God's time and most definitely not their own.* Look at Abraham. It took *25 years* between when God first promised to make Abram a great nation (Genesis 12) to the birth of Isaac (Genesis 21). Remember that Abraham was known as God's friend. Our natural man wants to rise up inside us and say, "Some friend! Twenty-five *years??*" But we must remember with whom we are dealing, and what friendship with God really means.

2) *God is God is God.* Do we really want a god (lowercase here on purpose) who, like the idols of the nations, is nothing more than a glorified mascot who performs for us on our terms? Do we want a petty patron deity who fits our ideas of the divine? There is a price to pay for worshipping the Lord of all the earth. There is a difference between "faithful" and "predictable." As C.S. Lewis said of his Christ figure in the *Chronicles of Narnia*, "Aslan is not a tame lion." God does things His way, and that is almost always inconvenient for human plans. On the other hand, He has real power to save and deliver.

3) *Waiting is a powerful form of positioning.* Of all the forms we might consider when it comes to bringing ourselves to a place where God can fulfill His word to us, waiting is one of the most powerful. A host of powerful things can happen in us when we wait on God. We are reminded that He is God and we are not. We have time to reflect and purify ourselves before Him. God, though timeless Himself, is able to work other things out that pertain to our situation. Waiting—which is an action, not a lack of action—is a very necessary aspect of discipleship.

Hebrews 6:12 says this...

We do not want you to become lazy, but to imitate those who through faith and patience inherit what has been promised. (NIV84)

We receive the promise through *faith*, as we have seen. But we also receive the promise through *patience*.

Let us be patient before the Lord, let us keep our eyes on Him, and let us hold on to His promises.

Day 65

The Apostle Paul tells us this...

Now you, brothers, like Isaac, are children of promise.
˜Galatians 4:28

Paul says something similar in Romans 9:8...

This means that it is not the children of the flesh who are the children of God, but the children of the promise are counted as offspring.

Remember the waiting of Abraham I wrote of yesterday? That waiting paid off, and the fulfillment is YOU. So while it may be easy sometimes to echo David's lament that *"my eyes fail, looking for Your promise,"* these passages help us remember that promise is not just something God gives us external to our being, but promise is actually intrinsic to our being. We are walking promises—the very children of promise. We are all spiritual Isaacs!

As you pray, looking for God's promise, positioning yourself by waiting on God and repenting, remember that you are beset by fulfillment itself because it is who you are. Every other promise pales by comparison with the promise of adoption into God's family, the promise of eternal life. For this reason, Paul also famously says,

*He who did not spare his own Son but gave him up for us all, **how will he not also with him graciously give us all things?***
˜ Romans 8:32

Look up, beloved of God. It is all yours.

We are to pray the promises of God by using the Scriptures. There are already many ready-made prayers in the Bible that include promises. When we read the psalms we find one beautiful prayer-promise after another, ready for us to read out, mix with faith, and offer to God as our own prayer. That is God's intention for us. Such prayers are found elsewhere in the Bible as well, in both Old and New Testament.

But we can take almost any promise, make it personal for our situation, and pray it to the Lord. There is great power in this, because we are praying the very Word of God, and God's anointing is already resting on the prayer. If there's a promise in the Bible that strikes your heart as you read it, and you feel the Holy Spirit quicken it to you, why not make it a prayer?

Here are some examples of how we might do this. Here's a beautiful and comforting passage in Isaiah...

But now thus says the LORD, he who created you, O Jacob, he who formed you, O Israel: "Fear not, for I have redeemed you; I have called you by name, you are mine. ² When you pass through the waters, I will be with you; and through the rivers, they shall not overwhelm you; when you walk through fire you shall not be burned, and the flame shall not consume you. ³ For I am the LORD your God, the Holy One of Israel, your Savior.

˜ Isaiah 43:1-3

If we are facing a difficult time, and feel the comfort of the Holy Spirit in this prayer, we might form this into a prayer we could pray whenever we want, or incorporate into our daily prayer time. It might read like this:

You created and formed me, O Lord. I will not fear, for You have redeemed me, You have called me by name, and I am Yours. When I pass through the waters, be with me; and through the rivers, keep them from overwhelming me; and when I walk through the fire, keep me from being burned and the flame from consuming me. For You are the Lord my God, the Holy One of Israel, my Savior.

Another powerful, comforting passage which is a personal favorite of mine is Isaiah 54...

O afflicted one, storm-tossed and not comforted, behold, I will set your stones in antimony, and lay your foundations with sapphires. [12] I will make your pinnacles of agate, your gates of carbuncles, and all your wall of precious stones. [13] All your children shall be taught by the LORD, and great shall be the peace of your children. [14] In righteousness you shall be established; you shall be far from oppression, for you shall not fear; and from terror, for it shall not come near you. [15] If anyone stirs up strife, it is not from me; whoever stirs up strife with you shall fall because of you. [16] Behold, I have created the smith who blows the fire of coals and produces a weapon for its purpose. I have also created the ravager to destroy; [17] no weapon that is fashioned against you shall succeed, and you shall refute every tongue that rises against you in judgment. This is the heritage of the servants of the LORD and their vindication from me, declares the LORD. ‾Isaiah 54:11-17

One might personalize the prayer into something like this...

O Lord, I feel afflicted, storm-tossed, and comfortless. Set my stones in antimony, and lay my foundations with sapphires. Make my pinnacles of agate, my gates of carbuncles, and all my wall of precious stones. May all my children be taught of the Lord, and may the peace of my children be great. Establish me in righteousness, take me far from oppression, and deliver me from fear; may terror be far from me. Cause those who stir up strife against me to fail. You are the one who gave the ability to make weapons, so I ask that You cause that no weapon fashioned against me might succeed, and may I refute every tongue that rises against me in judgment. This is my heritage from you, Lord, and my vindication.

Everyone will want to do this in a way they feel remains true to the original passage (we're not trying to change the Bible or come up with our own translation!), but also is "prayable" and expresses the sense of their own heart when they read the original promise. The sky is the limit on how we can incorporate God's promises into our prayer life as we do this.

Day 66

Before I move on from the subject of promise, I wanted to express one last thing that pertains to that subject, a thread that runs through all of God's promises and serves as an underpinning to the entire idea of promise. This simple but incredibly profound truth is that God is good. Although it sounds like a truth that might serve as a coloring project for a children's Sunday school class, if we do not embrace this truth we are crippled before we begin when it comes to prayer and promise.

The Scripture passages that speak to God's goodness are abundant and varied, even as they hold to that common truth. Here are some of them:

Psalm 119:68
You are good and do good; teach me your statutes.

Psalm 100:5
For the LORD is good; his steadfast love endures forever, and his faithfulness to all generations.

Nahum 1:7
The LORD is good, a stronghold in the day of trouble; he knows those who take refuge in him.

Psalm 25:8
Good and upright is the LORD; therefore he instructs sinners in the way.

Psalm 106:1
Praise the LORD! Oh give thanks to the LORD, for he is good, for his steadfast love endures forever!

These are not all of the verses that speak to the goodness of God. Others are barely modified versions of these. But collectively they pretty much cover the bases: God is good. He is not good by some standard known to Him and unknown to us, as if His goodness is a divine trick that we are forced to agree to but never benefit from. Furthermore, it is not as if God is good, but His actions towards us are *not* good, which would be another trick. No, He is good, and *what He does is good.* He is good relationally, meaning in a way that reaches out to us: *His steadfast love endures forever,* and *He knows us.* God is good in a way that makes us secure when we need it most—He is a stronghold in the day of trouble. He teaches us and guides us in His goodness. We ought to give thanks to Him for His goodness.

What of our trials? What of the difficulties we face and it seems like God is so distant? What of times when He disciplines us? His goodness can certainly seem so mysterious that by any human measure it's a stretch indeed to even call it goodness.

There are some hard truths we need to grapple with if we are to internalize the goodness of God. The reality is that if there is a disconnect on what goodness is all about, it's on the end of fallen human beings, not with the perfect, holy, sinless God who is the yardstick of everything that is worth anything. That isn't a slap down, it's healthy self-assessment. If we want to understand the goodness of God, we need to begin by a recognition that because we are fallen, a veil has also fallen over our understanding of God. It is by believing His word, it is by embracing His truth which is higher than ours, and yes, it is by declaring who He says He is even as the darkness of the veil covers us and we don't understand.

Some years ago, my family went through an excruciating crisis. It looked like everything was against us, like we were losing all we held dear in the face of forces too mysterious and powerful for us to even begin to fight. The crisis went on and on, and I came to the point that I felt God was actually torturing me. Disappointment was too weak a word to express my state of mind. But we ended up experiencing what so many people have said before: what the devil meant for evil, God meant for good. The very defeat we had suffered ended up serving as the nail in the enemy's coffin, and God turned the situation to ultimate and lasting redemption for our family. Lo and behold, God was being good—the whole time. It wasn't He that was blind to my pain, it was I who was blind to how good He really was.

When we make our prayers and our inner posture agree with God's Word, we position ourselves to receive the promise. The world is an evil place, and we have an enemy—the devil, who roams like a roaring lion, seeking whom he may devour. Knowing God is good is a foundation, a pillar for us as we fight the fight. Believe God is good. Believe His Word. Believe.

May God's goodness manifest to you today.

Day 67

We've covered matters having to do with worship, prayer habits, reading and applying God's Word, spiritual warfare, repentance and submission, and promise. Now with those matters behind us, I'd like to turn to the sticky issue of what many call "unanswered prayer."

The question of unanswered prayer as a matter of discussion between Christians (meaning, outside the scope of the Bible itself) is very old indeed. St. Augustine (think late 300s AD) tells what is, upon reflection, a truly heartbreaking story about his Christian mother, Monica. When he was a young man, not yet a believer and very given to the lusts of the world, he was determined to leave North Africa where he lived with his family and find his fortune in Rome. Monica was dead set against the move, fearful for Augustine's very soul in such a vast and decadent city, and literally followed him to his place of embarkation to plead with him and otherwise hinder his departure. Augustine wrote in his *Confessions* how he deliberately tricked his mother into going to a local shrine (i.e., a church) to pray, and while she prayed there for his soul he boarded a ship and left her behind. Imagine for a moment Monica's bewilderment and then despair as she left the church where she had been praying (and specifically praying that her lost son would have a change of heart), only to find that he had used her love for him and faith in God against her to frustrate those very prayers.

But, looking back, Augustine writes the following devotion to God about the episode (*Confessions*, Book Five, Section viii, 15):

Yet in your deep counsel you heard the central point of her longing, though not granting her what she then asked, namely that you would make me what she continually prayed for.

As things would go, it was in the decadent city of Rome that Augustine eventually found Christ. God did not answer Monica's prayers of that moment literally, but the *spirit* of those prayers were fulfilled beyond her wildest dreams. Eventually Augustine was to become one of the greatest teachers in the history of Christianity, and his thought extends deep into areas most Christians do not even realize (even Protestant Christians).

This is a very gentle introduction to the topic of "unanswered" prayer, to say the least. Augustine himself, and any reasonable mind reading his words, would conclude this is not unanswered prayer at all—it's just a misunderstanding on our end. Well and true, that. But that's the point. "Unanswered" prayer is about the *crisis of faith*—it's about how we feel, how we perceive our standing with God in respect to prayers we've prayed and how our life is (or is not) unfolding around us. In the broadest sense, we won't know if our prayers were truly unanswered until we stand before God, after this life is over. Until then, though, we need to deal with it as a reality we face (at least in our perceptions), and because the Word of God actually speaks to this issue in a number of ways.

As I see it, there are a variety of possibilities to consider when it comes to "unanswered" prayer, and I will list them here in shorthand form now but we will discuss them in more detail during the days to come.

I. God is really saying "yes," but it doesn't seem that way
    a. He's saying "yes" in a different way than we think.
    b. We are praying different prayers that actually conflict with each other, so He's saying "yes" to one prayer that is functionally cancelling out another.

II. God is making us wait
    a. He is working things out to answer the prayer (logistics).
    b. He is working in us to answer the prayer (character issues).
    c. He is working in others to answer the prayer (their will).
    d. All or some of the above.

III. He is actually saying "no"

    a. He is unable to answer and/or is chastising us for sin.

    b. He is actually blessing us by saying "no," because He knows better than we concerning our request.

    c. Our expectations conflict with God's word.

This is an overview, and some might argue that some of these ideas are really the same, or that other ideas might be added to expand what I have as single issues. Doubtless some have more eloquent and elaborate theologies on the matter than I have outlined here. But my goal for this study is clarity of thought, and the ability to move forward in faith and practice.

Day 68

In discussing unanswered prayer and different possibilities for this spiritual condition, my intent is not to try and tritely demystify what is fundamentally a mysterious, difficult, and deeply personal issue, but to provide a framework as a starting point so we can grapple with things, remain in faith, and draw near to God.

The first category I touched upon (and have actually discussed briefly in the life of St. Augustine) is the idea that, although our prayer appears unanswered, *in truth God is actually saying "yes."* The only way this can work is if God is answering us favorably, but He is doing so in a way that conflicts with our expectations, whether by timing, means, or degree.

This reality overlaps with previous things we have studied. An "ABC" of praying to the God of Abraham, Isaac, and Jacob— meaning the Sovereign Lord of the Bible rather than an imaginary mascot deity who jumps at our every passing whim—is that He rules over all, is holy, just, and loving, is authentically benevolent towards His creation (us and others), and is all-knowing, all-powerful, and all-present. By definition, such a God transcends us and will regularly do things in ways that fly clean over our heads. It amazes me, in respect to my own expectations and those of others, how hard a lesson this is to learn, and how resistant we are to accepting it. God telling us that He answers prayer is a promise that must be understood in light of these greater truths about Him. God does things His way, in His time, and conformed to the broad plan of His will, always.

Once we get past that rather big issue in principle, we need to apply it in practice. No matter how many times God has come through for us, *"exceedingly, abundantly above all we ask or imagine"* (Ephesians 3:20), we still act surprised and even disappointed when things come through so differently. Why? Because we attach our faith to preconceptions we summon within ourselves in respect to the resolution we need, rather than attaching those expectations to the Great Resolver Himself. We are so desperate for an answer we work up scenarios in our minds and become emotionally invested in them. But as I've said, God is obligated to His Word, not to our imaginations. So when our expectations rather predictably fall short of manifestation, we brand our prayers "unanswered" and our God unfaithful (let's be honest for a moment here about our inner attitudes sometimes, shall we?). God is very patient with these things, of course, as He is about teaching us His nature in the midst of all these trials. He can handle our frustration. But it will continue to be exactly that until we recognize what is going on. He wants our faith to be *in Him.* This is a very difficult truth for us very needy human beings to swallow: the heart of our faith consists in the truth that our God and our walk with Him is more important than what He might do for us in respect to our needs and wants as we perceive them at the moment—*even legitimate needs and wants.*

This is not an elaborate way to say that God doesn't really answer prayer. Our God is sovereign, but He is also personal and relational. He wants to answer prayer; He delights to answer prayer—for the very *sake* of answering our prayers. Jesus' First Coming (and all that goes with it) is the greatest proof of this, and, in fact, is a sort of proof that in a way the answer to every one of our prayers is "yes." But like Jesus Himself was the answer to countless prayers, in the end He was the answer on God's terms and not the terms of those who prayed. So God says "yes" to His faithful ones, He just says "yes" differently than we usually think. Sometimes the answer shocks us, sometimes exhilarates us, sometimes disappoints our preconceptions. But God answers.

I encourage you to read Romans 9-11. In these chapters, the Apostle Paul explains at length the standing of the people of Israel in relation to God after the coming of Jesus and the inauguration of the New Covenant. Great truths are explored, but running through the whole discussion is Paul's own disillusionment with how things have worked out for his people: how could it be that the Messiah has come, but the Chosen People missed the boat while the Gentiles get the deluxe cruise? Most of us simply do not have a reference point for the kind of disappointment someone like Paul felt over that disconnect.

Paul ends his Holy Spirit-inspired, brilliant treatise with these words:

Oh, the depth of the riches and wisdom and knowledge of God! How unsearchable are his judgments and how inscrutable his ways![34] "For who has known the mind of the Lord, or who has been his counselor?"[35] "Or who has given a gift to him that he might be repaid?"[36] For from him and through him and to him are all things. To him be glory forever. Amen. ¯ Romans 11:33–36

As we seek the Lord, let's not make the mistake of thinking we can ever understand Him to the point where he is not mysterious to us. Keep that mystery in perspective, even as you keep your faith.

Day 69

To continue with our reflections on "unanswered" prayer, I want to finish out the issue of what might be called a "masked yes." That is to say, a favorable response from God that doesn't look like it's favorable, at least not at the moment. [As an aside, before I continue, I would remark that reducing God's working in our life to a mere "yes or no answer," as if He is a politician responding to the testy questioning of a journalist; the wonders of a sovereign God can rarely be reduced to a mere "yes" or "no."]

I've already covered the matter of God saying "yes" in ways that we haven't expected or imagined. Today I'd like to touch upon a variant of that scenario, one in which our prayers actually conflict with each other.

Let's return to the "big picture" scenario I touched on yesterday...

Brothers, my heart's desire and prayer to God for them is that they may be saved.~ Romans 10:1

This, Paul's prayer in the midst of his monologue about the mystery of Israel's unbelief in Jesus, expresses not only his heart but (paradoxically in light of the story of Scripture) the very heart of God. God wants to redeem His people. Of course He does. Otherwise, why the Cross? God is not saying "no" to this prayer; He is not flat out denying Paul's intercession, for the rather obvious reason that Paul is doing nothing but praying God's Word and will.

The problem is that the very point of Romans 9-11 is that not only is Israel hardened to the gospel, but God has actually actively allowed that hardening for the time being so that the Gentiles might be saved. Since Israel's salvation is tied up with the end of time, and God isn't ready to end time yet, God has sort of "punted" on Israel until as many Gentiles as possible (a number known only to God) are saved. Then and only then will Israel be saved (in some expansive, collective sense that is still a mystery to us), and only then will the curtain fall and Jesus split the eastern sky.

So here's my point: Paul prayed for the Jewish nation to be saved. He prayed for Gentiles to be saved. And by the time he came to write Romans, some 20 years after he met Jesus on the Damascus Road, Paul had concluded that praying and getting the answer to the second of these meant the postponement of the answer to the first. I don't think it's an exaggeration to say it took 20 years for Paul to understand that—20 years, multiple heavenly visions, endless suffering in ministry, and he *still* struggled to work it out through three of the densest chapters he ever wrote for us.

Where does this put us? Where do we land when we pray for a job that looks perfect for us, but also pray that God uses us to minister in our local church? Well, God knows the job is going to eat our free time, frustrate our family life, compromise our ethics, and spin out of control in ways we cannot begin to see. He knows He cannot give us that job *and* give us the ministry—the worship, the giving of self that makes a life worth living, the souls won to Jesus—so He gives us the ministry and says "no" to the job.

Rinse, and repeat. He hears conflicting prayers uttered by the same lips, all day, every day. God knows it all. He is the prayer hearing, prayer answering God. He hears us pray, "Thy will be done." He loves us. So what is an all-knowing, all-wise, all-loving Heavenly Father to do with the precious prayers of His beloved children?

And He tells us to trust Him, and He answers in our best interest in a fallen world.

Day 70

After discussing the different ways God says "yes" to our requests—some of them not seeming to be "yes" at all, but in truth being manifestations of His goodness like everything else He does—we want to move on to the matter of *waiting*.

I've already talked about waiting on God and waiting for promises in a general sense. Now I'd like to address it in terms of our requests. That is, we have asked God for something, and the answer is not forthcoming in the timeframe we felt we needed; in the course of time we come to see this as *waiting* and not as "no." This isn't mere theory, because many Christians can testify that they prayed, heard nothing but crickets, but then, later than they expected or hoped, the answer came. And more often than not, even in our limited understanding of God's mysterious ways, we realize that the wait was not only worth it, but the delay was necessary and was actually part of God's answer.

Mortals waiting on God is a fundamental of our respective positions. As I've said, deep down we really want a God who can save, not a gumball machine that produces on demand. But in the moment, our attitude can be little better than that of a child who's dropped his nickel in and gets angry that the treat hasn't presented itself in our open palm. The injustice!

I am hardly making light of things. There have been plenty of times that I was praying a time-sensitive prayer, and I found myself in waiting mode. My state of mind and my very real circumstances were no joking matter.

The story from Acts 12:1-15 comes to mind. James the son of Zebedee had been martyred by Herod (Agrippa I), who then imprisoned Simon Peter. Peter's doom merely hours away, the church was praying fervently for him in the home of Mary, the mother of John Mark (the eventual author of the Gospel of Mark). We know the story: an angel came and delivered Peter in a salvation so supernatural even Peter thought he was having a dream. But it was no dream. When he came to Mary's home, they were still praying for his release. A servant girl answered the door to his knock, heard and recognized his voice, and reported what she heard, but they did not believe her. When she insisted, they concluded that what she heard was Peter's "angel"—a reference to a common belief at the time regarding a dead person's departed spirit. In other words, they thought Peter had already been killed as James had been; they thought their prayer was unanswered when, in fact, it had been answered beyond their dreams.

The truth is, the effectiveness of their prayers was lost on them due to the *waiting*—the delay in the answer, as brief as it was, was interpreted as failure because the state of their emotions was clouding their ability to discern. Sometimes that's just the way it is; we get so wound up we cannot think straight, we cannot handle the wait. But in this situation, God needed time to work things out. God is eternal, and transcends time, but He works within time to answer the prayers of time-bound human beings. At the end of the day, answered prayer comes down to logistics.

We must be prepared to wait. If waiting weren't a fundamental ingredient to answered prayer, why would Jesus encourage us to persist in prayer? Persistence *presumes* waiting. If we believe that God moves within time and space in answer to our prayers, we must be prepared to wait while He brings that answer to pass.

Waiting does not mean God is ignoring us.

Let us wait upon the Lord, patiently, while he brings to pass His plan.

Day 71

Yesterday we studied about the need to wait as God works things out in our situation in order for the favorable answer to come forth. Today we should talk about Him working things out in *us*.

The first thing that needs to be said here is that this is something of an academic exercise. Very rarely do we find ourselves in such a sterile situation that *either* God is working out logistics *or* He is working in us or others (the latter being something I will touch on tomorrow). Usually all of the above is happening at the same time. In fact, I'm not sure there is ever a time He is not working something out in us. God is very economical; He's always working for the "two-fer." His goal for us always has to do with us getting closer to Him, and us being forged into the image of His Son. Every situation we face will be bent to that ultimate goal.

That said, it is helpful to speak of this in a focused way. A simple passage comes to mind:

Before I was afflicted I went astray, but now I keep your word.
~ Psalm 119:67

As a missionary pastor, I wish badly I had some secret by which people could achieve character maturity without suffering. But I cannot. And I will not dangle a false, suffering-free gospel in front of would-be hearers to lure them in. We are the children of God, that is true, and God takes no delight in our pain. He delights to answer the "prayer of Jabez" ("Lord, free me from pain!" 1 Chronicles 4:10). But the other side of that truth is this:

*The Spirit himself bears witness with our spirit that we are children of God, [17] and if children, then heirs—heirs of God and fellow heirs with Christ, **provided we suffer with him in order that we may also be glorified with him**.* ~ Romans 8:16-17

No servant is above the Master. If Jesus suffered, we will suffer. If Jesus' prayers (apparently) went unanswered because God was working something in Him, it will happen to us as well. Read the Gethsemane passage beginning in Matthew 26:36. Jesus repeatedly prayed, and no answer was forthcoming; He had to persevere. The answer He got? A crowd with torches and clubs, approaching through the darkness, led by Judas Iscariot. And yet, in spite of appearances, God had answered His prayer. Hebrews 5:7-9 says this:

In the days of his flesh, **Jesus offered up prayers and supplications, with loud cries and tears,** *to him who was able to save him from death, and he was heard because of his reverence. Although he was a son,* **he learned obedience through what he suffered.** *⁹ And being made perfect, he became the source of eternal salvation to all who obey him...*

Think on that for a moment. The sinless Son of God "learned obedience" through suffering. He had never sinned—not even once. But God the Father had a work to do in His incarnate Son, a work to make Him "perfect" (meaning, bring to full maturity) so He could play the eternal role of high priest that lay in store for Him.

Now if God the Father made His spotless, sinless Son wait for an answer to prayer, put Him in a position to suffer and grieve and experience disappointment in the answer that eventually came, took Him at His word in the hardest way possible when He wept, "Thy will be done, Father, *Thy* will be done," where does that put *us?*

God is working things out in you. *You* are His big project, His most precious concern, as pressing as your need is right now (and I'm not saying it isn't). If you want to know if He will endure our frustrated accusations of faithlessness in favor of making us wait and working His will in us, the answer is an unequivocal *yes.*

Back to St. Augustine, he coined a phrase used through the centuries and up through C.S. Lewis: *"severe mercy."* The emphasis of the phrase is God's mercy, of course, not His severity, but the whole is a truth. Like the doe that wanders a few paces from her newborn fawn, denying it milk for a few moments so that its legs can grow strong for its own good, so God works His will with us. He *"leaves us to ourselves to test us and know all that is in our hearts"*(2 Chronicles 32:31). That's not a favorite bumper sticker Bible verse, right there, but it's the kind of verse we need to understand to reach maturity. God never leaves us or forsakes us, but the *feeling* of being left—"unanswered" prayer—tests us, reveals where we are in the Lord, puts us in a position to move the needle in the right direction.

Day 72

The last item I would like to cover under the subtheme of "waiting" as we discuss "unanswered" prayer is the question of God dealing with someone else. Logistics (God working things out in our circumstances) are inanimate realities of the natural world, and God working out things in us is something we have at least a modicum of control over, but *other people* is another question entirely. In this case, we are talking about a third party, made in God's image and (whether Christian or non-Christian) with a will of their own.

There are many reasons we might pray for someone else. We might be praying the "mother of all prayers"—that they might come to Christ and be saved. We might be praying that a brother in Christ get a new job, or that a sticky situation might work out in their finances. We might be praying for healing. But if it is true that God knows us better than we know ourselves, where does that put us in relation to someone else? Even if someone is being 100% transparent with us (something far more rare than is spoken), they might only *think* they are being transparent. In many respects we are flying blind when praying for another person. We are directed and indeed commanded to pray for each other, as we've seen. But more than ever, we need to realize the answers to prayer rest with God. And often—*very* often—the waiting has to do with God dealing with that other person's will.

When the early church prayed for Peter in Acts 12, they were indeed praying for a third party, but they were doing so in reference to a fairly clear-cut case of *external crisis*. Unless it were God's will that Peter be martyred (as it later was, but wasn't at the moment), the issue is straightforward, even if the means of deliverance were unclear. In this case the prayer was answered pretty much as miraculously as any prayer can be (an angelic visitation). Peter's will was not directly involved. But these situations are extremely rare.

On the other hand, if we are praying for someone's salvation (repentance and conversion to Christ), no matter how much we pray, God will not violate that person's will to answer our prayer. He can and will exert enormous pressure. He can bring situational forces to bear. He can respond to our prayer and fasting to clear away demonic forces that are blinding them. But in the end, God forces no one to repent and serve Him. That is not God's nature. As C.S. Lewis notes in *The Screwtape Letters*, God has limited Himself in such a way that he cannot "ravish"—that is to say, overwhelm us by a direct and unveiled revealing of His glory; His only option is to "woo" us into a relationship. Paul says this directly in reference to early Christians (very likely who came to Christ after they got married) praying for an unsaved spouse:

For how do you know, wife, whether you will save your husband? Or how do you know, husband, whether you will save your wife? ˉ
1 Corinthians 7:16

Simply put, Paul wouldn't be saying this if prayer worked like some sort of magic spell that "charmed" people into conversion. It doesn't. Paul is not questioning God's power, he is confirming the reality that God respects people's wills. God can deal with people's wills—He can "woo" them—but in the end He will not violate their decision.

I've heard remarkable stories of people coming to the Lord after decades of prayer by loving family members. Was God "not answering" those prayers for all those years? Of course He wasn't ignoring them. David says in Psalm 56:8 that God "stores our tears in a bottle." God remembers your prayers for your loved ones and cherishes them. He sees your sorrow, and He's working. And prayers for stubborn people do work, they do have effect. God has His ways of making things very, very clear. But it can take lots of time, depending on the person we are praying for. We mustn't accuse God of not caring—He sent Jesus to the Cross! We are being forced to wait because God Himself is being forced to wait.

In the middle can be other things. You may say, "But I'm praying for a Christian sister, and nothing I pray for ever works out, and everything keeps getting worse! God won't answer my prayers!"

You don't know the whole story, not by a long shot, whatever your friend is telling you. They could be acting in good faith and telling you all they know. But for all they know, they could be praying conflicting prayers (see my previous chapters), or God is exercising a "severe mercy" in their life. As you pray, "God! May Your will be done in her! Bless and guide her!" He might be saying, *I'm trying to do just that—let me!*

God is in heaven. We are on earth. Sometimes it's best for our words to be few. Pray, pray, pray, but know that we see through a glass darkly (1 Corinthians 13:12).

Day 73

Continuing with the subject of "unanswered" prayer, let's move to those times where there actually is a "no" of sorts, meaning, the answer is not forthcoming for a number of reasons. We'll touch on these successively, since learning that God isn't answering us favorably in spite of many promises to the contrary is a difficult issue.

The first reason for a "no" is that God's *unable* to answer us as we would wish. Naturally, this raises the immediate response, "Wait! Is God 'unable' to do anything? I thought He was all powerful!" Well, of course He's all powerful. But that very divine trait sets us up for a conflict. When I was in college a favorite dilemma people mooted was to ponder the impossible question, *"Can God create a rock too big for Himself to lift?"* This absurdity, posed by limited, mortal humans to an unlimited, immortal God illustrates just how we can paint ourselves in a corner when trying to grasp God's transcendent ways. We must understand that the only way God can even begin to deal with us (especially in our sinful state) is to *limit Himself*. God is self-limiting in respect to His own nature and self-limiting in respect to His commitments to us. To be God, God must remain true to Himself and true to His Word. If God were not self-limiting (itself an expression of His omnipotence) then all would be chaos, not to mention the fact that we'd all be toast because He would not be bound by His mercy.

It is part of God's goodness that He has bound Himself—limited Himself—in certain ways. But it also means that those self-limitations affect how He answers prayer. Over the next two days' reflections, I will touch on what I consider to the be the two "biggies" in this respect.

First, we have a situation in Daniel 10:12-14...

Then he said to me, "Fear not, Daniel, for from the first day that you set your heart to understand and humbled yourself before your God, your words have been heard, and I have come because of your words. [13] The prince of the kingdom of Persia withstood me twenty-one days, but Michael, one of the chief princes, came to help me, for I was left there with the kings of Persia, [14] and came to make you understand what is to happen to your people in the latter days."

For 21 days Daniel prayed with no response or breakthrough. He could very well have classified this as "unanswered" prayer. But when the answer came, he learned that God had responded immediately to his prayer. The delay was due to spiritual strongholds—the "Prince of Persia" (a demonic principality, see Ephesians 6) resisted God's deliverance, brought by angelic forces. The answer *couldn't* break through right away because of that warfare.

This is a tricky subject, and needs to be addressed carefully. All the devils in the world cannot compare to God's power—He can swat them like a fly. As C.S. Lewis notes, the devil is not the "opposite" of God; God has no opposite because His power is beyond compare. The closest thing to an "opposite" of the devil is the Archangel Michael. So how could a demon prince resist God's answer to Daniel's prayer?

The answer has to do with *authority,* and the very reason we pray at all. *The earth is the Lord's and the fullness thereof, the world and those who dwell therein.* (Psalm 24:1) But we also must consider that *The heavens are the LORD's heavens, but the earth he has given to the children of man.* (Psalm 115:16) Everything is God's; He's the owner. But He has *limited Himself* in respect to His own creation, His own earthly domain, by giving it to humanity when He created Adam and Eve. When humanity sinned, they compromised that authority in relation to the devil. Another illustration is that God rented us the house, but we (at least partially) signed the lease over to God's enemy. Until God comes back to take possession of His property (the Second Coming of Jesus) we have to deal with these realities.

Now, through submission to God we can still exercise the terms of the lease, the domain God gave us in the beginning. But if we want God to be involved—to overrule the mess we've made of things by inviting the devil in by sin—we have to *invite Him in*, just like a renter invites the owner of the house in to fix something. This invitation is called *prayer.*

Daniel's struggle was that of a submitted soul fighting against the demonic strongholds that were enthroning themselves on the sin of other people like spiritual parasites. God could have blown these demon princes away (just like Jesus could have called on His Father to send angels to rescue Him in Gethsemane, see Matthew 26:53) but that would have meant the *end of the world*—God revoking the lease of humanity on the world. So instead He worked through the prayers of the righteous—spiritual warfare.

Sometimes we are in a slugfest with the enemy. We battle not against flesh and blood. The delay has to do with God not just steamrolling creation. He will answer, but there's a battle to be waged. As a pastor, I can tell you many times where I was impatient for God to move, but He ultimately showed me that His patient, careful work—which seemed torturously slow to me at times—was about defeating the devil without nuking people in the process.

So persevere in prayer. Claim the authority of Jesus' name, rebuke the enemy by the Scriptures, bind the darkness and loose the light. By submission and word, invite the Lord by faith into all your doings. And the victory will come.

Invite the Lord into your life today.

Day 74

Let's go on with the next reason why God could be "unable" to answer our prayers. Yesterday I noted that through submitted prayer, we invite God into our situation; we yield the authority He had granted us by freewill, and He accepts that invitation. In short, just as God has self-limited in respect to His power so He can relate to us, we choose to self-limit, yield lordship over our lives so we can successfully relate to Him.

Thinking on this a moment, it doesn't take too long to figure a situation by which we pray but He is unable to answer: **we are in sin.**

If I had cherished iniquity in my heart, the Lord would not have listened. [19] But truly God has listened; he has attended to the voice of my prayer. ˉ Psalm 66:18-19

The wording of this passage is important. The psalmist is not saying God won't listen to sinners, period. If that were so, we'd all be done before we started. God listens to sinners, but they need to be *repentant* sinners. If we "cherish" sin—we continue in sin and refuse to give it up—that is active rebellion, and that lack of submission is going to *tie God's hands.* God *wants* to bless everyone, He *wants* all to be saved. So why aren't they? Because they refuse to repent. Being "in sin" is not a reference to the fact that we have all sinned, and that we all continue to make mistakes daily. Neither is it a reference to someone struggling with a character trait weakness that they are trying to conquer as they grow spiritually. It means someone is deliberately engaging in sinful behavior, they are not making an effort to turn from it, and that spiritual blight on their life is bigger than their devotion to Christ.

James tells us this:

You do not have, because you do not ask. [3] *You ask and do not receive, because you ask wrongly, to spend it on your passions.* ¯ James 4:2b–3

In other words, asking with wrong motives—asking from a rebellious, unsubmitted, sinful posture before God—*is the same as not asking at all.* We must invite God into our lives, but we must do so from a position of submission.

Consider also this famous passage:

He also told this parable to some who trusted in themselves that they were righteous, and treated others with contempt: [10] *"Two men went up into the temple to pray, one a Pharisee and the other a tax collector.* [11] *The Pharisee, standing by himself, prayed thus: 'God, I thank you that I am not like other men, extortioners, unjust, adulterers, or even like this tax collector.* [12] *I fast twice a week; I give tithes of all that I get.'* [13] *But the tax collector, standing far off, would not even lift up his eyes to heaven, but beat his breast, saying, 'God, be merciful to me, a sinner!'* [14] *I tell you, this man went down to his house justified, rather than the other.* ¯ Luke 18:9–14

The Pharisee was a "holy man"; the tax collector was a "sinner." Yet God answered the prayer of the tax collector, and rejected the prayer of the Pharisee. Why? NOT because the tax collector was "marginalized" and the Pharisee was "an insider." God has little use for modern political jargon and categories. No, God accepted the one and rejected the other for the very reason He also accepts or rejects any prayer: submission and contrition. If a Pharisee were submitted, and a tax collector rebellious (and you can bet there have been such cases), then the result would have been reversed. Jesus told this parable this way because He wanted to make a point: God judges on the merits, and according to the heart, even if that surprises us humans who tend to judge on appearances.

I encourage you not to beat yourself up over old sins. There is no condemnation for those who are in Christ. God doesn't hold grudges. If you have repented, and pray with a submitted, contrite spirit, the danger implied by Psalm 66:18 doesn't apply to you. But we should take caution: Jesus didn't tell the parable of the Pharisee and the tax collector for nothing. We need to search our hearts, repent of known sin, ask God to reveal any offensive way in us, and lead us in the way everlasting (Psalm 19:12-14, Psalm 139:23-24).

Let's remember that God is quick to hear the voice of the contrite heart. In Psalm 66, verse 19 follows quickly on the heels of verse 18.

Day 75

As of this writing, I recently returned from a couple of weeks in the Holy Land and Greece, retracing the steps of the biblical story, both Old Testament and New.

This was my second trip to Israel (9 years previous) and Greece (almost 2 years previous), but the spiritual encounter of it all was no less overwhelming. In some ways the trip took me to a new place, since the "newness" of some of the sites—the natural "wow" factor—had given way to the matter of those places' deeper significance. Jericho where Joshua parted the Jordan, the spring of Harod where Gideon tested and chose his 300 men, the hills of Bethlehem where David shepherded his flock, Mount Carmel where Elijah won his showdown against the prophets of Baal—these are exciting places to stand. The more sobering places, such as Mount Gilboa where King Saul and Jonathan fell, the high place at Dan where Jeroboam set up his abominable golden calf, or Megiddo where pure-hearted King Josiah was killed, well, these are no less impactful, though obviously in a different way.

But the queen of them all is, and must remain, Jerusalem. It is remarkable to be in that city just for the 3,000+ years that she boasts. But it is truly overwhelming to stand in a place—and specific places within that place—where, within a radius of mere yards, layer after layer of sacred history surrounds you. To stand in the Kidron Valley within mere footsteps of where David's men found the way into the Jebusites' fortress, and where Solomon was anointed king, and Isaiah delivered his stinging rebuke to Sennacherib's lackies, and Jeremiah shattered his jar, and Nebuchadnezzar's troops set fire to the city, and Nehemiah rode his horse, and where the Lord's prophecies were tragically fulfilled by the marauding Romans, and...well, it's all very overwhelming and next to impossible to process.

But if Jerusalem is the queen, Jesus is her One True King. There is a very good reason why places like the Pool of Siloam (where the blind man washed his eyes and was healed), the Church of Dominus Flevit (marking where Jesus wept over the Holy City), the Via Dolorosa, and the Garden Tomb are so visited and lingered in, even to the forgetting of many other profound events before and since that would be sufficient to mark any other place on earth as incomparable all by itself. Why? Because, for Christians, Jesus is the One who fulfills, completes, and gives meaning to all those other events. The event of David weeping, fleeing barefoot across the Kidron Valley from his son Absalom, then climbing the Mount of Olives with head covered takes on a whole new dimension when we stand in the very same spot, but now focused rather on how Jesus, Son of David, sweated blood in His own personal valley of the shadow of death called Gethsemane.

I have stood on Civil War battlefields, wondering what the men who fought there felt, what noble and base thoughts went through their heads, what they pondered about the meaning of their lives, the missed opportunities with their families, the hopes and jealousies, the mistakes and misunderstandings never resolved, or the victories and successes untold. Then my thoughts go to all such people all over the world, in peace or war, whether in modern history or ancient, men or women or children, and all the angst of human history summed up. What does it all amount to? The crushing reality communicated by the Book of Ecclesiastes is that, without God, the whole of it is chaff in the wind, no matter how passionately it is felt or told or fought for.

It is Jesus that brings meaning. It is Jesus who redeems. It is in Jesus that every promise is "yes" and "amen." He is the one who forgives our faults and sins, who makes sense of our puzzles, whether by answering them or by overwhelming them with a love that renders them irrelevant. So many seek from Jesus a blessing, and I do understand it. There were many such people in His own day. But the ones whom He called disciples and friends and who went on to mark other sites and make them holy by their deeds and deaths, these people consider *Jesus Himself* to be the blessing.

I know we have constant needs and concerns, all of us. But I also know that if we press into Jesus for Jesus Himself, we will not be disappointed. Let's do that, consecrating our hearts, our desires, even our griefs to Him. Let's love the Lord with all our heart and soul and mind and strength. And then let's see what He does with us.

Day 76

There is a corollary truth that goes hand-in-glove with the matter of miracles that I believe is essential for truly powerful living.

In Luke 10 we read the story of Jesus sending out the seventy-two (vv. 1-12). Later in the chapter we read about the results of their mission:

The seventy-two returned with joy, saying, "Lord, even the demons are subject to us in your name!"[18] And he said to them, "I saw Satan fall like lightning from heaven.[19] Behold, I have given you authority to tread on serpents and scorpions, and over all the power of the enemy, and nothing shall hurt you.[20] Nevertheless, do not rejoice in this, that the spirits are subject to you, but rejoice that your names are written in heaven." Luke 10:17-20

Here Jesus acknowledges the effectiveness of their work when they elatedly inform Him of their success. But in verse 20 He tenders an important qualifier: *Do not rejoice in the effectiveness of your ministry, but rather that your names are written in heaven.*

Now, most today would consider it a capstone experience to have healed someone in Jesus' name or cast out a demon. Verse 19 is still a powerful faith builder when engaging in spiritual warfare, and I have quoted it many times in prayer. But all that is Jesus laying the foundation to be able to grant these disciples an even greater gift— lasting joy.

If our joy is based in the results we get in Jesus' name, inevitably we put ourselves in a precarious position. Joy, says Nehemiah 8:10, is *strength*. Strength is needed to carry out ministry. But if we draw our joy from how our ministry is going for us at any given time, we upend God's economy—we turn what should be the *object* of our joy into its *source*.

Jesus has your name written in heaven. That is a settled issue for you no matter how you are doing, how well you think things are progressing for you in respect to what the Lord has put under your care. Your source of joy is outside of yourself, outside of anything you do; it's fountainhead is God's grace. Because of this, that joy is continuous, rain or shine, whether you get a quick victory or the battle drags on for you.

Rejoice in the Lord. Let me say that again: rejoice (Hhmmm...that sounds familiar). You belong to the Lord, and no one can snatch you from His hand. Snuggle in close to Him, enjoy Him and let Him enjoy you. That's why He created you! Feel that strength flow into you? Ah, *now* you can go and do what He's called you to do, and do it fearlessly, knowing that whatever that looks like during the battle or afterward, your joy is yours and depends not on how it all pans out, but on Him, and Him alone.

Day 77

There's a very simple but very profound not-so-secret secret that every Christian should know. It was known to the Lord Jesus and He made it known to us by His words and His actions. And we are taught to follow that lead. It has to do with the posture of our heart and our motives, which in turn affect our choices and our manner of carrying them out.

I am speaking of *pleasing God,* or rather, the *desire* to please God.

Jesus says this about the underlying motive, the inner "motor" for His ministry:

And he who sent me is with me. He has not left me alone, for I always do the things that are pleasing to him.¯ John 8:29

Clearly, Jesus is speaking of God the Father being "with Him" in a way that extends beyond mere omnipresence. Since God is everywhere, He is always "with" everyone, believer or not, obedient or not, pleasing or displeasing. No, but Jesus is speaking of the Father being with Him in the sense of *manifest favor.* The reason for this blessed presence is simple, even for Jesus: He does those things that *please* His Father.

For us, it could be tempting to interpret this as salvation by works. But it would be a mistake to see it that way. A passage like this doesn't call for such over-interpretation. Jesus is making a very straightforward observation. God favors those who live to please Him. We need to let that fundamental reality become a part of us, and not overwork the matter in our minds and hearts. To pray and determine within ourselves that we want to please God, and that everything from our devotional life to our business dealings to our family relationships should be moved by this sincere desire, can be very helpful amid all the complications that can arise in our lives. Living to please God is humbly inviting His favor into our lives.

Some might ask, "What's the difference between living to please God and living to do His will? Haven't we already addressed this through the prayer 'Thy will be done'?" In the end, that is of course true. But the very phrase "the will of God" can conjure a host of complications for us. At times I have struggled with the will of God as something mysterious and hidden, a long-term project, something that God needs to work in me as much as something He desires for me to do. But I have found great peace in telling God and telling myself, "Whatever the clouds surrounding His will, this I can say right now: *I sincerely desire to please the Lord.* I want to bless Him and I want Him to see me as poor in spirit, simplehearted, and submitted, even if I sometimes feel rather dense about the way forward."

C.S. Lewis observes that the desire to please God does, in fact, please God. So that's a start. The person who trains their inner person to desire God's pleasure over their own becomes increasingly attuned to God's will and receives the grace to do it; the person who loftily speaks of God's will but hasn't disciplined their inner man to desire God's pleasure with them as the highest good becomes easily entangled by little things, and misses the forest for the trees.

Consider this passage as you pray:

Beloved, if our heart does not condemn us, we have confidence before God; [22] *and* **whatever we ask we receive from him,** *because we keep his commandments and do what pleases him.* [1] John 3:21–22

Here John tells us what he relayed in another form through Jesus' own testimony. The clear conscience that can stand before God, the person who authentically pursues obedience, this is the person who pleases God and gets their prayers answered. It isn't magic, it's a relationship. Let's press in to please the Father.

Day 78

I would like to write today about the matter of *spiritual intensity*. I've touched on it before, at the outset of our journey, but think it is a good idea to come back now—after a sometimes weary road when intensity was more than we could muster and it was all we could do sometimes to keep at it. These discussions are the stuff of spiritual maturity.

Our emotions can certainly play an important role in the working of our spiritual fervor. That is part of loving the Lord our God with all we are. But even at their best emotions can be fickle. And if we allow them to be the driver of our spirituality we will find ourselves riding a constant rollercoaster, often based upon things like the weather, how well we slept last night, the moods of the people around us, and whether that meal we just ate is setting well on our stomach, among other things.

So how do we cultivate spiritual intensity if not through our emotions? A couple of passages are dear to my heart, and I believe speak to this issue. The first is Jeremiah...

For thus says the LORD to the men of Judah and Jerusalem: "Break up your fallow ground, and sow not among thorns.
                                                              ‾ Jeremiah 4:3

Hosea somewhat echoes the same thought...

Sow for yourselves righteousness; reap steadfast love; break up your fallow ground, for it is the time to seek the LORD, that he may come and rain righteousness upon you. ‾ Hosea 10:12

Both of these prophets use the same metaphor: *plow up the fallow ground in your life*. In other words, areas that are potentially fruit bearing, but currently uncultivated, should be surrendered to God. But plowed ground must be sown with seed. So together the prophets give us further counsel: do not sow among thorns (i.e., repent of displeasing things); make sure you sow unto righteousness (i.e., use those fallow areas for God's service).

My sense is that by asking God to speak to us, asking for guidance on fallow areas, these things will present themselves to us with remarkable speed and clarity. Time frittered away, frivolous interests, vain pursuits, entanglements if not outright sins, worldly appetites that dull our edge and cool our passion for Christ...all these things are fallow ground, and all will show themselves for what they are when we ask the Holy Spirit to reveal them.

Now, once we begin to plow that ground, that means that much more of us is surrendered to God and begins to bear fruit unto Him. As Jesus noted, the crops grows and flourishes "of itself" (Mark 4:28). There's no straining, there's no fussing. Surrender to God leads to an increase of spiritual flow and intensity that is authentic rather than drummed up or manufactured by our emotions. What we seek is not mere enthusiasm; what we seek is *revival*. And while we seek God for that, it is something that only God can do.

Day 79

Therefore, since we are surrounded by so great a cloud of witnesses, let us also lay aside every weight, and sin which clings so closely, and let us run with endurance the race that is set before us, ² looking to Jesus, the founder and perfecter of our faith, who for the joy that was set before him endured the cross, despising the shame, and is seated at the right hand of the throne of God.˘
Hebrews 12:1-2

This passage from Hebrews is one of the most preached on in the New Testament, and for very good reasons. Having just rattled off the "Hall of Fame of Faith" in chapter 11, the author of Hebrews invokes those witnesses as if they were cheering fans in the stands, urging us on towards our goal. And what is our goal?

Our goal is Jesus. Only keeping Jesus as our goal—or reminding ourselves that he is our goal—will give us the strength to finish the race, will suffice as a motive to shed the sins and weights that hinder our forward progress. Only Jesus' example is pure enough for us and by His Holy Spirit imparts the much-needed strength that sustains us.

Almost all faiths feature and encourage spiritual disciplines. And obviously I am a huge proponent of them, else we wouldn't be on this journey together. But disciplines aren't enough. Disciplines like prayer and Scripture study can weary us if we lose our focus on Jesus. They become an end in themselves, lead to perfectionism and despondency, and in worst case scenarios, can become idols in themselves—sources of spiritual pride, despondency, and fruitlessness.

What? Am I discouraging prayer and time in the Word? Absolutely not. I am simply reaffirming our focus on the Lord Jesus. We are Christians; we serve *Jesus*, not abstract truths, not a denomination, and not an impossible standard to live by. It is Jesus who is the founder of our faith—He who birthed us by His Holy Spirit into new life, He who is our hope of perfection, it is

He who faced down the agony and shame of the cross for the joy that awaited him (and us).

As we finish this race strong, let us shake off the weariness that can sometimes take hold of those who have stretched their spiritual muscles and maybe gotten a bit stiff in the process. Let's remind ourselves why and *for Whom* we are doing all this. It isn't (ultimately) for our families or ourselves. We are pressing on toward the goal for the prize of the upward call of God *in Christ Jesus* (Philippians 3:14). Losing sight of the goal brings on spiritual atrophy; having the right goal in mind and heart gives us a second wind.

I'm doing this whole thing for Jesus. Human praise is vain and empty, but to hear, "Well done, good and faithful servant" from Jesus is what we live for. Let's refocus on Him, think of His reward and joy, and press towards the finish line.

Day 80

Continuing briefly in the theme of our pilgrimage in the Lord as an athletic competition, consider this passage from 1 Corinthians:

Do you not know that in a race all the runners run, but only one receives the prize? So run that you may obtain it. [25] Every athlete exercises self-control in all things. They do it to receive a perishable wreath, but we an imperishable. [26] So I do not run aimlessly; I do not box as one beating the air. [27] But I discipline my body and keep it under control, lest after preaching to others I myself should be disqualified. [24] 1 Corinthians 9:24-27

Paul was appealing to the Corinthians' immediate context. In ancient Greece, the most famous athletic competition was of course the Olympic Games, held every two years (in those days) in honor of Zeus. But in the off years, the second-most prestigious competition was held near Corinth in honor of the god Poseidon, and were known as the *Isthmian Games* (after the Isthmus of Corinth, the land bridge connecting upper and lower Greece).

Like all competitions of that day, the games included running, boxing, other martial exercises like the javelin throw and discus, chariot races, and even poetry reading and oratory. The winner would be crowned with a wreath. Many know that the wreath given at the Olympic Games was the bay laurel, but at Corinth the crown was made of soft long-needle pine. Pine trees were sacred to Poseidon and grow abundantly around Corinth, even today.

The message Paul is sending becomes all the more powerful when we consider how the Corinthians would have understood this. The pine, of course, is an evergreen. Of all the crowns one could win in those days, a *pine crown* would last the longest—lasting many days whereas the laurel would fade in a day or two. But Paul is using this very fact to drive his point home: **even the most enduring glories and rewards of this world fade quickly.** Only the glory of God is worth the trouble, and only the eternal life He offers justifies the discipline we invest in the journey.

We run for Jesus, eyes on the prize. He is the goal. And what is the alternative? The vain pursuits the world offers today are no better than Zeus or Poseidon, fickle, lustful idols who must be appeased, who change with the wind, and who fill their followers with dread rather than hope. The gods of this age are cruel and demanding, and require no less than the God of Israel, except they grant no mercy and do not keep faith. No thanks.

Let's press on. Jesus is worth it. He's the only thing in this world that is.

Day 81

I'd like to mention what I consider one of the most powerful forms of poetry in the Bible: *the lament.*

A lament is a cry for help, a spiritual complaint to God about our situation, but from a sincere heart rather than a grumbling one. The psalms are full of laments (Psalms 22 and 88 immediately come to mind, although there are many others), but we also find them sprinkled throughout the prophets, and an entire book of the Bible, written by Jeremiah, is titled "Lamentations."

The laments are a bit of a paradox for us today, because they cut across the grain of what most people consider faith talk, or edifying speech, even by the Bible's own standards. How can "lamenting" our circumstances do us any good? But that perspective is seriously flawed, because the Bible's laments are anointed of the Holy Spirit. Their writers expressed themselves *in the pleasure of God, even in their complaints.* The result is a work that has a powerful comforting effect. After all, if David, or Jeremiah, or Habakkuk felt this way, and it's in God's Word, it means that God understands me, too.

Some of the most powerful encounters I've had with Scripture have been through the laments. When I'm on top of the world, it's easy to read a psalm of praise. But when I am crushed in spirit, a different kind of reading is in order. Knowing that God inspired those laments touches me deeply because as my spirit responds to them I know that God hears and sees me, too. Knowing that God sees us in our troubles and knows us in the midst of our situation is often the only thing we need to make it through.

Remember my affliction and my wanderings, the wormwood and the gall! [20] *My soul continually remembers it and is bowed down within me.* [21] *But this I call to mind, and therefore I have hope:* [22] *The steadfast love of the LORD never ceases; his mercies never come to an end;* [23] *they are new every morning; great is your faithfulness.* [24] *"The LORD is my portion," says my soul, "therefore*

I will hope in him." [25] *The LORD is good to those who wait for him, to the soul who seeks him.* [26] *It is good that one should wait quietly for the salvation of the LORD.* [27] *It is good for a man that he bear the yoke in his youth.* [28] *Let him sit alone in silence when it is laid on him;* [29] *let him put his mouth in the dust— there may yet be hope;* [30] *let him give his cheek to the one who strikes, and let him be filled with insults.* [31] *For the Lord will not cast off forever,* [32] *but, though he cause grief, he will have compassion according to the abundance of his steadfast love;* [33] *for he does not afflict from his heart or grieve the children of men.* ¯ Lamentations 3:19-33

May God comfort you today.

Day 82

And they were on the road, going up to Jerusalem, and Jesus was walking ahead of them. And they were amazed, and those who followed were afraid. And taking the twelve again, he began to tell them what was to happen to him, [33] saying, "See, we are going up to Jerusalem, and the Son of Man will be delivered over to the chief priests and the scribes, and they will condemn him to death and deliver him over to the Gentiles. [34] And they will mock him and spit on him, and flog him and kill him. And after three days he will rise." – Mark 10:32-34

Today, I'd like to shift focus and begin to look at the passages of the Gospels that directly address the events that unfolded leading up to Jesus' suffering and resurrection. Something we need to understand about the Gospels is that from the earliest days, people understood from the witness of the Apostles that many of the events the Gospels record were not presented in chronological order. When Mark (or Matthew or Luke, who largely follow Mark) says "then" at the outset of a particular episode, early readers took that to mean, "and then there was the time that..." Most scholars today understand that the arrangement of these stories is meant to build our faith in Christ by presenting themes and truths one after the other and were never intended to present a complete and chronologically precise history.

For the most part, that shifts in Mark chapter 11 (and parallels in Matthew and Luke), because it is at that point that the chain of events begins to unfold that leads to the culmination of the book. We see that in the passage I wrote above. Here we read that Jesus, even after repeated threats from His enemies, begins to head resolutely to Jerusalem. Those around Him react variously, their emotions ranging from *fear* to *amazement*. To punctuate it, and remove all doubt from the minds of any who might think this was all overreaction, Jesus takes the Twelve aside and lays it out for them: He predicts—now for the third time (see Mark 8:31ff, 9:30ff)—that He will be taken by the chief priests, handed over to the Gentiles, cruelly mocked and killed, but then rise on the third day.

The disciples don't get it, and I think we still don't get it, we who are children of the resurrection.

There are many layers of truth here, as Christ's passion is unfathomable. But I see one right on the surface here. Wherever we land emotionally in respect to Jesus' iron will to give Himself for our sake, that emotional reaction falls short of the glory of God revealed in Him. "Perception is reality" is a commonly used phrase in our age of social media, Yelp ratings, and online reviews. Everyone has an opinion, and in our consumer-driven society (even for churches!), the favor of the buyer is constantly curried. Perception can indeed become reality for the business owner—if everyone that bothers to post a review says that his roast beef sandwiches are awful (even though they are really delicious), then his business can really suffer for it. The problem with all of this (aside from the distress of a very good roast beef sandwich vendor) is that it goes to our heads: we really believe that perception is reality.

But the phrase is just a figure of speech to make a point about dealing with a crowd. Perception really isn't actually reality, it's just perception. And given our fallenness and God's transcendence, that perception is inevitably flawed—either far short of the mark, or downright skewed. Jesus' redemptive works, every word He speaks and every decision He makes in the final hours of His earthly ministry, are above our likes and dislikes, are above our feelings, are beyond our comprehension. We see but slowly, we grasp bit by bit. Our fear is not fearful enough; our amazement falls far short of the awe that God has coming to Him. In truth, there is no emotion within the range available to us that is capable of responding properly to what Jesus has done for us. How we feel does not somehow define Jesus' death and resurrection. The Christian life is a journey of conforming our lives to that which is presently beyond us, *not* settling for a powerless form of religion that we have created after our own thoughts, senses, and image.

So how do we move forward? The Scriptures are not written to discourage us or to paralyze us. They are written to take our breath away, to fill us with awe and bring us to our knees. May I suggest worship? Yes, let's focus on worship as we draw near to the cross. Jesus is enthroned on our praises, and in the light that comes with a submitted, worship heart, we can begin to see Jesus (again to quote C.S. Lewis), *not as we have imagined Him, but as He knows Himself to be.*

Day 83

I'd like to bring something out that we find in John chapter 14. It begins with the famous verse often quoted regarding "mansions" in heaven:

*In my Father's house are many **mansions**: if it were not so, I would have told you. I go to prepare a place for you.*
~ John 14:2 (KJV)

Of course, nearly any modern English Bible will render the word the King James translates as "mansions" very differently...

*In my Father's house are many **rooms**. If it were not so, would I have told you that I go to prepare a place for you?* ~ John 14:2

The Greek word in question is *monē*, which is best understood as a "abiding place," "dwelling," or "habitation." In this context it implies a cozy and secure home within the Father's heavenly house. It turns out that in 1611 when the King James Version was first published, "mansion" was a legitimate rendering for this concept, but over the course of centuries "mansion" came to mean a grandiose and opulent dwelling. In other words, the *English language shifted* in respect to the semantic meaning of the word "mansion," but, the *King James remained the same*, as did (of course) the underlying Greek concept in the word *monē*. So folks unwittingly began to think in terms of a "mansion" in heaven—*a big material reward*—rather than what Jesus clearly means here, which is *an eternal relationship*.

The incredible thing that both confirms and develops this is that *monē* only occurs one other time in the entire New Testament—twenty-one verses later in John 14:23...

*Jesus answered him, "If anyone loves me, he will keep my word, and my Father will love him, and we will come to him and make our **home**[monē] with him." * ~ John 14:23

These two occurrences of the word *monē* within the same discourse are obviously connected and are meant to be understood in relation to each other. Simply put, the heavenly promise of John 14:2 is contingent upon how we live out our earthly life in respect to John 14:23. If we live in such a way as to make our life a cozy home, an abiding place, a "mansion" for the Father and the Lord Jesus, then they will come and take up residence with us. We do this by loving God and keeping His word. Living this way prepares the way for a heavenly dwelling to await us in the hereafter.

I say these are the only times this noun occurs in the New Testament, and that is true. But related words abound. For instance, from the opening verses of the next chapter...

"I am the true vine, and my Father is the vinedresser. [2] *Every branch in me that does not bear fruit he takes away, and every branch that does bear fruit he prunes, that it may bear more fruit.* [3] *Already you are clean because of the word that I have spoken to you.* [4] ***Abide***[meno] *in me, and I in you. As the branch cannot bear fruit by itself, unless it* ***abides***[meno] *in the vine, neither can you, unless you* ***abide***[meno] *in me."* ~ John 15:1-4

Here we find another angle on the same truth: If *monē* means "abiding place," the verb *meno* means "to abide." If we spend our lives abiding in Christ, He will also be with us through our lives by abiding in us.

Let's abide in the Lord. Let's press in, and determine that abiding will be a way of life for us and not just something we will do for a season and then let go. Let us conform our lives the Jesus' words. Let us be Christians.

Day 84

Perhaps it is a bit gratuitous at this point to say what I am about to say, but the more I think on it the more necessary I think it is. It has to do with *daily prayer and Scripture reading*; this includes the practice that the wisdom literature in the Bible calls "meditating" on the Word—that kind of prayerful thoughtfulness in passages of Scripture that the Holy Spirit quickens to us.

What I mean to say is that I do not believe there is any way to be a Christian in any meaningful and effective sense without these disciplines in our lives. As I've said, discipline as an end in itself becomes dead religion and even idolatry; discipline as a helpful, divine gift applied to empower our drawing closer to God in Christ Jesus by the power of the Holy Spirit is life and peace. To spurn the stark and repeated commands and counsel of Scripture to pray and stay in God's Word continually is to walk away from the very means of appropriation God has given us. Promises are ours in abundance, but we *must* position ourselves to receive their fulfillment.

When I first came to the Lord, I made lots of mistakes. But of all the teachings I fumbled, one of them took: you must have a "quiet time"; you must set a space aside in your schedule for daily prayer and Scripture reading. I was choppy at this when I was in high school, but the fire and solitude of college brought me to my knees, and it became unthinkable to me to miss my daily time with Jesus. When I began, this time was perhaps 15-20 minutes. But it grew so that by the time I graduated and went into ministry, I was spending several hours a day with God. This discipline changed my life.

As I stepped into the larger world of ministry, I was surprised and even shocked to learn that many Christians just didn't see things that way. Church once or twice a week was not only enough, it was a badge of honor to them. But I also noticed that such folk seemed to go from crisis to crisis, and leaned heavily upon the faith of others to get through hard times. They were "thermometer"

Christians rather than "thermostat" Christians; they were low-fruit followers rather than fruitful leaders.

I find it especially ironic and even tragic that now, decades later, even fewer people consider it fundamental for the Christian walk—for all Christians, not just "ministers"—to pray and read large chunks of Scripture on a regular basis. Today's culture is darker, the spiritual perils more frightening, the threat to our families greater than ever. Yet we are consumed by entertainment and social media, yet we are too busy to pray at length and experience the deep, dredging cleansing that we desperately need. We are confused, but we don't read more than but a few verses at a time, and so our faith remains tepid and feeble in the face of increasingly strong challenges from the enemy.

The devil is not letting up. But then again, neither is Jesus. Where sin abounds, grace abounds all the more. It is ours to be had. But we must avail ourselves of it.

This passage from Hosea has been such a blessing to me, a promise,

"Come, let us return to the LORD; for he has torn us, that he may heal us; he has struck us down, and he will bind us up. ² After two days he will revive us; on the third day he will raise us up, that we may live before him. ³ Let us know; let us press on to know the LORD; his going out is sure as the dawn; he will come to us as the showers, as the spring rains that water the earth."

~ Hosea 6:1-3

Much blessing awaits us, but we must press in to take hold of it. I encourage you to begin to prepare yourself with hard questions about what your life will look like after the unbroken prayer challenge ends.

Day 85

We return to Jesus' approach to Jerusalem, just before Passion Week...

And they came to Jericho. And as he was leaving Jericho with his disciples and a great crowd, Bartimaeus, a blind beggar, the son of Timaeus, was sitting by the roadside. ⁴⁷ And when he heard that it was Jesus of Nazareth, he began to cry out and say, "Jesus, Son of David, have mercy on me!"⁴⁸ And many rebuked him, telling him to be silent. But he cried out all the more, "Son of David, have mercy on me!"⁴⁹ And Jesus stopped and said, "Call him." And they called the blind man, saying to him, "Take heart. Get up; he is calling you."⁵⁰ And throwing off his cloak, he sprang up and came to Jesus. ⁵¹ And Jesus said to him, "What do you want me to do for you?" And the blind man said to him, "Rabbi, let me recover my sight."⁵² And Jesus said to him, "Go your way; your faith has made you well." And immediately he recovered his sight and followed him on the way. ¯ Mark 10:46-52

This is a beautiful, well-known story. It is one of three stories (not counting parallel accounts) in which Jesus heals a blind person—each time a man. The first is the healing of the man at Bethsaida in Galilee, when He spits on the man's eyes (Mark 8:22-26), the second is the healing of the man born blind, where He makes mud and sends the man to the Pool of Siloam to wash (John 9), and then there is this one, the healing of Blind Bartimaeus outside of Jericho and on His way to Jerusalem to suffer for us.

Many in Jesus' day considered it the definitive sign of the Messiah that He should heal the blind (based upon the Greek translation of Isaiah 61). If you look at each of these stories, it is pretty clear that the Gospel writers concur: the story in Mark 8 is followed by Jesus asking "Who do men say that I am?" and Peter's famous response that Jesus is the Christ; the story of John 9 is shot through with messianic implications and is followed (and topped) by Jesus raising Lazarus from the dead. The same is true here: this healing of Bartimaeus is a drum roll and cymbal crash ahead of all that happens in Jerusalem in the following days, cementing Jesus as Messiah for all time.

But what I want to point out here is the faith of the blind man himself. He was not merely asking for a healing, like so many others. *By asking* he was confessing that he believed Jesus was the Messiah. He was asking what would have been impossible for anyone *but* the Messiah to do. It was a startling confession of faith. To confirm this powerful truth, he calls Jesus "Son of David"—the Messiah's title by right.

Well, you might say, talk is cheap. He was taking a chance. What did he have to lose? He was already blind and couldn't end up any worse if Jesus failed him. Ah, but that's where we'd miss it. Look at verse 50: "*And throwing off his cloak, he sprang up and came to Jesus.*"

There is little doubt that the man's cloak was his choicest and most important possession. A cloak not only served as warmth from the cold and shelter from the wind and the heat, it was essentially a poor man's bed. The Law of Moses (Exodus 22:26-27) had strict rules about taking a poor man's cloak from him, and there are writings found in ancient Israel proving this very thing (i.e., a poor man appealing to a magistrate because a powerful man had taken his cloak in pledge and had not returned it).

The question is this: when a poor, blind man flings away his cloak and leaves it behind, how does he expect to recover it unless he fully expects to be able to turn around and *see it?* Bartimaeus not only believed Jesus was the Messiah and therefore *could* heal him, he believed He *would* heal him. And he demonstrated that faith by his actions. He had no Plan B, no safety net.

We are to walk in faith. We want to see the results only faith can bring. But very often we build so many safety nets into our actions that by the time we get through there's little need for faith. The irony is, such an approach is actually a form of *spiritual blindness*—it is failing to see Jesus for who is actually is.

Let's believe God for great things. Let's toss our cloaks aside, cry out to the Son of David, and wait for Him to call our names.

Day 86

After the healing of Blind Bartimaeus, Jesus continued into Jericho. And there is where His famous encounter with Zacchaeus occurred...

He entered Jericho and was passing through. ² And behold, there was a man named Zacchaeus. He was a chief tax collector and was rich. ³ And he was seeking to see who Jesus was, but on account of the crowd he could not, because he was small in stature. ⁴ So he ran on ahead and climbed up into a sycamore tree to see him, for he was about to pass that way. ⁵ And when Jesus came to the place, he looked up and said to him, "Zacchaeus, hurry and come down, for I must stay at your house today."⁶ So he hurried and came down and received him joyfully. ⁷ And when they saw it, they all grumbled, "He has gone in to be the guest of a man who is a sinner."⁸ And Zacchaeus stood and said to the Lord, "Behold, Lord, the half of my goods I give to the poor. And if I have defrauded anyone of anything, I restore it fourfold."⁹ And Jesus said to him, "Today salvation has come to this house, since he also is a son of Abraham. ¹⁰ For the Son of Man came to seek and to save the lost."⁻ Luke 19:1-10

This is a very colorful story for a number of reasons, comical, really. A short, wealthy man with a bad reputation climbs a tree to see a penniless but celebrated holy man, then wins an evening with the guy.

One thing that strikes me is something I know about a theme that runs through Luke—his emphasis on the socially marginalized of his day. These include women, children, the poor, and the ceremonially unclean like lepers and foreigners. But just before Jesus suffers, we have this inclusion of a rich tax collector who doesn't seem to fit any of those categories. What makes him fit is that he is despised and marginalized in another way; he is seen as beyond redemption. Zacchaeus helps us understand that God is not a social activist, He is a *redeemer.*

It is important to follow the sequence of the story, else we will misinterpret the last three verses. In those verses we see Zacchaeus declaring his penance—financial reparations for those he has harmed and alms for the poor; this declaration is followed by Jesus' pronouncement of salvation. Do Zacchaeus' "good works" result in his salvation?

The answer is no. The salvation was already happening when Zacchaeus wanted to see Jesus—when he stirred spiritual desire in himself for something other than wealth. A wealthy man up in a tree? Not very dignified. But he counted knowing Jesus as something more valuable than his dignity. But Jesus did the real saving when He invited Himself into the tax collector's home. Zacchaeus had to say yes, of course, but we take for granted that Jesus also humbled Himself, also made Himself the target of scorn for associating with this dirty little man.

Jesus came to seek and save that which is lost. "Jesus" *means* salvation—it is the DNA of the Lord's name. But we are Christians, and we are supposed to imitate Jesus in all things. We, too, should seek and save that which is lost. Sometimes we have to go a distance to find the lost; sometimes the lost are closer than we dare to admit.

My desire and vision for us all is that we would focus fiercely on three things: Scripture, prayer, and soul-winning. These three are bound together in a functioning unity by love—love for God and love for each other. If we can do these things, we will be His disciples.

Day 87

Today, I'd like to focus on Luke 19:30-31 (the gist of which is also found in Mark 11:3 and Matthew 21:3)

"Go into the village in front of you, where on entering you will find a colt tied, on which no one has ever yet sat. Untie it and bring it here. If anyone asks you, 'Why are you untying it?' you shall say this: 'The Lord has need of it.'"

That little phrase, *"The Lord has need of it,"* as natural as it seems in the context as an appropriate answer for why the disciples were absconding with a stranger's donkey, is actually a matter of significant debate. A little bit of thought leads to the (rather deep) question, *"Does God really **need** anything from human beings?"*

Consider these passages...

...Every beast of the forest is mine, the cattle on a thousand hills. [11] *I know all the birds of the hills, and all that moves in the field is mine.* [12] *"If I were hungry, I would not tell you, for the world and its fullness are mine.* [13] *Do I eat the flesh of bulls or drink the blood of goats?"* Psalm 50:10-13

Who has measured the Spirit of the LORD, or what man shows him his counsel? [14] *Whom did he consult, and who made him understand? Who taught him the path of justice, and taught him knowledge, and showed him the way of understanding?"* Isaiah 40:13-14

Both of these passages tell us in no uncertain terms that God Almighty doesn't need mortal man for anything, whether materially or spiritually. And a quick glance at the Lord's words starting in Job 38 confirms this truth. In the grand scope of things, God doesn't need us. He makes pretty clear that He wants us (incredibly)—but He doesn't *need* us.

Or does He? Here is this troublesome passage about Jesus needing a little donkey. The Son of God is about to enter Jerusalem and fulfill the Destiny of the Ages, the redemption of all humanity hangs in the balance, and He has to bum a ride off a stranger. What gives?

Of course, we can appeal to what is known as *kenosis*, the "emptying" of divine glory Jesus experienced just by becoming fully human, described in Philippians 2:5-11. But that doesn't explain passages like this, which we've touched on before:

I sought for a man among them who should build up the wall and stand in the breach before me for the land, that I should not destroy it, but I found none. [31] *Therefore I have poured out my indignation upon them. I have consumed them with the fire of my wrath. I have returned their way upon their heads, declares the Lord GOD."* ~ Ezekiel 22:30-31

This passage, while not explicitly saying God *needed* a person, states that God *looked* for someone to carry out His purposes—and found no one. This is remarkably similar to the passage about Jesus needing a donkey. How?

Well, Jesus didn't *need* that donkey any more than God *needed* an intercessor. That is to say, the need being expressed by God in these passages is not the kind of fundamental need that we experience—need for food, or healing, or even love. Our needs are absolute, or to be more lofty in our language, they are *existential needs*: if they aren't met, we're done. In the big picture, God doesn't suffer existential needs. God-made-man in Jesus certainly did, because He was fully human so He could redeem us, a great wonder and mystery in itself. But glorified, He is beyond those existential needs now. So the divide between our needs and God's "needs" remains stark.

But that isn't the whole story. Because of God's love for us, His care for us, and His purposes for us, He has bound Himself into a covenant relationship with humanity. This covenant, which by His Almighty power He has formed, *limits* the exercise of that selfsame Almighty power. In other words, God's commitment to us, His desire to be in relationship with us, causes Him to need us—not in the sense that we need Him, but nevertheless in a very real way. The nature of that covenant is that in order for God to redeem, *He must involve His people.* So to exist, God doesn't need us like we need Him for *us* to exist. But on the other hand, for Him to execute His plan of salvation, He *chooses* to need us— He needs us to pray, He needs us to give, He needs us to bear witness and share His love and His Word.

The Lord needs your donkey. Let Him use it. By the time it gets back to you, that donkey's going to have a boast that will last forever.

Day 88

Today I'd like to take a look at a powerful (long) passage from Mark, which follows on the heels of the Triumphal Entry.

On the following day, when they came from Bethany, he was hungry. [13] And seeing in the distance a fig tree in leaf, he went to see if he could find anything on it. When he came to it, he found nothing but leaves, for it was not the season for figs. [14] And he said to it, "May no one ever eat fruit from you again." And his disciples heard it. [15] **And they came to Jerusalem. And he entered the temple and began to drive out those who sold and those who bought in the temple, and he overturned the tables of the money-changers and the seats of those who sold pigeons. [16] And he would not allow anyone to carry anything through the temple. [17] And he was teaching them and saying to them, "Is it not written, 'My house shall be called a house of prayer for all the nations'? But you have made it a den of robbers." [18] And the chief priests and the scribes heard it and were seeking a way to destroy him, for they feared him, because all the crowd was astonished at his teaching.** *[19] And when evening came they went out of the city. [20] As they passed by in the morning, they saw the fig tree withered away to its roots. [21] And Peter remembered and said to him, "Rabbi, look! The fig tree that you cursed has withered." [22] And Jesus answered them, "Have faith in God. [23] Truly, I say to you, whoever says to this mountain, 'Be taken up and thrown into the sea,' and does not doubt in his heart, but believes that what he says will come to pass, it will be done for him. [24] Therefore I tell you, whatever you ask in prayer, believe that you have received it, and it will be yours. [25] And whenever you stand praying, forgive, if you have anything against anyone, so that your Father also who is in heaven may forgive you your trespasses."* Mark 11:12-25

The setting for this passage is Mark 11:11, which clarifies an important detail about Jesus' famous actions upon arriving in Jerusalem that week: after the Triumphal Entry, Jesus simply surveys the Temple courts; He doesn't carry out His famous "cleansing" until the following day (what we would call Monday morning).

But Mark presents Jesus' actions in the Temple courts in a very special fashion that helps us understand what He is up to. As Jesus goes to the Temple, He sees a fig tree. Finding it fruitless, He curses the tree. Mark then tells the story of Jesus overturning the tables and driving the vendors from His father's house. Why? Because the Temple is supposed to be a *house of prayer.* But after telling this story, Mark goes back to the condition of the fig tree—now withered from the roots. Upon seeing the tree, Peter remarks about its demise. Jesus responds...with a lesson about *faith and prayer.*

Scholars call this kind of literary structure an *inclusio.* The opening episode about the fig tree—an incomplete story—couples with the concluding episode to *frame* a feature story found in between the two of them. The opening and the closing serves as literary "arrows," pointing the what is found in the middle. Together, the opening, the centerpiece story, and the close form a unified whole that communicates something. Mark, under the inspiration of the Holy Spirit, is offering us an invaluable lesson. What is he saying?

1) Spiritual fruitlessness is brought on by treating the holy things of God casually and as if they were meant for our personal benefit rather than for His greater purposes.

2) God will fiercely defend His interests, even if the short term result of that defense is any number of overturned tables and upset pigeon salesmen inside His house.

3) Those who yield to God's discipline receive life; those who refuse are rendered forever fruitless, just like the fig tree.

4) Fruitfulness has to do with faith and prayer.

My takeaway from all of this is that God is not interested in mere *activity* in His name. The moneychangers and animal sellers, in cahoots with the priesthood, were all very *active* in God's house. But the problem is they didn't have any faith, and they weren't doing what God had called them to do—indeed, God's whole purpose for even *having* a Temple: communion with Him. They were active about their own business, not God's. More specifically, His people's distraction was muting His witness to the nations, so that His salvific purposes were being utterly distorted.

Jesus uses the fig tree as an illustrated sermon. Peter is amazed by the miracle itself, but true to form, Jesus focuses on the point: Have faith. Believe God. Pray. Seek God. In a divine irony, Jesus reveals that His demonstration of faith in cursing and killing the fig tree was more fruitful than the empty tree itself—that fruitless fig being a symbol of the fruitless spiritual leadership in Jerusalem that He was challenging.

Here's what I want to do: I want to clear my own Temple courts *before Jesus has to do it Himself.* Just like He was then, Jesus is hungry to see fruit today. I want to be fruitful when He comes looking. I want to imitate His faith, I want to submit to His teaching, I want my life to be a house of prayer, empty of profiteering and self-interest.

Jesus, reveal to us our own hearts, and have mercy. Help me lift these heavy tables I've set up here; help me clear out all the junk I've allowed to accumulate. And don't stop until the courts of my heart are clean by Your standards and not just what I have thought is "good enough." Amen.

Day 89

I'm reminded of Holy Tuesday. By my reckoning it would have been the day that Jesus, leaving Jerusalem for the day as was His custom to lodge at Bethany, delivered His famous "Olivet Discourse" (Matthew 24-25, and parallels in Mark and Luke) from the summit of the Mount of Olives, looking over Jerusalem as the sun went down; it would be His last time to so behold the Holy City at sunset before He suffered. This is one of Jesus' longest sermons, comparable to His Sermon on the Mount (Matthew 5-7, with another version in Luke 6ff), and His Last Supper Discourse (John 13-17).

There's no way all He says could even begin to be summarized here. A brief overview would be that Jesus' disciples ask Him about the "end of the age" and the "sign of His coming," which rather remarkably He answers with a thoroughness I can only guess surprised even them. Jesus knew His hour was near, and it was time for full disclosure. Matthew's version is divided into two sections: chapter 24 predicts the events in prophetic fashion (complete with assurances, startling warnings, and ambiguities), while chapter 25 illustrates and drives those points home by means of three parables now famous to many but often taken out of their context and (therefore) sadly stripped of a great deal of their meaning (these are *The Wise and the Foolish Virgins*, *The Parable of the Talents*, and *The Sheep and the Goats*).

I would like to focus on just a couple of Jesus' statements and responses:

First, the conversation that began it all. While still in the city with His disciples, Jesus responds to His disciples' glowing remarks about the Temple with a brief and harsh statement recorded in all three Synoptics: *Do you see all this? Not one stone will be left upon another.* Note that Jesus did not take issue with His disciples' admiration. The Jewish Mishnah, a codification of Jewish law written centuries later, stated, *"He who has not seen Herod's temple has not seen beauty."* In other words, by all

317

accounts the Temple was every bit worthy of the praise it received. Even today, the Western Wall—a retaining wall and all that remains of the huge platform upon which the Temple rested—is magnificent. But can you imagine what would happen if a church member praised God for the beauty of a newly finished church building project (and the Temple wasn't even fully completed until years later, so it was new, too), and the pastor said, *"Yeah, it's all going to burn...*"? Let Jesus' words hit you as they hit those men.

The Temple was leveled in AD 70, and all its rubble shoved by the Romans off the western side of the platform; those who pray at the Wailing Wall today stand on 50-60 feet of holy rubble. Jesus wasn't kidding, and He wasn't exaggerating.

God is not interested in monuments, relics, or museums. He is not interested in His holy house being turned into testimonies to human resourcefulness, wealth, culture, or ingenuity. Where He lives in heaven—where He has promised us a home—makes anything we do on earth seem truly humble by comparison. I believe we ought to glorify God with our place of worship. We shouldn't have glorious homes but a cast-off church building. The Prophet Haggai has plenty to say about that. But the truth remains: a pretty building is no substitute for a heart on fire for Christ.

In Matthew 24:12 Jesus delivers a warning that makes His words about the Temple seem mild, to me anyway: *"And because lawlessness will be increased, the love of many will grow cold."*(ESV) The NASB and NIV interpret this passage to mean that the love of *most* will grow cold, making the verse even scarier.

Many wept over the disaster at the Cathedral of Notre Dame, Paris. Hundreds of millions of dollars were pledged for her restoration. Well and good; may she be rebuilt.

But what about our *hearts?*

Jesus gives warning because He expects us to take warning. Let us seek God fervently, ask for a second wind, plead that He reveals to us where we are so that He can rectify us. Because at the end of the day, sooner or later, every last work lifted by human hands will fall, and all that will remain will be what we've offered to Him. We are His house, or we have nothing at all.

When the Son of Man comes, will He find faith on the earth? Lord have mercy, and let the answer be "yes" in each of us.

Day 90

Let's evaluate a rather cheap character contrast: Simon Peter and the Lord Jesus Himself. The time is the night the Lord is betrayed, and the setting is the Garden of Gethsemane.

The lead up to this situation is clear to us: Jesus' repeated predictions that He would suffer, the announcement that one of the Twelve would betray Him, and His sad declaration that all of His disciples would abandon Him. In other words, His task was clear to Him, including the many painful obstacles and letdowns that would mark His way.

Heading into Gethsemane, Peter's path forward was also fairly clear. Jesus warned him that he would deny Jesus thrice before the rooster crowed, a prediction that Peter balked at (in his defense, he wasn't alone: the rest of the disciples talked that way, too).

Here's how things unfolded:

Then Jesus went with them to a place called Gethsemane, and he said to his disciples, "Sit here, while I go over there and pray."³⁷ And taking with him Peter and the two sons of Zebedee, he began to be sorrowful and troubled.³⁸ Then he said to them, "My soul is very sorrowful, even to death; remain here, and watch with me."³⁹ And going a little farther he fell on his face and prayed, saying, "My Father, if it be possible, let this cup pass from me; nevertheless, not as I will, but as you will."⁴⁰ And he came to the disciples and found them sleeping. And he said to Peter, "So, could you not watch with me one hour?⁴¹ Watch and pray that you may not enter into temptation. The spirit indeed is willing, but the flesh is weak."⁴² Again, for the second time, he went away and prayed, "My Father, if this cannot pass unless I drink it, your will be done."⁴³ And again he came and found them sleeping, for their eyes were heavy.⁴⁴ So, leaving them again, he went away and prayed for the third time, saying the same words again.⁴⁵ Then he came to the disciples and said to them, "Sleep and take your rest later on. See, the hour is at hand, and the Son of Man is betrayed into the hands of sinners. ⁴⁶ Rise, let us be going; see, my betrayer is at hand."

The skinny is that Jesus—flawless, sinless Son of God—prayed fervently and repeatedly regarding the trial He knew was coming. He didn't lean on His status with the Father, His past performance, or His righteousness. In short, *Jesus presumed nothing* as He appealed to the Father in gut-wrenching spiritual agony.

Peter slept. That sounds harsh, but it's the truth. (Again, he wasn't alone in his negligence, but there it is.)

Now, what are the consequences, the end result of these actions?

Jesus:

And the high priest said to him, "I adjure you by the living God, tell us if you are the Christ, the Son of God."⁶⁴ Jesus said to him, "You have said so. But I tell you, from now on you will see the Son of Man seated at the right hand of Power and coming on the clouds of heaven."-- Matthew 26:63-64

Peter:

Now Peter was sitting outside in the courtyard. And a servant girl came up to him and said, "You also were with Jesus the Galilean."⁷⁰ But he denied it before them all, saying, "I do not know what you mean."⁷¹ And when he went out to the entrance, another servant girl saw him, and she said to the bystanders, "This man was with Jesus of Nazareth."⁷² And again he denied it with an oath: "I do not know the man."⁷³ After a little while the bystanders came up and said to Peter, "Certainly you too are one of them, for your accent betrays you."⁷⁴ Then he began to invoke a curse on himself and to swear, "I do not know the man." And immediately the rooster crowed.⁷⁵ And Peter remembered the saying of Jesus, "Before the rooster crows, you will deny me three times." And he went out and wept bitterly. ˉ Matthew 26:69-75

Jesus and Peter both knew what was coming their way—there weren't any curve balls in this game. The pitches were right over the plate. Both were asked questions, quite literally yards from each other and essentially simultaneously. The difference is that Jesus faced the high priest in his rage who had the power to put Jesus to death, while Peter faced a slave girl—someone of low social station and no power at all.

What's the difference? *Jesus prayed through,* while Peter didn't pray at all. It is easy for us to shrug and say, "Well, Jesus was the Son of God, of course He was tough as nails." That statement is not untrue, but it's truer than most people who say it realize, and in different ways. Jesus was sinless indeed, but that purity of soul gave Him the wisdom to know He needed to call on His Father for strength. There was no presumption in Jesus. Peter, in contrast, thought that his zeal and love for the Lord would be enough to carry him through, and he was proved terribly wrong. The sad truth is that Peter *did* love Jesus, and *did* have genuine zeal for Him. But love and zeal and good intentions—to say nothing of strong words and promises—aren't enough.

All of us face spiritual mountains. Often we know they are coming at us as we move through life. Let's take a lesson from Jesus and Peter: those mountains have to be moved *before we actually reach them.* Presuming nothing, taking no chances, putting no confidence in the flesh, we pray, pray, pray and we allow God to achieve the victory in us first, so that the battle is won before we step onto the battlefield. Agonize now in prayer and reap God's peace later, or sleep now and agonize later at a price you cannot afford. Jesus was cool as ice facing the Sanhedrin because (in the Spirit) He'd already bashed in the Serpent's head in Gethsemane. Peter failed to deal with a squeaky little girl because he hadn't done what he needed to with the window of opportunity he'd been given.

Day 91

I'd like to take one last look at Gethsemane before we step into even more difficult events. Yesterday we read Matthew's version; today we'll see how Mark and Luke tell things:

And they went to a place called Gethsemane. And he said to his disciples, "Sit here while I pray."³³ And he took with him Peter and James and John, and began to be greatly distressed and troubled.³⁴ And he said to them, "My soul is very sorrowful, even to death. Remain here and watch."³⁵ And going a little farther, he fell on the ground and prayed that, if it were possible, the hour might pass from him.³⁶ And he said, "Abba, Father, all things are possible for you. Remove this cup from me. Yet not what I will, but what you will."³⁷ And he came and found them sleeping, and he said to Peter, "Simon, are you asleep? Could you not watch one hour?³⁸ Watch and pray that you may not enter into temptation. The spirit indeed is willing, but the flesh is weak."³⁹ And again he went away and prayed, saying the same words.⁴⁰ And again he came and found them sleeping, for their eyes were very heavy, and they did not know what to answer him.⁴¹ And he came the third time and said to them, "Are you still sleeping and taking your rest? It is enough; the hour has come. The Son of Man is betrayed into the hands of sinners.⁴² Rise, let us be going; see, my betrayer is at hand." ⁓ Mark 14:32-42*

And when he came to the place, he said to them, "Pray that you may not enter into temptation."⁴¹ And he withdrew from them about a stone's throw, and knelt down and prayed,⁴² saying, "Father, if you are willing, remove this cup from me. Nevertheless, not my will, but yours, be done."⁴³ And there appeared to him an angel from heaven, strengthening him.⁴⁴ And being in agony he prayed more earnestly; and his sweat became like great drops of blood falling down to the ground.⁴⁵ And when he rose from prayer, he came to the disciples and found them sleeping for sorrow,⁴⁶ and he said to them, "Why are you sleeping? Rise and pray that you may not enter into temptation." ⁓ Luke 22:40-46*

Again, there are so many painful beauties in these passages, but I am focused on one of them right now: *the will of the Father.* Jesus teaches us a great deal about the will of the Father, and the truth that Jesus is sinless and already more submitted than any human being has ever been only highlights what He has to show us.

First, submitting to the will of God is not automatic, and it is not an easy thing. This might not be a popular message today, when "being in the will of God" is often treated as the same thing as sort of winning the spiritual lottery—*here come them blessings!!!* Well, it *is* a blessing, and a fountain of blessings, but there's a lot more to it in our lives than just laying back and receiving. Jesus had walked a long road of perfect obedience, and now at the end, He still had to do battle in the spiritual realm to bring Himself into the realm of God's perfect will and fully submit to it.

I've asked many Christian people if they desired God's perfect will for their lives; never has anyone ever waffled on the matter. On the contrary, the query is usually met with a fervent affirmation. I believe this response is sincere as far as people understand. It's just that I don't believe people usually really understand. Stepping into the center of God's plan for us is not just us saying yes, it's us saying yes over and over, and as we go—if we are truly submitted—the bar gets *raised* for us, *not lowered.* Submission leads to God getting a firmer grip on us, then asking more of us, demanding deeper surrender still, until Gethsemane after Gethsemane leads us into the image of Jesus Himself. If it wasn't easy for Jesus, how can we expect it to be easy for us? The Lord Himself said a servant is not greater than his master.

The second matter to be addressed is how the will of the Father is absolutely non-negotiable. I used to hear people say, "Well, it's one thing to call Jesus Savior, it's another thing to call Him Lord." Hhmm. I think I know what they are *trying* to say, but the problem is such a dichotomy is found *nowhere* in Scripture. It's all one for Jesus—there are no "tiers"—no optional levels of commitment. What He does with us in the end is up to His mercy, but *my Bible* tells me He wants it all and isn't the least bit interested in second skimmings. So the will of the Father is the one and only way forward for the disciple of the Lord. Until we submit, we'll be stalled out, waiting on the Lord when the entire time He's the one waiting on us.

I am grateful—beyond grateful—that Jesus pressed through, fought the fight, and rode His desire to do God's will above all else. Because at the end of the day it really is about what we want to do, what we long for. If we really want to please God, really want to obey Him, really want to do exactly what He wants, we'll sweat blood just like Jesus did to make that happen.

Day 92

Today I want us to consider Jesus' self-sacrifice for us, meaning His atoning death. We've already looked at Gethsemane from different angles as the battleground upon which Jesus fought the fight beforehand. Now we'll see how things played out, and for my purposes I want to look at three episodes within the larger drama.

First, Jesus before the high priest just after He is arrested:

And the high priest stood up in the midst and asked Jesus, "Have you no answer to make? What is it that these men testify against you?"[61] But he remained silent and made no answer. Again the high priest asked him, "Are you the Christ, the Son of the Blessed?"[62] And Jesus said, "I am, and you will see the Son of Man seated at the right hand of Power, and coming with the clouds of heaven."[63] And the high priest tore his garments and said, "What further witnesses do we need?[64] You have heard his blasphemy. What is your decision?" And they all condemned him as deserving death. ¯ Mark 14:60–64

This passage begins with the high priest's frustration, which has been building during the entire hearing: conflicting witnesses are undermining his efforts to condemn Jesus. It looks like the whole attempt to railroad Jesus is going to founder. But then, in v. 62 an unlikely witness comes to the high priest's rescue: *Jesus Himself.* If Jesus would have remained silent (which was His right), the whole thing would have fallen apart. But Jesus effectively condemns Himself.

Jesus' self-indictment by the standards of the Council triggers their next step: take Him to the Romans.

But here we see Jesus follow an inverse strategy when dealing with Pontius Pilate...

And as soon as it was morning, the chief priests held a consultation with the elders and scribes and the whole council. And they bound

Jesus and led him away and delivered him over to Pilate. ²And Pilate asked him, "Are you the King of the Jews?" And he answered him, "You have said so." ³ And the chief priests accused him of many things. ⁴ And Pilate again asked him, "Have you no answer to make? See how many charges they bring against you." ⁵ But Jesus made no further answer, so that Pilate was amazed. ˜ Mark 15:1–5

Here we see Jesus says just enough to be true to Himself and to show Pilate he is not ignorant or obstinate. Then He falls silent. In contrast to the audience before the Council, here it would have behooved Jesus to *speak*—to explain Himself and why the priests were after Him, to tell how all He does is help people, how He isn't against paying taxes and isn't challenging Caesar. This was Jesus' second chance to shut the whole thing down—but now He chooses to remain silent, which allows the priests to dominate the floor (for an example of how this could have gone, see Acts 24-25 and read how Paul handled such a situation). In other words, both the trials Jesus stood through needed *His help* to condemn Him.

Now we come to the crucifixion itself:

And they offered him wine mixed with myrrh, but he did not take it. ˜ Mark 15:23

Just before they nailed Him to the cross, the soldiers offered Him a drug—"myrrhed wine" is the exact phrase—to dull the pain. Some have considered this a "backhanded mercy," since such an anesthetic (ingested, myrrh had a mild narcotic quality) would have only prolonged the torture by reducing the effect of shock from severe pain, which in itself can hasten death. Others consider that this was a practice of pious women, a true mercy by intent; though the text seems pretty clear that His executioners were the ones doing the offering, it may have been something Jewish women handed off to them and that they would grudgingly agree to. In any case, Jesus turned the drug down. Added to the previous details, this is most telling.

Jesus in not a masochist; He is not embracing agony for its own sake, as if suffering in itself holds value. Jesus was determined to carry our sin and all its consequences to the cross. The hard truth is that there is no wiggling out of the consequences for sin and there is no way to adequately numb the terrible grief it brings. By God's power, by praying through, Jesus *took control* of His situation *in order to surrender control* to the Father. He died for our sins under the kind of terms we must face, rather than terms He could set for Himself. In this way He fully atoned for our misdeeds, in order to restore life and freedom to us.

The result?

For if, because of one man's trespass, death reigned through that one man, much more will those who receive the abundance of grace and the free gift of righteousness **reign in life** *through the one man Jesus Christ.* ‐ Romans 5:17

Because of Jesus, we have been translated from a place where we were at the mercy of consequences beyond our control to a place where we experience so much freedom that "reigning" is the only way to describe it.

Thanks be to God for His indescribable gift! (2 Corinthians 9:15)

Day 93

One of the most telling details of the crucifixion accounts is what happens inside the Temple upon Jesus' death...

And Jesus uttered a loud cry and breathed his last.[38] *And the curtain of the temple was torn in two, from top to bottom.*
~ Mark 15:37-38

This event is also recorded in Matthew 27:50-51 and Luke 23:45, demonstrating that the Synoptic Gospel writers all considered it fundamental to the meaning of the story.

The curtain, of course, is the heavy, elaborate veil that separates the Holy Place from the inner sanctum, the Most Holy Place. It is first mentioned in Exodus 26:31-33 when Moses receives instructions about the Tabernacle, but then is made again to fit the Temple in Solomon's day (2 Chronicles 3:14). The point of the curtain was to separate and therefore communicate the unique holiness of God, letting people know that God is not accessible to them. Once a year, on the Day of Atonement, the high priest would enter the Most Holy Place to offer sacrifice for sin (Hebrews 9:7); otherwise access was completely forbidden. Why? Because of our sinfulness.

This veil being rent—and being rent from *top to bottom* especially—therefore carries great significance. It wasn't some sort of divine vandalism, as if God the Father is getting back at the priests who ran the Temple for what they had just done to His Son. We've already seen from what Jesus did by cleansing the Temple courts that He considered the Temple *His house* already—not the priests. No, what God was doing was what He had always wanted to do, but never could because of our sin: He opened the way into His most holy presence so that we could freely come.

Therefore, brothers, since we have confidence to enter the holy places by the blood of Jesus, [20] **by the new and living way that he** *opened for us through the curtain, that is, through his flesh,* [21] *and since we have a great priest over the house of God,* [22] *let us draw near with a true heart in full assurance of faith, with our hearts sprinkled clean from an evil conscience and our bodies washed with pure water.* ¯ Hebrews 10:19–22

Upon His death, Jesus accomplished by divinely appointed priesthood what generations of priests could never do: He *permanently* cleared the way for us to enter into God's presence. Now there is no veil, no separation, because there is no condemnation. By the blood of Christ we have been adopted into God's household. We can now call God "Father" and have it be true, not presumption or worse.

Paul puts it even more directly, but says the same thing:

For through him we both have access in one Spirit to the Father.
¯ Ephesians 2:18

I could go on and on about Luke's theology in Acts, about how *we* are the Temple now, and John's theology in Revelation about the New Jerusalem being a *cube*—the same shape as the Holy of Holies—meaning that eternally God's presence is both our abode and our identity, or Peter saying we are together being built into a temple for the Lord, but it's all the same: a seismic shift has happened at the cross in respect to the relationship between God and humanity. No wonder there was an earthquake!

I fear our non-Jewishness really hurts us here. Since our minds are not saturated in Leviticus and Deuteronomy, we struggle to appreciate what it means to live on the other side of that veil. We sort of internally say, "Well, *of course* He's my Father. *Of course* I can approach Him so easily"—when there's no "of course" about it; Jesus paid the highest price for us to be so naïve. On the one hand, like a father who is happy that his child has no sense at all about what it took for her to have her own room and clothes and food, God is pleased that we think this state of affairs is normal. Because according to His plan, it *is* normal. But we need the power of the Holy Spirit to work in us, lest familiarity breed contempt. If we really appreciated this access the way we should, we would pray more, and longer, and more fervently. If you could, at will, spend your morning coffee time on the porch of a château gazing up at the Swiss Alps, and your evenings walking the beaches of Fiji, wouldn't you? And yet riches untold await us in God's presence, the way opened for us through Jesus' body, and we'd rather do other things.

As Paul says, this is not said to shame or guilt anyone—I include myself as first—but to take stock. This is the time for it.

Day 94

In lieu of our recent studies concerning the days leading to Jesus' crucifixion, I want to share a passage of a favorite book of mine, C.S. Lewis' *The Lion, the Witch, and the Wardrobe*. For those who haven't read it (and you really should), I will give a brief backstory to catch you up to the point I will share...

Four children in World War 2 era England are sent to a country manor house to escape the Blitz in the city. There, under the care of a mysterious and eccentric professor (hey, that's a major selling point for the book right there!), they discover a wardrobe that acts as a door to another world called *Narnia*. After an uneven beginning (Lucy, the youngest, gets into Narnia alone at first, followed by Edmund, then finally all of them together when Peter and Susan, the eldest two, are mysteriously granted entrance), the four of them wander into the beautiful but evilly enchanted land. Narnia, you see, is a good place but is sad and oppressed because a terrible witch (symbolic of the devil) has cursed it so that it is always winter but never Christmas—obviously a nightmare scenario for any child. In the end, Aslan the Lion (Christ) comes and destroys the witch's power, but that is afield from what I'd like to share.

An exchange between Peter and Lucy struck me in my most recent reading, and I'd like to share it. It takes place just after all four children walk through the wardrobe together for the first time. Faced with the bitter cold of Narnia's terrible winter, they ponder how to keep warm (they wore light clothing back in England, and were, after all, indoors), and decide that taking the long fur coats from the back of the wardrobe would be OK, since they weren't even taking them out of the closet!

At this point, Lucy pipes up, suggesting that they could all pretend to be explorers. Peter's response is a classic. He simply says that things will be plenty exciting without having to pretend.

Lewis is saying more than he appears to be in this apparently infantile little book; he always has a purpose in saying what he says. When I look back on my Christian experience—now completing 40 years—I think about countless personal encounters, church settings, and ministry experiences. I also think of all the different theories and angles I have heard and read when it comes to how we should "do church" in the postmodern era, especially in America. And today I compare them with the raw, stunning power of the resurrection of Jesus, the running back and forth, the breathless testimonies and the tears, the awe and fear and elation...and I wonder: *are we pretending when there is absolutely no need for it?*

Walking through the back of a wardrobe into a magical land. Hhmmm. Well, that is a child's story. But it seems to me that even a child's story like Lewis' comes closer to the truth than a lot of the antics I've seen done (and sometimes that I found myself doing) in the name of the Lord. And Lewis' story—as every story must—falls far, far short of the shift that took place with the resurrection of Jesus Christ. The new dimension we walked into as the human race when the Lord looked the devil in the eye, took the keys of Hades and death from him, and rose from that grave, well, no amount of metaphors, fantasies, illustrations, poems, or songs will ever tell the whole of it this side of glory.

We don't need to pretend. We don't need to pretend to have joy, pretend to have peace, pretend to be blessed. We don't need to pretend to have God's favor. We have Jesus, alive, breathing, and smiling upon us. And in Him, we have it all. This is exciting enough without pretending.

Welcome to Narnia in high summer—for the rest of your life.

Day 95

I'd like to share something that came to me as I was doing some leisure reading this week. While in Israel, I picked up a guide booklet while visiting a national park bookstore. This particular booklet details the archaeological dig at Bet She'an (the biblical Beth-shan, where the Philistines hanged King Saul's body as a trophy), but which was known as *Scythopolis* in Jesus' day. The city isn't mentioned in the Gospels by name, but it is indirectly implied in the Parable of the Prodigal Son, since Scythopolis was the capital city of the pagan *Decapolis*, Gentile urban centers straddling the Jordan River and known for pagan sinfulness.

What struck me as I read the brief history of the city and looked over the photos of the ruins was the paradox between the vast time span of the city's saga and what it has come to now. Basically, the city (located on the west side of the Jordan River south of the Sea of Galilee) was a significant urban center on-and-off for roughly 2,500 years—from the time of Egyptian domination before the Exodus all the way through the Crusades—*ten times* the age of the United States of America. During that period it experienced desolations that lasted centuries, control by multiple empires and kingdoms, boom periods that led it to urban glory, then crashes that led to poverty, more praise and restoration, and then catastrophes both military and natural. As I read the story—which would encapsulate several centuries at a time—something struck me: *This is a **human description** of human life.* What does *God* say about us by comparison?

Come now, you who say, "Today or tomorrow we will go into such and such a town and spend a year there and trade and make a profit"— [14] *yet you do not know what tomorrow will bring. What is your life? For you are a mist that appears for a little time and then vanishes.* ~ James 4:13-14

Some of the rulers' names mentioned in the brief that I read were barely familiar to me; names left as memorials or dedicatories in mosaics—put there so people would appreciate the wealthy people who paid for the decorations—are names only, their meanings forever lost. Scythopolis was home to thousands and thousands of people over the millennia, and now if an archaeologist can unearth the record of a single one of them it is a major victory. Add to this that up until a little over 50 years ago, Scythopolis was buried by the sands of the Middle East; only during the last lifetime is there any sense of what she was. But she was full of people made in God's image, full of hopes, jealousies, fears, aspirations, disappointments, conquests, and pains—just like us. Now Scythopolis is barely a memory; she is a ruin where tourists stop to take pictures for a few minutes before they hurry on their way.

The story of this once-glorious city can be repeated over, and over, and over again, and multiplied by millions—nay, *billions* of souls across all of human history. It is a grim picture for us to take in. But Scripture speaks to us, gives us perspective to warn us:

There is no remembrance of former things, nor will there be any remembrance of later things yet to be among those who come after... Their love and their hate and their envy have already perished, and forever they have no more share in all that is done under the sun ~ Ecclesiastes 1:11, 9:6

What are we to do with this? Throw up our hands? Well, maybe in respect to vain pursuits that is exactly the appropriate thing to do. A great deal of grief in the world would have been spared the children of men if some had decided to give up their vain pursuits instead of seeing them through to their bitter end. But not all is vanity...

I have seen the business that God has given to the children of man to be busy with. " He has made everything beautiful in its time. Also, he has put eternity into man's heart... ~ Ecclesiastes 3:10-11

God has put eternity in your heart. Everything that pertains to this life and its ambitions will be buried like the sands buried

Scythopolis, and none of our fretting, or sleeplessness, or striving, or fear, or vainglory will remain. But what we do unto Jesus, what we submit to Him and for His glory, *that* will remain. It is easy to reduce this to stereotypes and simplistic tropes—evangelism and prayer will last, earning a living won't. But it isn't that easy. Two men may to the naked eye be doing the same task, but God judges the motives of each one. Worse, one may seem to be doing something "holy," but have unholy and selfish motives, while another might seem to be doing something secular, yet the whole time they are dying to themselves and submitting to God's greater purposes.

We are not the judges of another, but we should examine ourselves, and ask God to search our hearts. However we proceed, let us realize that the only thing that will outlast this creation and make it into the next is that which is done sincerely in the name of the Lord.

Day 96

What better way to conclude our unbroken time with God then to celebrate *freedom.*
Jesus tells us,

...if the Son sets you free, you will be indeed free. (John 8:36)

Paul tells us in Galatians 5:1a...

For freedom Christ has set us free...

Both of these passages, in their references to our freedom, feature what is called "tautology"—the repetition of an idea in different words to drive a point home. Another way to look at these passages is that they are basically *truisms*—along the lines of saying that water is wet or the sky is up. John's account of Jesus' words and Paul's declaration of Christian freedom both bend under the weight of the circular thinking behind them: God wants us free *just because.* We are made in God's image, we are created for freedom, and all other things aside, being *unfree* is an unnatural state of being for human beings.

So Jesus has set us free for the express purpose of *being*—again, *just because*...because it's who we are supposed to be, and He loves us, and He takes pleasure in our freedom for its own sake, as a good in itself apart from any usefulness we might serve in the aftermath of that liberation. In reference to freedom, *being* matters to God far more than *doing.*

But from where we stand as children and servants of Christ, we do have something to *do,* even if that something flows from who we *are.* That something is that we are to spread the news of our liberation. Someone once said that sharing the gospel is essentially one beggar telling another beggar where to find bread: I've been freed from spiritual famine, and you can be, too.

Here Isaiah 61 kicks in...

The Spirit of the Lord GOD is upon me, because the LORD has anointed me to bring good news to the poor; he has sent me to bind up the brokenhearted, to proclaim liberty to the captives, and the opening of the prison to those who are bound;² to proclaim the year of the LORD's favor, and the day of vengeance of our God; to comfort all who mourn;³ to grant to those who mourn in Zion— to give them a beautiful headdress instead of ashes, the oil of gladness instead of mourning, the garment of praise instead of a faint spirit; that they may be called oaks of righteousness, the planting of the LORD, that he may be glorified.

This was the passage Jesus preached from in Nazareth when He first inaugurated His ministry (Luke 4). It conveys great truths— that Jesus was the Great Liberator, setting the captive free. But there's more...

And as you go, preach, saying, 'The kingdom of heaven is at hand.' Heal the sick, raise the dead, cleanse the lepers, cast out demons; freely you received, freely give. ˉ Matthew 10:7-8 (NASB)

Freely we have received, freely we should give—the very liberation we have received we should pass along to others. In setting us free, He also commissions us to set others free. This, of course, requires us to walk in the freedom He has given us. For this reason, among others, the whole of Paul says in Galatians 5:1 is this...

It was for freedom that Christ set us free; **therefore keep standing firm and do not be subject again to a yoke of slavery.**
ˉ Galatians 5:1 (NASB)

Similarly, Jesus prefaces His statement about the Son setting us free with this word...

"If you abide in My word, then you are truly disciples of Mine;³² and you shall know the truth, and the truth shall make you free." ˉ John 8:31-32 (NASB)

I believe God wants to use His church as a place where people can be set free—free from depression, free from deceptions, free from chemical dependency, free from spiritual bondages and sins. The Lord Jesus wants to use His body—His hands and feet—as partners (not slaves) in that mission. But for us to do that, we must walk free.

I encourage you, from another angle but essentially in repetition of my last reflection, to seek the Lord deeply and invite the conviction of the Holy Spirit into your life. The Lord convicts to *liberate*, not to *alienate*. I know I sound like a broken record here, but it is what the Spirit keeps whispering to me, urgently, urgently. We must walk free and in the light in order to help others see the light. We have to get past the basics of petty slap fights with old sins and break into a walk that God can bless with His Holy Spirit. Because where the Spirit of the Lord is, there is freedom (2 Corinthians 3:17).

THE END AND THE BEGINNING

I bless you as you continue in your journey of intimacy with God. Allow the Holy Spirit to complete the good work He began in you and continue to draw near to Jesus daily. Do not let your season of unbroken time with God end. He is too good for you to be drawn away by anything else. Nothing else matters. Continue to be a surrendered worshipper. Worship the Lord. Sing to Him. Lift your hands. Tell Him you love Him. Tell Him you trust Him. Tell Him you want Him. Ask for grace to be more surrendered to Him than ever. Saints of God, if you do nothing else in His presence, do this each day.

Made in United States
Orlando, FL
09 January 2025